Hollywood and History

Hollywood and History

What the Movies Get Wrong from the Ancient Greeks to Vietnam

Jem Duducu

ROWMAN & LITTLEFIELD
Lanham • Boulder • New York • London

Published by Rowman & Littlefield
An imprint of The Rowman & Littlefield Publishing Group, Inc.
4501 Forbes Boulevard, Suite 200, Lanham, Maryland 20706
www.rowman.com

86-90 Paul Street, London EC2A 4NE

British Library Cataloguing in Publication Information Available

Library of Congress Cataloging-in-Publication Data

Names: Duducu, Jem, author.
   Title: Hollywood and history : what the movies get wrong from the ancient
   greeks to Vietnam / Jem Duducu.
   Description: Lanham : The Rowman & Littlefield Publishing Group, Inc.,
   [2023] | Includes bibliographical references and index. | Summary: "A
   fun but informative look at Hollywood's more-than-a century long love
   affair with historical figures, events, and places. This book delves
   into what really happened in history, as opposed to the Hollywood
   interpretation of events, and reveals why the movies don't usually
   reflect the reality of our known history"-- Provided by publisher.
   Identifiers: LCCN 2023008066 (print) | LCCN 2023008067 (ebook) | ISBN
   9781538177068 (cloth) | ISBN 9781538177075 (epub)
   Subjects: LCSH: Motion pictures and history. | Historical films. | Motion
   pictures--History.
   Classification: LCC PN1995.2 .D83 2023 (print) | LCC PN1995.2 (ebook) |
   DDC 791.43/658--dc23/eng/20230414
   LC record available at https://lccn.loc.gov/2023008066
   LC ebook record available at https://lccn.loc.gov/2023008067

∞™ The paper used in this publication meets the minimum requirements of American
National Standard for Information Sciences—Permanence of Paper for Printed Library
Materials, ANSI/NISO Z39.48-1992.

Dedicated to Gavin and Greg, thanks for all the support!

Contents

Introduction

Hollywood is sometimes referred to as "the dream machine." It excels at creating compelling stories, supported by stunning visuals, and transporting us to worlds we could never imagine. But the people making movies set in historical contexts must face the realities of time and place. Most history has no satisfying narrative arc. Political scenarios can be complex, sometimes involving a dozen key players in multiple countries. Nobody is going to follow that in a two-hour movie. This is compounded by the fact that almost all the dialogue at the time of great events has never been recorded and is forever lost. And all of that comes before the simple fact that some historical eras are more visually pleasing than others. The result is tension between what factually happened and the way Hollywood wants to tell the story.

Hollywood's goals are to entertain and make money; moviemakers are not required to be slavishly loyal to historical facts. So, real events and characters are merged and moved around to create a satisfying two-hour story of good guys and bad guys, which is nothing like how real life works. I have done some work as a historical adviser. The emphasis here should be on *adviser*: You can explain the facts and sometimes they are listened to, but if the facts diverge too far from what's needed to tell the story or have a certain look, then it will not be used. The reality is that more people will see a movie than will ever read a history book, and when millions of viewers believe that distorted images are historical fact, the few voices on the sidelines raising concerns that it didn't happen that way are ignored.

In Christopher Booker's *The Seven Basic Plots: Why We Tell Stories*, he points out that we have been telling the same stories over and over again since the dawn of writing:

Overcoming the monster
Rags to riches
The quest
Voyage and return

Comedy
Tragedy
Rebirth[1]

And he's correct. Overcoming the monster is the basic structure of the oldest extant story we have, the Epic of Gilgamesh, and it is the same narrative structure of a James Bond movie written more than four thousand years later. The problem is that real life is never this simple, so we get hugely complex events distilled into a straightforward linear story of, for example, a pauper becoming emperor (in essence, rags to riches).

To avoid the criticism that Hollywood ignores history, it has come up with a couple of ubiquitous disclaimers, so we see "Based on a true story" or "Inspired by real events" at the start of films. There is an important difference between the two: "Based on" means (usually) names, dates, and events are true. Sometimes multiple characters are condensed into one, and events may be concentrated into a shorter time frame. "Inspired by" is very different: Something happened and we are taking that idea and running with it. A number of famous horror films are "inspired by real events" (perhaps most notably, *The Exorcist* and *The Texas Chainsaw Massacre*), but these movies in no way reflect what happened in real life. Quite simply, the facts have been repurposed into whatever story the filmmakers want to make, facts be damned. There is no specific formula or source to this, it has just become accepted Hollywood shorthand that to add "based on" means the film is closer to accurate than a film that is "inspired by."

Finally, there is the motivation and level of deception to consider in the making of these movies. Three examples that will be discussed in more detail later are *300*, *Braveheart*, and *Hero*. *300* is based on a Frank Miller comic book that was inspired by *The 300 Spartans* (a 1962 Hollywood movie) that was based on actual Ancient Greek history. That's a lot of filters to get to real events. However, the stylistic choices and the fact that it has actual monsters in it should indicate to the casual viewer that this is not to be taken as a historical drama. Because of this, I think it's being more honest with its audience that this is entertainment and not history than many other so-called historical movies.

Braveheart, however, has a veneer of historical authenticity, and it appears that the moviemakers have done their homework. The actors talk in a semi-Shakespearean language (you know, like everyone did in the "olden days"), and most importantly, it has dates and locations right up there on screen. The fact that the very first date is wrong sounds a loud alarm bell to any historian, but the average viewer doesn't know it is wrong, so *Braveheart* is not being honest with the viewer. It looks legitimate and serious and yet it's as big a fantasy as *300*.

Then there's the Chinese movie *Hero* (directed by Yimou Zhang and starring Jet Li). It would be hard to ever see a more beautiful movie. The fight choreography is perfection, the visuals are stunning, and the story of an assassination attempt on the first emperor of China is real. But unlike the other two films it has governmental interference. Chinese movies must put China in a good light and have to have messages that make the Chinese Communist Party look good, and so the message behind the film is that China needs strong centralized power. This is propaganda and is a prime example of history being repurposed for political means. China did not invent propaganda movies, but what I found interesting when it first came out in 2002 was how the British press gushed over the film, ignoring the unsavory political undertones, particularly the left-leaning *Guardian* which would normally recoil at such totalitarian messages. Reassessment of the film didn't happen until years later, when people began to confront head on that this was an example of China projecting a very specific message to its people, and perhaps more importantly, to the rest of the world.[2]

This book aims to give the reader the ammunition needed to spot the clichés that Hollywood falls back on, to correct some of the most egregious errors, and to have a look at the behind-the-scenes stories of some of these historical dramas. There are thousands of them. For brevity's sake, I will focus mainly on English-language films. Other countries' films will get mentions, and there is a chapter on Asian cinema.

NOTES

1. Christopher Booker, *The Seven Basic Plots: Why We Tell Stories* (London: Bloomsbury Continuum, 2019), 5–6.
2. www.theguardian.com/about.

Chapter 1

It's All Greek to Me

The Ancient era is one of the rare periods of history that works around the world. Ancient China or Ancient Egypt are acceptable historical terms as is Ancient Greece. The issue is the time frame is vast. Looking at Europe, the Ancient era starts with the Minoans (whose civilizations began to emerge around 3500 BC) and goes all the way up to the fall of the Western Roman Empire at the end of the 400s AD. So, this era spans about four thousand years, more than the rest of the eras described here combined. To give you an idea about this length of time, you are closer in time to Cleopatra than she was to the building of the Great Pyramid.

With that said, most movies set in the ancient world tend to be over a roughly seven-hundred-year period, from the Persian invasion of Hellenic Greece around 500 BC up to the reign of Emperor Marcus Aurelius or Commodus, who died in 192 AD. Unless you know your history, the look and style of these films tend to merge vastly different time frames. For example, Alexander the Great could never have met Julius Caesar as they were separated by nearly three hundred years.

THE TEN COMMANDMENTS (1923)

In 2014 archaeologists in California discovered a sphinx statue. The strange thing is that they had been looking for it. This is the curious tale of Cecil B. DeMille's gigantic 1923 epic *The Ten Commandments*. DeMille understood that in the silent era, cinema was a purely visual art form, and as such, the more expansive, the more lavish, the larger the scale of the production, the more likely people would be to come and see his motion pictures. So, he put the story of Moses on film and nearly bankrupted himself in the process. The centerpiece was the City of the Pharaohs. Built in the Guadalupe Dunes on the California coast, the set featured four thirty-five-foot-tall statues of the pharaoh, twenty-one five-ton sphinxes, and a city wall 120 feet high. At its peak there were 2,500 actors, extras, carpenters, and laborers on set, with an additional 3,500 animals.[1]

Everything about this film was crazy. In the chariot-racing scenes, every crash was real and unscripted; those were real stuntmen (and horses) getting hurt. When DeMille ran out of money, he was forced to get a $500,000 loan (a huge sum of money at the time). In the end, the production cost $1.5 million, but it grossed more than $4.2 million, so it made its money back and more.

When filming was over, the problem was what to do with the gigantic set. The answer: bulldoze the sand dunes over it and bury it. And so, nearly a century later, archaeologists were looking for ancient Egyptian artifacts in California. None of these were meant to last; the props and sets were all paper, plaster, and plywood, but the fact that they were buried in sand and kept away from the elements and that California is hot and dry meant that there were remains all these decades later. This strange tale has itself been immortalized in the Peter Brosnan documentary *The Lost City of Cecil B. DeMille*.

DeMille was not about ensuring historical accuracy; he was all about getting the biggest bang for the buck. Scenes shot on the set are stupendous, and it is worth remembering that this was more than half a century before CGI sets and enhancements. The reason why someone looked like they were standing beside a giant statue is because they were. So, while DeMille delivered on the stupendous front, historically, it's a mess of dynastic styles mixed in with anything that looked exotic to the casual viewer. No historical care had been taken, and as such, it has no historical merit.

There is an important side note to this: When Egyptian hieroglyphs began to be translated in the nineteenth century, the Vatican had an attack of nerves because it realized that after two thousand years of hearing biblical stories from one perspective, people could hear them now from another. As more Egyptian texts were translated in the twentieth and twenty-first centuries, among many surprising discoveries was that there have been precisely zero references to Moses in all translated Egyptian texts, and that the pyramids were built by artisans and stonemasons (we've even found many of their tombs) and not by slaves. There is no mention of a great exodus, and unhelpfully in the Bible, only one Egyptian ruler is named (Shishak, actually Shoshenq I) and not Ramesses the Great. It seems Moses to the story of the foundation of the Jewish nation is a bit like King Arthur is to the story of Britain. Therefore, we can probably give DeMille something of a pass as he was basically filming a legend rather than hard history. However, just because moviemaking was in its infancy doesn't mean it wasn't ambitious, and historical dramas were one of the first genres created. Indeed, what is widely considered to be the very first proper movie with a narrative structure is *The Great Train Robbery* (1903), a cowboy movie. There will be more on it in two chapters to come; the film is that important. Pretty impressive for a film that lasts less than a quarter of an hour.

BEN-HUR: A TALE OF THE CHRIST (1925)

Two years after *The Ten Commandments*, the first (full-length) film adaptation of the book *Ben-Hur: A Tale of the Christ* arrived in theaters. This 1925 production dwarfed Cecil B. DeMille's in terms of ambition, with a budget just under the entire gross of *The Ten Commandments* (it went on to gross more than $10 million, and once again, showed the public's insatiable appetite for spectacle). The story of a Jewish prince called Ben-Hur, whose boyhood friend was the son of a Roman tribune (official), the film has action and excitement, but ultimately it all leads to the real star of the show, Jesus. It's a parable for the modern age about the era when the parables were created. Again, anything that looked vaguely era appropriate was carted onto the set, but now there was also an impressive working model that enabled depictions of naval combat.

BEN-HUR (1959)

Ben-Hur was made again in the 1950s, now in color, with sound, and starring Charlton Heston. Is it epic? Yes, the famous chariot race still holds up; it's a very well-made action set piece. Did Roman chariot racing look like this? Not really. The stadium (hippodrome) is pretty accurate, with the metal dolphins used to count off the laps being an unusually accurate detail. But bladed wheels (a real Hollywood fixation) are a flat no, and without getting too technical, the chariots themselves and the techniques to drive them are also inaccurate. For example, the riders tended to have the reins lashed around their body in the real races. But again, the film was based on a novel evoking tales from the Bible, so is it history in the first place? But like its silent predecessor, it caused a huge amount of excitement, and more importantly, it was a monster hit. Its initial release grossed more than $140 million and that was in 1959 dollars.

The exuberance from the crowds, however, could be said to be underplayed. A second century AD charioteer called Gaius Appuleius Diocles is justifiably regarded as the richest athlete who ever lived. His lifetime earnings amounted to roughly six thousand pounds of gold and over thirty-four thousand tons of wheat.[2] But there was a dark side to chariot racing, best illustrated in the Nica riot of 532 AD. As in the film, team names were colors:

the Blues, Greens, Reds, and Whites. Fans of the age were as fanatically loyal to their color as modern football fans are to their teams. Cutting a long story short, Emperor Justinian worried that fans were becoming politically organized (particularly the Greens and Blues). Small-scale riots led to murders but not the apprehension of the suspects, all of which culminated in a massive riot in January. Areas of Constantinople were burned and looted, and in the end, Justinian sent in the imperial bodyguard to quell the rioters. By the time the dust settled, there had been substantial damage to his capital, and around thirty thousand race fans were dead on the streets. This is the first example of real history being more interesting than the Hollywood story, and yet it has never been made into a film. Many great historical tales have yet to be told in the medium of cinema while the same old stories continue to be trundled out over and over again. *Ben-Hur* was remade yet again in 2016. I'll save you two hours: It's terrible and bombed at the box office.

The 1959 *Ben-Hur* really annoyed Kirk Douglas because he wanted the juicy title role but lost out to Heston.[3] So, he made it his business to find a similar story, a "sword-and-sandals" epic, where one man stands up to the might of an empire.

SPARTACUS (1960)

Enter the story of Spartacus in a novel by Howard Fast. Douglas loved it but had difficulty getting the script into shape and hired Dalton Trumbo to work on it. The basic story (and what really happened) was that Spartacus started a slave revolt in a gladiatorial school against the Romans. He and his fellow gladiators picked up support from other slaves until he eventually had an army capable of beating the Roman legions. His luck eventually ran out, and he and his men were captured and crucified.

The problem with Trumbo was that he had been blacklisted. In 1950s and 1960s America, there was real concern about the threat of communism, the "Red Menace." It was regarded as the antithesis of everything a God-fearing capitalist in America loved. The House Un-American Activities Committee (HUAC) was led by Senator Joe McCarthy, whose mission was to root out communist agitators in the moral rats' nest that was Hollywood. Careers were destroyed as people, who were true Americans but with communist sympathies, were grilled in committee hearings as if they had been spying for Stalin himself. Trumbo was a talented writer and Douglas was a big enough star not only to get him for his project, but to give him an onscreen screenwriting credit. So now we have a historical film that reflects real Hollywood history. *Spartacus* is the perfect allegory for the McCarthy years.

Anthony Mann was hired to be the director, but he was fired after just a week of shooting on Douglas's orders. Douglas had already worked with up-and-coming director Stanley Kubrick on the highly controversial *Paths of Glory* and wanted him for his very own *Ben-Hur/Spartacus*. For Kubrick, *Spartacus* was his midpoint movie. While he was still a director for hire on major motion pictures and hadn't yet reached the obsessive heights of his later career, his care for historical accuracy and attention to detail set him apart from his peers and everything that had come earlier. Kubrick clashed with the cinematographer Russell Metty who, at one point, threatened to quit, but Metty was convinced to stay and won an Oscar for his work.[4] *Spartacus* won a total of four Oscars, but *Ben-Hur* won a joint best-of-all-time with eleven.

The thing about slaves is that they aren't seen as important, and their stories are not recorded. However, Spartacus was a slave who led an army that threatened Rome itself, which meant he got a mention in various manuscripts, but for the most part, his story is guesswork. Plutarch describes Spartacus as "a Thracian of nomadic stock," but he was writing about seventy years after the events.[5] One immediate area of historical inaccuracy was that Spartacus was a type of gladiator known as a murmillo. In the film we see him fighting as a stereotypical gladiator because a murmillo had his head in a big brass helmet with a face grille, armor on one arm, sword and shield on the other. In other words, dressed authentically, viewers would not have been able to see Kirk Douglas's face. Spartacus's gladiatorial role was switched for practical reasons of box office: Douglas's face was too handsome to be caged.

After leading a slave rebellion and defeating multiple Roman armies, Spartacus could have left the Italian peninsula and gone on to settle down anywhere he pleased, but he didn't. He stayed and fought and eventually lost. What was his motivation? We don't know, but that answer isn't good enough for Hollywood. Critically, the Roman writers all agree that he died in the final battle and his body was never identified. But the most famous scene of the film occurs when the Romans want to know who Spartacus is, and as Douglas stands to reveal himself, so do the other slaves, who all declare, "I am Spartacus." It's a great ending to a movie, but it never happened in real life, although it is true that the remaining six thousand slaves and gladiators were crucified along the Appian Way. This unity in the face of adversity is clearly a metaphor for Trumbo's victimization over his socialist ideals and, perhaps, a yearning for the kind of support Spartacus had that Trumbo never received when facing the HUAC.

The events of what has become known as the Third Servile War were all happening in 1970s BC, so the executions had no Christian connotations at the time. Crucifixion was a horrible way to die, and the executions acted as a warning to others, but of course, a modern viewer can't help but see them as a religious sacrifice. It's also worth pointing out that prior to the movie *Spartacus*, the Roman slave was not a well-known figure in popular culture. Indeed, this is one occasion when the movie made the historical figure famous.

CLEOPATRA (1963)

Ben-Hur came out in 1959, *Spartacus* in 1960, and then there was *Cleopatra*, which began filming in 1960 . . . but wasn't finished and released until 1963. Cleopatra VII of the Ptolemaic dynasty had already been the subject of four other films, stretching back into the silent era. Once again, as her title implies, there were a whole bunch of other Cleopatras that movies could have fixated on, but instead, Hollywood went straight to number VII. To be fair, Cleopatra VII marks the end of the Egyptian dynasties, a way of life that stretched back three thousand years. Also, her story intertwines with one of the most famous people in history, Julius Caesar, and it's always helped that Shakespeare wrote a play about this. Cleopatra was genuinely important in history, and events around her were exactly the kind of epic clash of armies and civilizations that everyone since Cecil B. DeMille had been looking for.

Cleopatra was Walter Wanger's baby. Wanger had been a major studio producer since the silent era. He went into coproduction with 20th Century-Fox, and after years of wrangling, writing, and complex negotiations with some of the biggest stars in the world, they were ready to shoot in 1960. Initial filming was in Pinewood, England, but with the weather bitingly cold and Elizabeth Taylor in costumes suitable for the hot Egyptian sun, the star got a cold that developed into full-blown meningitis. At this point 20th Century-Fox was forced to shut down production after sixteen weeks of filming at a cost of $7 million (not adjusted for inflation) that had resulted in only ten minutes of film.[6] To put that into context, the budget for an average movie at the time was less than that—and Wanger was just getting started. After recovering from meningitis, Taylor caught pneumonia and had to have a tracheotomy. The whole production was moved to somewhere warmer (and presumed to be cheaper) in Cinecittà in Rome, but the entire project was moving from historical drama to disaster movie.

Why is Richard Burton in the World War II movie *The Longest Day*? Because he was literally doing nothing during the time he was meant to be filming *Cleopatra* and wanted to work (his cameo is awesome). *Cleopatra* eventually came out to big box office and good reviews in 1963 and won a total of four Oscars at the 1964 ceremony. The colossal costs, estimated to be $50 million, made it the most expensive movie ever made; it probably still is if adjusted for inflation. Eventually the money was made back, but careers were ruined, and finances were shattered.

So, how historically accurate is it? The answer is, it's not bad, but there are plenty of problems. Perhaps the greatest moment is the amazing arrival of Cleopatra in Rome. It was a sight to behold in 1963, and the real entrance by the real woman in the first century BC was just as impactful. In both instances the whole point was to impress, to dazzle and distract. It is a moment of pure Hollywood that the impact of the filming of this occasion exactly matches the intended impact of a moment two thousand years old.

Of course, the costumes are all historically incorrect: For example, we have Romans wearing armor when there was no battle. Many of the costumes are made from modern fabrics and do not reflect that period textiles would have been coarser as they were all hand woven. And we know what Cleopatra VII looked like as we have a bust which shows an impressive nose, so the producers weren't going for accuracy by duplication, more for a means to show off Elizabeth Taylor.

And then there's the whitewashing: Richard O'Sullivan, who played the young pharaoh Ptolemy XIII, would later become best known for his role in the British sitcom *Man About the House*. While he was not ethnically Egyptian, the same could be said about Elizabeth Taylor in the title role. Although the Ptolemy dynasty descended from one of Alexander the Great's Greek generals, today there would be a huge conversation about the lack of ethnic representation.

Spartacus used subtle racism to good effect. Everyone in the film spoke English (which was not, of course, the language of the era), but Spartacus and his friends were all played by Americans with their familiar and, therefore, "friendlier" accents, while the Romans were played by Brits, who with their "foreign accents" (to the intended American audience) conveyed "difference" and "otherness" in a negative way. Brits being used to denote the bad guys can be said to have started here with *Spartacus*. This kind of racial slurring came to a crescendo of cliché and brilliance in the action movies of the 1980s and 1990s, perhaps best personified by Alan Rickman in *Die Hard* (although a theater actor for years, that was Rickman's first-ever film role).

The next big issue with *Cleopatra* arises because of the film's budget and scope—everything looks fabulous. The same can be said of *The Ten Commandments* and earlier films. Enormous amounts of money were spent to build impressive sets, so everything would look as good as possible. In other words, nothing looks lived-in. These are the practical reasons why everything is clean and shiny, but it could be argued that we are seeing the inadvertent visualization of something more profound. Since the fall of the Western Roman Empire in the fifth century AD, there has been a constant yearning for a return to the old days. Renaissance painters revolutionized the arts in the late medieval era, but as sensational as the works of Michelangelo or Da Vinci are, they are looking to the past not the future. Tales from the Bible or the Roman era permeate the great Renaissance works. In central Europe there was the rise of the Holy Roman Empire, essentially a group of states that wanted to emulate the lost empire of "civilization" (although it is worth pointing out that the Romans themselves thought the Germanic tribes across the Rhine were the very definition of barbaric). The reality was, as the historical joke goes, it wasn't holy, it wasn't Roman, and it wasn't an empire. But apart from that it was a really good name. Paris, Berlin, and even Washington, DC are all awash with civic buildings designed to resemble the pagan temples of Athens or Rome, built two thousand years earlier. Westerners, whether they know it or not, worship the ancient civilizations of Hellenic Greece and Rome. With all that in mind, when we hear "Middle Ages," we tend to think of mud and superstition; by contrast, "Hellenic Greece" conveys images of philosophers and white marble Doric columns. So, cover the sets of ancient Rome with dung and dirt . . . never!

A final error so common in any film featuring armor is men wearing it when they are not on the battlefield. This is a cardinal sin for historians, one frequently committed in movies. Anyone who has ever worn armor will tell you that it's good to have for protection, but it is also extremely uncomfortable; it's metal, so the wearer is either too hot or too cold, plus it's bulky and restrictive. No one would wear it unless they had to, so only in battle. While Rex Harrison may look great as Julius Caesar in full battle regalia, there is no way this portrayal is historically accurate.

After *Cleopatra*'s eye-watering costs, the sword-and-sandals epics began to decline in popularity. There aren't any of note from the 1970s to the 1990s, when they were regarded as too expensive or too old-fashioned. If you had a choice to see *ET* or *The Fall of the Roman Empire*, it's clear which one the moviegoers of the 1980s would choose. But then, in 1999, Ridley Scott decided to update the genre for the modern generation.

GLADIATOR (2000)

A few years earlier Scott had been shown a copy of *Pollice Verso* (Turned Thumb), by the French artist Jean-Léon Gérôme. It's an oil painting of one of those murmillo gladiators standing over a defeated enemy, looking up at the emperor, who is turning his thumb. Scott, who studied at the Royal College of Art, was always a visual person (which explains why his films, even the less successful ones, always look beautiful) and became inspired to make a movie about gladiators which, apart from *Spartacus*, had not often been done. So, after filming in the muddy forests of England and the baking heat of

Malta with talented but difficult leading man Russell Crowe (originally it was meant to be Antonio Banderas, which is why he's called "the Spaniard" in the movie) and Oliver Reed inconveniently dying during the shoot, Scott pulled together one of the greatest sword-and-sandals epics of all time, *Gladiator*.[7]

Gladiator is the perfect example of fun before facts. Is this film historically accurate? In some ways, yes, but in many ways no. But is it a thrilling ride where we are transported to ancient times and put right at the heart of the action? Absolutely. Even the tagline screams "gripping": "The general who became a slave. The slave who became a gladiator. The gladiator who defied an emperor." Who wouldn't want to see that? When Maximus screams at the onlookers, "Are you not entertained?" the cinema audience mentally shouts back, yes! Maximus Decimus Meridius (the hero of the story) is made up, so he can't be historically accurate, but he does interact with two real Roman emperors. It was said that Richard Harris was so mesmerizing as Marcus Aurelius that his performance won him the role of Dumbledore in the Harry Potter franchise (Harris did the first two films before he died, and as good as Michael Gambon is, he's #notmyDumbledore). Harris is contemplative and positively drips charisma. This is completely on point for the real Marcus Aurelius as, apart from being an emperor and general, he was also a Stoic philosopher. It's a pretty accurate depiction right down to the fact that he did, indeed, die on campaign in the Rhine area, although it's important to note that not since Vespasian had there been an emperor with a legitimate son groomed as the heir to the throne. So, for his final two years, he and Commodus were joint rulers. Commodus didn't have to kill his father to become emperor, nor did he go on that campaign.

Gladiator starts with a battle. The accompanying music could be Hans Zimmer's most rousing piece of music ever, and this is an epic scene showcasing the might of the Roman legions in their prime. Or is it?

I have two friends who were extras in that battle, and they told some stories I'm not sure have been captured before: The extras were cold and bored and started to play soccer. When the props manager saw what was happening, he told Scott to stop them, something they were reluctant to do until it was pointed out that the ball being used was the $10,000 prosthetic head that would be the trigger for battle. The game quickly came to an end, but I didn't find out who was winning the match.

A second story comes from just before the filming of the battle (I am getting this secondhand, so I can't verify). Scott approached the "Germanic barbarians" and reminded them that this was just a film. They were to run down the hill, screaming and shouting and waving their weapons, to make it look good for the cameras, but once they got to the Roman line, they shouldn't go in too hard; it's make-believe after all. Then he went to the extras playing

Roman soldiers and explained that the barbarians were going to come rushing down the hill and to really let them have it.

Meanwhile, back to what's on screen, and while the battle is awesome, it's a mess historically. The heavy ballistae and similar engines of war all existed, but they were almost always used in sieges. It was a lot of heavy equipment to drag around the forests of Germany on the off-chance you might come across an enemy tribe. So, no, they weren't a standard sight on a field of battle at the time.

This is the first, but definitely not the last mention of fire arrows. Cinema is many things, but it is first and foremost a visual medium, and arrows don't film very well; they tend to get lost against the background of sky. Did fire arrows exist? Yes, but this is where I'm going to get technical. The short bow of the Roman era had a limited range. This was still a time when slingshots were used because they could, at times, outrange the bows. The later composite bows, crossbows, and longbows were the ones that had real range. Next, arrows had multiple different heads for multiple different targets. The standard diamond-shaped arrowhead was perfect for hunting and for use against lightly armored infantry. In the Middle Ages they also had arrowheads in the shape of a crescent moon. These were anti-horse. Arrows spin in flight (something you never see even with the special effects shots); if a spinning crescent hits a horse, well, let's just say it's going to hurt. The anti-armor arrows of the longbow in the Middle Ages needed penetrating power and, as such, looked like six-inch spikes stuck on the end of an arrow. Finally, fire arrows: Behind the head is what looks like a wire cage where cloth or gauze is lodged and lit, but there are two problems:

1. How do you get the cloth to stay on?
2. A big ball of cloth will make the arrow less aerodynamic and so reduce effective range.

With that in mind, there is no reason to use fire arrows over a normal arrow unless it is a siege, and the attackers want to set fire to the target in front of them. Further, every time the leader in a film orders archers to "fire," it's anachronistic. That's what you tell a bunch of guys with guns to do. The correct term is to "loose." Now you know more than you ever wanted to know about arrows.[8]

A final strange point on *Gladiator*'s opening battle: It uses sound effects from another historical, but very different movie. The war chants of the barbarians are genuine, except they are from Zulu warriors in the 1964 movie *Zulu*. Once you notice it, it's a distracting choice.

The beating heart of this movie is the Colosseum, and it is name-checked several times, but that was not its name. Everyone at the time called it the

Flavian Amphitheater. It's roughly 50 percent too big in the film, but the retractable shades at the top were a real feature. And it's here that Scott shows his British roots and the influence of the British Museum's armor collection, an impressive array of artifacts. The trouble is that the museum's pieces are from the wrong time and place for this film, or in the case of the famous helmet Russell Crowe throws away to reveal his identity to Commodus, completely made up, with no archaeological evidence for such a spiked, full-face helm. There is, however, a real Roman artifact in the movie: the signet ring Connie Nielsen wears she bought in an antiques shop in Britain, which turned out to be genuine.[9]

Then we come to Joaquin Rafael Bottom, early on in his career called Leaf Phoenix, brother to River Phoenix and now better known as Joaquin Phoenix. Aged twenty-five, he knew this was his big break but was intimidated by the giants of the industry around him. This was apparently resolved when Harris, Reed, and Phoenix got drunk (which was, sadly, both Harris's and Reed's main flaw). Phoenix plays Commodus, a sniveling, spoiled brat, who fixes a fight in the Flavian Amphitheater and is wary of his scheming sister Lucilla. This isn't far from the truth, particularly about the sister, who did seem to be part of a plot to overthrow Commodus. Phoenix put in an incredible performance, after which he never looked back and went on to star in such great films as *Her*, *Walk the Line*, and his Oscar-winning role, *Joker*.

However, Commodus ruled for twelve years, not the year or so implied in the film. By the 190s he was displaying ever more erratic and megalomaniacal behaviors. He had statues put up everywhere comparing him to Hercules (Heraclius), and he did fight in the Flavian Amphitheater against weaker foes, sometimes having his body coated in gold leaf before he did so.[10]

Eventually the Roman aristocracy had had enough, and he was assassinated. But unlike the film, he was poisoned (which he vomited up) and then strangled in his bathhouse by a wrestler named Narcissus. However, what happened next may come as a surprise because in 193 AD, known as the year of the five emperors, different factions vied for the title of emperor. Commodus may have been outrageous, but he was better than civil war.

Two brief points: First, the core of the movie is the argument of the emperor versus the senate. This was a huge conversation in the first century BC, but by 180 AD the imperial system was too ensconced to be considered optional. Indeed, had Maximus's last wishes been carried out, the whole of Roman history would have changed. Second, the thumbs and the fate of gladiators: We know that thumbs up and down were signals in the games, but it is a surprisingly contentious issue among historians as to what they signified. The simple answer is we will never know for sure, but to a modern audience thumbs up would only mean a good outcome, so that's the way it's used.

Gladiator was a huge box-office hit and won five Oscars, including Best Picture and Best Actor. Hollywood took note; it looked like a dead horse needed flogging. And so, after decades of hibernation, the sword-and-sandals epic returned, and this time it went even further back in time.

TROY (2004)

Four years after *Gladiator*, Wolfgang Petersen released *Troy*. The story of the Trojan Wars has two main sources: the *Iliad*, attributed to Homer and written in about the eighth century BC about events happening around 1200 BC, and the *Aeneid*, written in the late first century BC. We are closer in time to Chaucer than Virgil was to Homer when writing the *Aeneid*.

Even in Ancient Greece there was debate about whether the Trojan Wars marked the end or the beginning. Was this the last time the gods interfered in the politics of man, so marking the end of the age of myth—or were the wars the first historical records of the deeds of the Greeks and, as such, the start of the age of history? The fact that this debate has been going for a long time is important because the 2004 moviemakers were so heavily influenced by *Gladiator* that they tried to make a legend "historically accurate," so much so that there was even an exhibition of the armor and costumes at the British Museum to give it a kind of historical stamp of approval.[1112] They also decided to take out all the stuff about the gods, therefore, taking out many key moments and motivators and entirely misunderstanding the story.

That is not to say that there aren't some noteworthy moments. Peter O'Toole turns up to do a Richard Harris and has one electrifying scene with Brad Pitt, a masterclass in acting, before promptly dying in the movie. Both Brad Pitt and Eric Bana worked exceptionally hard to build their physiques to become the embodiment of Achilles and Hector, and their battle correctly uses spears and shields as the main weapons. The reason for this is a technical one (and worth remembering when we come to the final movie in this chapter). Unlike the Roman era, all these Greek stories happened in the Bronze Age, and bronze is much softer than iron. As such, swords of the time were quick to dull and could even bend. They were a weapon of last resort; the spear and shield were infinitely better weapons.

The story of Troy is integral to the story of Europe. Children learn about the Trojan horse in primary school; it's even in the 2014 animated film *Mr Peabody & Sherman*. In 2022, British theater company Punch Drunk introduced their most ambitious production yet, and it is based on the aftermath of the Trojan Wars, only updating the styling to be a kind of neo-noir.

Troy was not only important for European culture, but archaeology was literally invented by Schliemann in his search for the site of Troy. The reason why the Iliad is called that is because the Greek for Troy is Ilium, and yet we know the Hittite satellite town it refers to was called Wilusa by the locals. This story is constantly being retold, and if someone wants to do a version without the gods, why not? Okay, the result is unsatisfying, but now we know why people keep the gods in the story.

Trying to make the story of Troy historically accurate is like trying to make King Arthur historically accurate (which they also tried in the 2004 film *King Arthur*, and that didn't work either, but more on that in the next chapter). It was doomed to fail because it's a legend, and the point is to tell a tale, not to make sure the helmets are the right shape. Also, alpacas are from South America, so if the aim is to get the facts right, don't bring in an animal from a different continent, unknown to the locals for another 2,500 years.

And now we come to the Trojan horse. There is a line in the *Iliad* that says the Trojans had to dismantle part of the gate to allow the wooden horse to enter. Let's be honest. I think once we've all heard the story of the Trojan horse, we tend to think the Trojans were pretty dumb. How did they fall for it? It has also led to the phrase "beware of Greeks bearing gifts." But this one line from the text can mean a different, less fun but more likely explanation: the Trojan horse was a siege engine. And what the *Iliad* could be describing is the first catapult or maybe a battering ram with a canopy. Siege engines were often given names. My favorite is a trebuchet, constructed under the orders of King Edward I of England, called War Wolf. The idea of the Trojans succumbing to never-before-seen innovative siege technology is perhaps a more satisfying story idea than a city tricked by a suspiciously large "we're sorry" present.

ALEXANDER (2004)

In the same year, there was yet another historical epic, *Alexander*, directed by Oliver Stone and starring Colin Farrell, amply supported by the scenery-chewing Angelina Jolie as his mother. Much was made of Farrell keeping his Irish accent, which I think Stone deflected brilliantly because Alexander was from Macedon, a territory to the north of the Greek city-states, which was looked down on by the citizens of Athens, Thebes, and Sparta. So, Farrell having a different regional accent to others in the film was a clever device because, once again, if they were going to do it absolutely authentically, they would all have to be speaking Ἑλληνική. Another interesting anachronism is the fact that the mosaic map of the world was annotated in Latin, again so everyone's brains didn't explode, but it is, of course, the wrong language. Further, eight years of campaigning are condensed into a few hours. The main battle scene is reasonably close to what happened, and the use of an eagle to give, literally, a bird's-eye view of the battle is a genius flourish by a director who has created some electrifying movies.

Another interesting decision was to be upfront about Alexander's bisexuality (Achilles in *Troy* didn't have a male lover). This completely agreed-upon fact sparked the people of modern Greece to protest furiously and threaten to ban the movie on the grounds that it was denigrating Alexander.[13] This is a classic example of uncomfortable facts annoying . . . someone. Good or bad, love it or hate it, that's the way it was. To pretend otherwise makes you the bad guy.

The noble gestures to one side, the film is a disaster. There have been numerous versions released on DVD and Blu-ray, including one that's nearly three and a half hours long, but no amount of additional material can save this well-meaning but hopeless mess. Perhaps at least some of the problems can be explained by the fact that Stone was in a race with Baz Luhrmann, who was also trying to get his version of the great man, starring Leonardo DiCaprio, into production. Best intentions do not lead to the best film. All of these 2004 films underperformed or flopped. Suddenly *Gladiator* looked like something of an anomaly. But then, one modestly budgeted film in 2006 tore up the sword-and-sandals playbook and showed that there was still life in the old dog yet.

300 (2006)

I was lucky enough to co-present with Tom Holland (the historian, not Spider-Man) a showing of *300* in front of an audience, with a Q&A afterward. Holland always likes to tweak the noses of established theories and when asked, "What's the most historically accurate film made?" he replied, "This one." What he went on to say was that trying to be 100 percent historically accurate in a film is folly: It can't be done. So instead, the director's job is to make the film feel the way the people in the story felt at the time. And with that in mind, *300* does just that. In terms of the events and what happens when, it's surprisingly accurate, and the introduction explaining the Spartan way of life and the Agoge is about as good a summary as there can be in three minutes. To the Greeks at Thermopylae (the hot gates), fighting these different armies from places they had never heard of, wearing outfits they had never seen before, all of this was completely alien; the enemy might as well have been orcs and trolls. And as for the historically inaccurate Spartan outfits, swords, and tactics (they start off in the correct phalanx formation, but that isn't very cinematic, so very quickly, they are doing slow motion

Spartan-fu), it's all just pure fantasy. Would the Spartans have loved their depiction? Yes, absolutely. Gerard Butler is every inch what a Spartan wanted to be and how he wanted to be seen (and Butler worked hard to get the right body). But obviously Ancient Greece was lacking in the protein shake, baby oil, and waxing salons.

Once again, a movie of events from thousands of years ago irritated the people of a modern country. This time it was Iran, saying that it did not reflect history and was Western propaganda.[14] They were right, but in a way, that's what the events from 480 BC were all about. Had Xerxes sent in a smaller army, perhaps cavalry based, it could well have outflanked the fissiparous Greeks and beaten them before they could get into their armada of ships or set up holding actions at Thermopylae. But Xerxes wanted to intimidate his enemies into submission, and while there was a period of success (don't forget, the Spartans lost and Athens burned), he ultimately had to retreat to Anatolia. So, the West earned the right to do what it wanted without Persian interference.

The film does make one practical adjustment: The Spartans are delayed from going to war because of a religious festival referred to as the Carnea. This is correct, but the Carnea was, in fact, the Olympic Games and they were sacred; it was unthinkable to wage war while they were taking place. I'm guessing the Carnea reference was introduced because "you can't fight while the Olympics are on" makes it sound as if the Spartans are all at home, sitting on the sofa, eating handfuls of chips, watching TV.

The film does point out that there were other Greeks fighting, but the reason it's all about the three hundred Spartans is because once it was obvious they were surrounded, the others left, and the Spartans remained to be finished off.

The movie is peppered with genuine Spartan comments, almost as if they had anticipated the invention of the action movie one-liner:

Persian: "Our arrows shall blot out the sun."

Spartan: "Good, then we fight in the shade."

This is a real exchange from 2,500 years ago, preserved by Herodotus and now in a modern film.

The whole tale is told in flashback by Dilios, one of the three hundred Spartans who had to leave the battle due to a wound in the eye. He is treated with reverence in the film, but that is a case where liberties have been taken and the reality is even more interesting. Toward the end of the battle, two Spartans were told to leave by Leonidas because both had problems with their eyes. They were Eurytus and Aristodemus (Dilios is made up). Eurytus was totally blind, but he turned back and fought to the death with the other 298. Aristodemus made it back home and was promptly mocked, for had not a blind man turned back to fight? He had an infection in just one eye, so why didn't he go back? The movie shows, correctly, Aristodemus (or in the movie's case Dilios) there at the Battle of Platea a year later, itching for revenge, part of the phalanx of an entire Spartan army (plus thousands of Greek allies). However, in reality, Aristodemus, having been mocked for a whole year, was so eager to get into the fight and prove himself that he broke ranks and got into the Persian front line first and was eventually cut down. The Spartans did not see this as an act of bravery but as a breakdown in discipline, his solitary actions endangering the Spartan phalanx formation with a dangerous gap. As such, the mockery of poor old Aristodemus continued even after his death.[15]

300 is perhaps the only example of a film with a gritty view of the ancient world. As mentioned earlier, if a fortune is spent on a film set, the makers want all the money there on screen and they don't want scruffy. *300* looks tired and worn, like an actual place where people lived and died . . . whatever its other inaccuracies.

I'm not sure I agree with Tom Holland's thesis about historical accuracy, but what I can say is that *300* is clearly hyperstylized and does not reflect reality. The film was cheap to make as everything was done on a small soundstage with a lot of greenscreen. It is not meant to be taken as a historical documentary, but more a graphic novel come to life.

MULAN (1998, 2020)

Even Hollywood can recognize when a subject has been mined to exhaustion and it is time to turn its attention to another ancient civilization: China. Even better news toward the end of the twentieth century, China was becoming a bigger and bigger market for movies. So, it was inevitable that at some point ancient Chinese stories would be remade for Western audiences, and the most famous is the "Ballad of Mulan," a story first recorded around 400 AD during the Northern Wei era of Chinese history. Mulan has been a perennial favorite in Chinese folklore, perhaps reaching its zenith in the sixteenth century. The story is simple: Chinese lands are under attack, so the emperor must conscript men into the army. But Mulan's father is old and will inevitably die in battle, and her brother is just a child, so to save the family, Mulan disguises herself as a man and joins up. Various hijinks and heroics ensue.

In 1998 Disney was on something of a roller coaster with its animation. This was the decade of megahits like *The Lion King*, *Beauty and the Beast*, and *Aladdin*, but there were also box-office disappointments like *The Hunchback of Notre Dame*. The usual Western fairy tales had all been done; it was time to look farther afield, and this story of female bravery worked well with the Disney formula.

The largely Asian voice cast was a progressive step, and the animation was sumptuous peak Disney. There were no real attempts to make things look like they were specific to the Northern Wei dynasty; anything "Chinese" was good enough. But let's not be too harsh. This is a movie where Eddie Murphy voiced a small dragon called Mushu, so it's not trying to be real history.

1998's *Mulan* was a hit, not as big as the likes of *The Lion King*, but it had a fan base, and people returned to it over the years. In the 2000s, Disney started creating live-action versions of their classic animated movies. We can debate how "live action" something like *The Jungle Book* or *The Lion King* could be, but *Mulan* was an obvious one to do. The story of female empowerment with a non-white central role had aged well. So in 2020, we got live-action *Mulan,* starring Liu Yifei. Mushu the talking dragon was out, but martial arts were in. No expense was spared, and Disney was expecting big things from the tale of the warrior woman. This time things did not go well.

Undeniably, a key issue was COVID-19: many movie theaters around the world were closed, so in most markets its main release was on its streaming service, Disney+. But other controversies surrounded it: Liu Yifei had been vocal in her support of the Chinese government's crackdown on the Hong Kong protestors, and Disney never wants to be in the midst of a political debate.[16] It got worse. Some of the movie was filmed in the Xinjiang province where the Uyghur minority lived. The Chinese government wants uniformity, and an ethnically different Muslim minority is regarded as something to suppress, not embrace. As a result, there are multiple allegations of human rights' violations, many carried out in the so-called reeducation camps.[17] One of those camps is mentioned in the "special thanks" section of the movie and caused a PR nightmare.

Disney was hoping for a theatrical release in China (a major movie market by 2020), but its potential audiences didn't exactly flock to see it . . . not because of any of the controversies, but because, from a Chinese perspective, it was a rather average retelling of a well-known story, with mediocre martial arts. No country likes another country telling their stories as they will never feel authentic. That was the problem here.

NOTES

1. Peter Brosnan, *The Lost City of Cecil B. DeMille* (documentary), 2016.
2. Jem Duducu, *The Romans in 100 Facts* (Gloucestershire, UK: Amberley Publishing, 2015), 30.

3. Kirk Douglas, *I Am Spartacus!: Making a Film, Breaking the Blacklist* (New York: Open Road Media, 2012), 15.

4. Douglas, *I Am Spartacus!*, 27.

5. Plutarch, *Life of Crassus*, Loeb Classical Library edition, 1916, 8–11.

6. Dina Gachman, *George Lucas's Blockbusting: A Decade-by-Decade Survey of Timeless Movies Including Untold Secrets of Their Financial and Cultural Success* (New York: HarperCollins, 2010), 21.

7. Ridley Scott, director, "Making of" documentary, *Gladiator* (Dreamworks, 2000, 2001), DVD.

8. Jem Duducu, *Slinkys and Snake Bombs: Weird but True Historical Facts* (Gloucestershire, UK: Amberley Publishing, 2021), 129.

9. Scott, "Making of" documentary, *Gladiator*.

10. Duducu, *Romans in 100 Facts*, 28.

11. Wolfgang Petersen, director, "Audio Commentary," *Troy* (Warner Bros. Pictures, 2004, 2005), DVD.

12. *The Myth of Troy* exhibition, British Museum, 2004.

13. Helena Smith, "Legal Threat Over 'Gay' Alexander," *The Guardian*, November 22, 2004.

14. Associated Press, "Iranians Outraged Over Hit Movie '300,'" nbcnews.com, March 13, 2007.

15. Tom Holland, *Persian Fire*, new ed. (London: Abacus, 2006), 407.

16. Hannah Sparks, "'Mulan' Star Liu Yifei's Support for Hong Kong Police Sparks Disney Boycott," *New York Post*, August 16, 2019.

17. *OHCHR Assessment of Human Rights Concerns in the Xinjiang Uyghur Autonomous Region, People's Republic of China*, August 31, 2022.

Chapter 2

Ye Olde Middle Ages

The term Middle Ages is a much-contested one. They usually refer to a period that starts around the fall of Rome (late 400s AD), although the first few centuries can be referred to as the Dark Ages (it's a deliberately derogatory term that belies a pro-Roman bias, but you get the idea). But roughly from 500 AD to 1500 AD, Europe tended to be run as a feudal system. The monarch's powers were absolute, and there was tension between royal power and the religious power of the Church.

Warfare was largely fought the same way throughout this period, with heavy cavalry, archers, castles, and increasingly complex armor the usual order of the day. While gunpowder was first decisive in a military campaign in 1453 at the Siege of Constantinople, guns and cannons were still a novelty at this time. Similarly, the Church's stranglehold on religious truth began to be questioned from 1515, with Martin Luther challenging the theological validity of the Pope's position of primacy.

To further compound this, there is the problem of the Renaissance. There is an argument that while the beautiful art of the late 1400s and 1500s is awe inspiring, it did nothing to change the world. The Sistine Chapel is spectacular, but other than a few hundred fabulously rich and powerful men, who saw it? It wasn't a tourist attraction in the 1500s, and Michelangelo's art didn't change the lives of France's peasantry.

In the previous chapter, there were a lot of enormous film sets, a lot of Oscars won, and a lot of serious topics. The one genre never mentioned was comedy. I will add one comedy fact to that chapter right now. With all the huge delays and changing of location for *Cleopatra*, some of the sets were left just lying around and were eventually reused for the British bawdy Carry On team for one of their best films, *Carry On Cleo*. The film makes no attempts to be historically accurate (people outside of the Roman Empire appear to be living in the Mesolithic and not the Iron Age), but it's a lot of fun and has that great line from Kenneth Williams (who was a better Julius Caesar than Rex Harrison), "Infamy, infamy, they've all got it in for me."

MONTY PYTHON AND THE HOLY GRAIL (1975)

So, let's start with a classic comedy about the Middle Ages, *Monty Python and the Holy Grail*. In 1969, a group of comedians who had been working on British TV for years came together with an American animator to create the cult surrealist show *Monty Python's Flying Circus*. Nobody had ever seen anything like it. John Cleese left after three seasons on the grounds that they had begun to repeat themselves, and he felt the job was done. There was a fourth season that was okay, but it did have a Cleese-shaped hole in it. After this, the supremely talented group broke up to start their own projects, but they kept meeting up and almost accidentally wrote a shooting script for a movie. At the time, some successful TV shows did go on to release film versions, but they were usually the same scenario as the original show, just on holiday (usually to lure the actors into doing the film and getting a nice holiday at the same time). And they were almost always terrible disappointments. But as Python had no overarching plot and very few returning characters, that wasn't an option. So instead, they wrote a comedy based on the legend of King Arthur.

Getting funding for the film is the coolest story ever because it didn't involve boardroom meetings with Hollywood executives where phrases like "points on the gross" were used. Instead, the Pythons reached out to their very rich friends in the music industry to raise the capital. Pink Floyd stepped up. They had stopped recording their seminal album *Dark Side of the Moon* to sit down and watch Python, so they couldn't wait to support a project with more Python. Led Zeppelin also were huge fans with colossal sacks of cash, and they agreed to back it; so, too, did Genesis. Despite substantial funding, the budget was still small, and to make matters worse, Terry Jones and Terry Gilliam (the codirectors and members of the Python team) had never directed a movie before. It looked like a disaster in the making.

One of the best gags in the film was created by necessity. Arthur and the knights pretended to ride horses as their squires banged coconut shells together. This was a reference to that same technique traditionally used on radio shows to create the sound of a horse, but it was also, in Python's case, a practical necessity because they didn't have the budget for a dozen horses. Would people find it funny or just cheap?

As in the TV show, each cast member played multiple roles, and all of them had at least one moment to shine. But the production was plagued with problems: Graham Chapman as King Arthur had to hold the film together, but he was fighting alcoholism and was in no fit state to do so. One castle was used as a stand-in for every castle. Shooting in Scotland created an almost World War I atmosphere of constant cold and damp, with mud everywhere and the ever-present threat of running out of money. The whole thing should have been a catastrophe.

Instead, *Monty Python and the Holy Grail* was one of the best-reviewed comedies of all time, which also made it big at the box office. The film is set in 932 AD, during the reign of the very real first king of England (and technically overlord of Scotland and Wales) Æthelstan. But when a film starts with subtitles, allegedly in Swedish, and they keep getting distracted by moose, and the title makers are fired mid-credits to be replaced by an alleged South American company which then starts going on about llamas . . . well, this is clearly not a documentary. There is no "history" to be taken from this film and to go line by line through it to say it's wrong for this reason is to be an utter killjoy. The madness resulted in this gloriously insane comedy that is one of the most quotable films of all time.

"Who's that then?"

"I dunno, must be a king."

"Why?"

"He hasn't got shit all over him."

Another truly unique point about the visual style of Terry Gilliam is his fascination with repurposing art from the past. On this occasion he looks at the art of the illuminated manuscripts of the Middle Ages, and to be fair to Gilliam, they are weird. Nobody can say what was going on in the mind of someone in the past, but clearly the monks, whose endless daily task was to copy out the gospels and other religious works, sometimes got bored and began to doodle in the margins. That's when we get imagery of everyday life, like peasants working in the fields, showing us the realities of life at the time.

But we also get lots of craziness too. The dog-headed men were a staple of the time. Everyone in Europe knew they existed, just not here. When explorers traveled across Asia, the locals would always agree that these creatures were real but were always somewhere to the east, over the horizon. There are images of knights fighting giant snails, a famous one of a woman picking "fruit" from a tree . . . except that every fruit is a penis. In another, a man is firing an arrow into the bare bottom of another man. These are all the kinds of incoherent, fantastical things you'd expect to find scrawled on a workbook in school. It's a very human part of the study of medieval manuscripts and rich soil where Gilliam could sow his surrealist ideas.

Monty Python was hugely influential. It inspired a host of American comedians in the 1970s but also has been fully embraced by geeks (including me), so much so that jokes like the holy hand grenade are still being referenced in the video game series *Fallout* or in miniature games like Warhammer.

KING ARTHUR (2004)

Monty Python and the Holy Grail is loosely based on the legend of King Arthur, a legend that is continually reinvented. In the previously mentioned *King Arthur*, the filmmakers do not only present Clive Owen as the King of Camelot, with a round table of knights in shining armor, but instead attempt to get to the history behind the legend. And just like *Troy*, which also came out in 2004, it completely misses the point of Arthurian legend and so satisfies no camp.

In the 2004 film, Arthur is a Roman and Guinevere, played by Keira Knightley, is some kind of Celt archer wearing a leather bra (because that's sensible clothing in British weather). This is also the first film mentioned that has a Black director, Antoine Fuqua, and it's intriguing that a thirty-eight-year-old guy from Pittsburgh, who had made the music video for "Gangsta's Paradise," was interested in making a film that deconstructed the Arthurian myth.

When I was studying for my degree in archaeology and medieval history, historians finally confirmed that the last piece of evidence thought to be contemporary to Arthur was indeed written later. Quite simply, King Arthur doesn't fit British history, and this is why: King Arthur is a feudal king with knights, castles, and fiefdoms. All of this came to England after 1066. Feudalism was invented in France. Prior to 1066 England was ruled by an Anglo-Saxon culture (England is derived from the name Angle lund—land of the Angles, and as they were German, you could say that England actually means Germany). The Anglo-Saxons fought as infantry in battle; a knight was not a type of warrior they came across until the Battle of Hastings in 1066.

Modern historians know this and have tried to push the tale of Arthur as early as possible, claiming there may have been a Roman cavalry officer called Artorius who fought against the Saxon invaders after the legions left. Could that have happened? Yes. Does that make a Roman cavalry officer the same thing as King Arthur and his knights, with Camelot and everything else you associate with the legend? No. The whole point is the legend. The main sources for Arthur, Morgan le Fay, and the quest for the Holy Grail (which is never actually described) in *De gestis Britonum* or *Historia Regum Britanniae* by Geoffrey of Monmouth or *Le Morte d'Arthur* by Sir Thomas Malory were all written after 1066. The tales are dripping with the ideals of the age and not of an earlier time. A good way to think about the tales of Arthur is that they represented a pinnacle, an ultimate and almost unobtainable level of chivalric perfection. A modern analogy might be a police officer watching *Die Hard*, knowing it's not real but yearning to be John McClane just once in their career.

Arthur keeps getting made. In 2017, there was an attempt by Guy Ritchie to kickstart a fantasy franchise with *King Arthur: Legend of the Sword*. It was average and forgettable. Then there's 1995's *First Knight*, starring Sean Connery as King Arthur, with Richard Gere as Lancelot and Julia Ormond as Guinevere. It was an interesting decision by Connery to play Arthur as Scottish, but despite the stellar cast, the film was dreadful. In a way, it was back to the sword-and-sandals epics: Everything was pristine, with not a speck of mud to be seen, and the population of Camelot all wearing the same blue tunics and hats, with the crowd scenes making it look like Connery was King of the Smurfs. Unbelievably, it turned a profit, but it certainly didn't deserve to.

THE GREEN KNIGHT (2021)

Finally, for the world of Arthurian legend, we come to *The Green Knight*, based on the anonymous fourteenth-century poem "Sir Gawain and the Green Knight." It tells the tale of a supernatural green knight arriving at King Arthur's court at Christmas and challenging anyone to land a blow on him; in a year's time that blow will be returned. Gawain steps forward and takes the knight's head clean off. The knight then puts his head back on, and now Gawain knows he has a year to live before he will be beheaded by the Green Knight. The film stars Dev Patel as Sir Gawain and that led to complaints that Gawain was white and shouldn't be played by a man of Indian heritage. Well, as this is a medieval legend and knights aren't green nor able to reconnect their heads, perhaps the director simply thought to cast the right actor for the role. Dev Patel is utterly compelling and convincing as Gawain.

In the era of superhero movies and indie darlings, this mid-level budget film that takes its time in an odyssey of self-discovery is both refreshing and retro. It shares its pacing and contemplative style with the likes of *Apocalypse Now* and *Aguirre, the Wrath of God* and is unlike anything more modern. Again, like *Monty Python and the Holy Grail*, you can almost smell the foul atmosphere and see the dirt under the fingernails. Interestingly, there's a scene with Saint Winifred, a genuine Welsh saint from the early Middle Ages, where Winifred, after turning down a prospective suitor, had her head cut off. The story has it that a holy spring came out of the ground where her head fell, and her uncle (who was also a saint) reattached her head, after which she spent the rest of her life founding convents. This is all as unlikely as the story of the Green Knight, but it was widely believed at the time. The people of the Middle Ages were superstitious: At the Battle of Antioch during the First Crusade (which we know happened), eyewitness accounts describe the battle but also Saint George fighting with the Christians. To this day you can visit Saint Winifred's spring at the aptly named site of Holywell in Wales. The Green Knight got into the mindset of a medieval person, something we rarely see.

After the era of Angle, Jute, and Saxon invasions, there was calm for a time until 793 AD. "This year came dreadful fore warnings over the land of the Northumbrians, terrifying the people most woefully: these were immense sheets of light rushing through the air, and whirlwinds, and fiery, dragons flying across the firmament. These tremendous tokens were soon followed by a great famine: and not long after, on the sixth day before the ides of January in the same year, the harrowing inroads of heathen men made lamentable havoc in the church of God in Holy-island, by rapine and slaughter."[1]

This is the first reference in British history to the Scandinavian incursions by those who became known as the Vikings. There is genuine history to the history of the Vikings. From the start, everyone who was attacked by them wrote of the horrors of the dragon ships and the heathen men who poured out of them. Then in the nineteenth century, the emphasis became more about their adventures and exploits, moving away from the violence and raping and enslaving. In the 1950s and 1960s the focus moved to Scandinavian innovations. A longboat is an amazingly crafted ship in which these great navigators were able to cross the North Atlantic. They were highlighted as traders and builders who founded (somewhat counterintuitively) Dublin (which in old Norse means Blackpool) and Kyiv in Ukraine. But by the 1980s, there was pushback to remind everyone that while, yes, they were great naval engineers and traders, let's not forget the raping and pillaging stuff.

THE VIKINGS (1958)

Kirk Douglas certainly didn't forget these as he strode onto screen as the one-eyed Einar in *The Vikings*. The only thing historically accurate in this deeply misogynistic and culturally insensitive romp is the fact that they did film some of it in Norway on longships that were based on original eleventh-century designs. This is ironic as the director, Richard Fleischer, claimed to have spent years researching Viking culture and history. It has all the tropes, including castles before there were castles, fire arrows (because it seems to be some kind of law to have them in a movie with archers), and completely incorrect weapons and armor. It's essentially a grab bag of anything that looks "old" according to Hollywood, although the helmet Douglas wears does look like a replica from the era.

THE 13TH WARRIOR (1999)

It is odd that the Vikings are such a source of interest in general pop culture but not so much in movies. There are lots of low-budget affairs, and even Terry Jones of Monty Python fame adapted his book into *Erik the Viking*, a pale imitation of the likes of *Monty Python and the Holy Grail* or *The Life of Brian*. But the next proper stab at the culture is 1999's *The 13th Warrior*. Based on the mega-successful writer Michael Crichton's novel *Eaters of the Dead*, directed by John (I directed *Predator*, *Die Hard*, and *The Hunt for Red October* back-to-back) McTiernan and starring the superhot Antonio Banderas, it had to be a hit. It was even based on real history as Ahmad ibn Fadlan recorded his firsthand account of pagan Nordic culture when traveling in the early 900s in the Volga region.

Banderas played Fadlan, and the film uses the same device as *The Hunt for Red October*, where everyone speaks their mother tongue, before the camera zooms into the speaker's mouth, then pulls back, and they are speaking English. It's a great conceit to please the purists but make it accessible. It was an interesting decision by Sean Connery, in *The Hunt for Red October*, to play a Lithuanian submarine captain as Scottish.

The 13th Warrior had a kind of supernatural element to it as the only thing scarier in the dark wood is a group of animallike men. It's more a horror survival film than anything as historically epic as *The Vikings*. It didn't just fail; it bombed spectacularly. The production budget spiraled out of control, and nobody went to see it. Except me. It's okay, by no means unwatchable, but it is thought to have lost about $129 million in total.

In 2010 comes the popular but hardly historically accurate (Horned helmets? No! Undisclosed location and time? No! Dragons and magic? No!) *How to Train Your Dragon* series of animated films. They are a lot of fun for kids, but I have a question: Why do all the adults have Scottish/Northern English/Irish accents and all the kids sound like they come from California? What happens at puberty?

THE NORTHMAN (2022)

Let's move swiftly on to the truly astonishing *The Northman*. Directed by the indie horror director Robert Eggers, the film stars a staggeringly muscular Alexander Skarsgård as Amleth. Like *Gladiator* the plot can be simply summarized: "I will avenge you, Father! I will save you, Mother! I will kill you, Fjolnir!" It's based on the Amleth saga, which in turn was the inspiration for

Hamlet. It's taken Hollywood over one hundred years, but finally we get an accurate depiction of a Viking berserker and the world he lives in.

In *The Northman*, we see a visceral raid in the lands of the Rus (so linking it to the Kyiv-based Vikings mentioned above). Filmed on location in Iceland, it accurately reproduced ships, dwellings, and even tombs. In his writings Ahmad ibn Fadlan recorded a firsthand account of a Viking pagan burial so accurately reproduced in the film that the moment I saw a woman's head appear from the bottom of the screen, talking about how she can see her family, I knew exactly what I was seeing.

The mythical elements are accurate to Scandinavian religious beliefs, and it was, of course, historically accurate to show that it's cold standing in a field in Iceland. It is now and was a thousand years ago, which is easy to reproduce: just get your actors to stand in a field in Iceland.

While the entire endeavor hangs on Skarsgård's immense frame, everyone is totally committed, with a special mention of the deliciously complex performances turned in by Anya Taylor-Joy and Nicole Kidman.

There is one understandable error: When they talk about the Gates of Hel [*sic*], they are referring to a volcano and lava. And while the Scandinavians did believe in an undesirable place in the afterlife, it was not boiling hot. Hot is desirable, fire is good. Life in Scandinavia meant you were cold all the time, so their version of hell was freezing cold, with a perpetually howling wind. This makes sense from their perspective.

The Vikings, in terms of their history, haven't had a great run of luck in Hollywood (*The Northman* didn't set the box office on fire) except in one area: It has always seemed strange to me that despite Christianity having erased so much of the pagan past in Europe, it is still sitting there in plain sight. We have months of the year named after pagan Roman emperors (July for Julius Caesar and August for Augustus), but the days of the week are all named after pagan gods. Take Thursday, Thor's day. It seems to be a missed opportunity that some of the Thor movies were released on a Friday, Freyja's day, from a Norse goddess who had a chariot pulled by cats (she must be truly mighty to get cats to do what she wants). Release Thor movies on his name day—obvious, right?

THOR RAGNAROK (2017)

What I find interesting is how much people think Marvel made up but didn't. The rainbow Bifrost Bridge that takes the gods to Earth is in the Norse legends. Odin loses an eye, which he plucked out for knowledge, according to the Icelandic sagas written eight hundred years ago. Thor has always wielded a hammer called Mjolnir. Kenneth Branagh was the director of the first Thor film and found saying Mjolnir almost impossible, so he asked if they could change the stupid name. To the Marvel producer's credit, they said no.

Scandinavian paganism is still big business. *Thor Ragnarok* (a reference to the Scandinavian name for the end of the world) was the third and biggest-grossing of the initial trilogy of Thor movies. Thor has appeared in all the Avenger films up to *Avengers Endgame*, and those four films have grossed more than $7 billion. Odin and Hel are now dead in the Marvel movies, but Loki and Thor appear to be in good health, and it's strange that today little kids in the United States can say Mjolnir, a word from a religion that died out a thousand years ago on another continent.

THE ADVENTURES OF ROBIN HOOD (1938)

If there's one British legend from the Middle Ages that has been filmed more often than Arthur, it must be Robin Hood. Ask anyone from Nottingham if he was real, and they will have no sense of humor about it and assure you he was. But he wasn't . . . like Arthur. Were there bandits in the forests around Nottingham? Yes. But were any of them called "Robin Hood," with friends like Friar Tuck and Will Scarlet, fighting against the evil Prince John, stealing from the rich and giving to the poor? No, so if all the legend is stripped away, what's left is the standard banditry that was the same across the globe. An uncomfortable fact is that the very first mentions of Robin Hood are set against the reign of King Edward I, the grandson of John. Everything else was added later.

The Adventures of Robin Hood is perhaps the greatest depiction of Robin on screen. Errol Flynn is at his most dashing, Olivia de Havilland is at her most beautiful (sorry, this is the 1930s and the women rarely got to do much apart from looking pretty). It is everything you could want from a Hollywood movie: action, romance (it was marketed as "the most glorious romance of all time"), impressive sets, and a villain everyone could boo. Is there any care in recreating twelfth-century England? No, but at least they aren't driving cars and firing pistols at each other. It's interesting to note that King Arthur was always fighting those pesky Saxon invaders, but Robin Hood was busy upholding noble Saxon traditions against the opposition of Norman nobility.

This 1938 film falls into all the traps of the sword-and-sandals epics where the goal was never to "do" history. Instead, it was to whisk moviegoers off to an exotic time and place, featuring all the new technology of color film-making. It's glorious entertainment, and one of the finest pieces of escapism created in the Golden Age of Hollywood. Go see it now.

ROBIN HOOD: PRINCE OF THIEVES (1991)

The same cannot be said of *Robin Hood: Prince of Thieves*. This tries to have its cake and eat it too. You know you are in trouble with the opening credits. The glorious music swells (Michael Kamen's rousing score is still used in Disneyland parks) as we get . . . footage of the Bayeux Tapestry, the famous depiction of the events of 1066 and the Battle of Hastings. These have absolutely nothing to do with the film and are from about 130 years earlier. Then, the opening scenes of the film take place in Jerusalem in 1194. Robin, played by Kevin Costner, has been on the Third Crusade with King Richard I and has been captured . . . except Richard never lost a battle on that crusade so how he was captured isn't explained.[2] Also, 1194 is two years after the crusade was over, not to mention that the crusade never got to Jerusalem. The entire setup makes Robin an incompetent idiot, not a hero we should be rooting for.

But Robin escapes with Morgan Freeman, and the next shot shows them arriving at the White Cliffs of Dover. Yes, the entire trek through hostile territory in the Middle East and across the whole of Europe is omitted. Now that would be a film. Even the real King Richard found that part tricky as he was captured and held for ransom—which is kind of the backstory of most Robin Hood tales, including this one. But never mind. Robin then declares that they will be in Nottingham the next day (apparently he had access to better roads and running shoes than everybody else in 1194), only for the next shot showing the two of them on Hadrian's Wall, meaning they have overshot Nottingham by about half the country, reinforcing the notion that Robin was an idiot, not a hero.

I could go on, but I won't. You get the idea. But I will finish with Sean Connery's turn at the end as King Richard, interesting because Connery decided to play Richard as Scottish.

ROBIN HOOD (2010)

About twenty years after Costner, Ridley Scott tried to reboot Robin Hood by doing it grittier and more realistic, with Russell Crowe in the title role. It's a solid film and shows the genuine threat to England at the time of a new French takeover around 1216 (thanks to the unpopularity of King John), but the arrival of the French in landing craft that look like they've just come from *Saving Private Ryan* is disarming. Unfortunately, this one lacked the fun of the other two, so what could have started a franchise failed to take off.

KINGDOM OF HEAVEN (2005) AND EL CID (1961)

Ridley Scott does appear to have a fascination with the Middle Ages, perhaps most ambitiously in *Kingdom of Heaven*. This film concentrates on the events that eventually triggered the Third Crusade and the capture of Jerusalem by Al-Nasir Salah al-Din Yusuf ibn Ayyub, better known as Saladin. It's interesting to compare *Kingdom of Heaven* with *El Cid*. Rodrigo Díaz de Vivar, aka El Cid, was an eleventh-century Spanish Christian warlord who fought against the Muslim Moors of Spain. He died at the siege of Valencia in 1099, where legend says he was strapped onto his horse and sent out with the knights of the city to push back the attackers. It worked for a time, but the Moors eventually won. Charlton Heston saw the 1961 film *El Cid* as his follow-up to *Ben-Hur*. Like the previous film, it leaned heavily on every cliché that existed around the era. The joust (not likely in eleventh-century Spain), the conical hats for the ladies, and period-inappropriate armor were all there. It looked "medieval" so that was okay. However, the Moors are the undisputed bad guys. El Cid is merciful to the Moors (true), but his soldiers are exclusively Christian (not true) and see the Moors as a force to be feared, a great host of evildoers. The movie shows the legendary end of El Cid, his body strapped onto his horse, going out alone to push back a whole army. The reality is that the role of Islam in the Middle Ages, particularly on the Iberian Peninsula, is substantially more complex than that. Indeed, if anything, the Christians were the barbarians of the era, while the Muslims made breakthroughs in mathematics, science, and the translation of Ancient Greek texts.

By comparison, *Kingdom of Heaven* is very much a post-9/11 movie. There are good guys and bad guys on both sides. Islam is not a monolithic threat. Everyone had seen on TV how the extremists of both Islam and right-wing Christians tried to turn events into a clash of civilizations. After the events of 9/11, President George W. Bush used the term *crusade* once (but only once as his advisers pointed out that many countries denigrated the Crusades and that the Christians ultimately lost in the Holy Land). It was a sign that bridges needed to be built and divisions needed to be cast aside, a little awkward when Hollywood is always looking for a story where the heroes are the good guys, and the villains are definitely bad. So, in the film, the most charismatic character is Saladin, played by Ghassan Massoud. With all due respect to the lead, Orlando Bloom, Bloom comes across as a great supporting character (think *Lord of the Rings* or *Pirates of the Caribbean*) to Massoud, who steals every scene he's in. In this role Bloom simply isn't leading man material, but the most onerous role in the film is arguably that of Reynald de Chatillon, played by Brendan Gleeson. The real Reynald seems to have been a sociopath; every story about him in the annals is about violence, and so, when he was captured after the Battle of Hattin, he was executed by Saladin (as depicted in the movie). Even the Christian chronicles didn't think this was an unjust end to such a man. Reynald did, however, have power, and his clashes with Guy de Lusignan are a good approximation of the tensions in the Christian Kingdoms of the Middle East at the time. Baldwin IV is resurrected (he died just before the events of the film), but this leper king, who did indeed wear a silver mask to cover his disfigurements, was integral to the creation of the situation. The armor is largely accurate, the events play out close to what really happened, and it's probably the best depiction of the Crusades ever put on film . . . but there are problems:

First, a technical one: The film is too long, and its release to theaters was cut to ribbons. Many of the hanging plot points are resolved in the superior director's cut, which while longer, feels shorter.

Second, during the final siege, Hollywood rears its head and gets involved (spoiler alert for real history that happened more than eight hundred years ago): Saladin does capture Jerusalem, but in the film he does it with an army far larger than he could field. Once again, reality isn't glamorous enough to pass muster. The defenders use flaming catapults in the film, but as already discussed, flaming weapons were incredibly rare; in reality, plain old stones were hurled at the oncoming army.

There also needs to be a brief mention of the gambeson. Almost every film set in the Middle Ages makes the same mistake. Metal stops cutting wounds, but it can also harm the wearer with no padding. A gambeson is a padded jacket worn under the armor. It is almost never seen. Also, and critically, a similar padded hood is worn underneath the chain mail on the head. The medieval manuscripts make it look like the knights are wearing crash helmets because, in every way that mattered, they are. With nothing but metal mesh directly on the head, any damage will only be increased. However, because this padding looks "wrong" no film shows it; without it, authenticity is lost, no matter how accurate the rest of the armor may be.

The Crusades led to a cultural exchange between East and West, and some of that has been preserved in stone. Castle technology greatly improved in the two hundred years of Christians in the Middle East, so this is where there has to be a section on real castles versus Hollywood castles.

A castle is the fortified residence of a lord or monarch. A fort is a defense structure for a garrison. A castle is a home with seventy-foot-high walls and guards armed to the teeth, but a home nonetheless. As such, castles tend to be quite small and depend on the effectiveness of their defenses in the event of a siege. A fortress has basic defenses and depends on the garrison to be the deterrent.

Looking at *The Adventures of Robin Hood*, the stone hallways in the castle are huge, with lots of space for dozens of people to fight. No castle has that space. In *Robin Hood: Prince of Thieves*, Kevin and Morgan fight their way through an entire castle complex only to come up to the gates of even more castle, one that seems to be weirdly big. (Another note of realism: When the two of them escape by launching themselves from a catapult, both would have died on impact. Like I said, Robin Hood in that movie is an idiot.)

Because of their defensive nature, castles didn't have windows; they had arrow slits as a window is an obvious weakness. Some castle ruins today have window frames, but these were added from the 1500s onward because castles, while great places for defense, were cold, damp, and gloomy. And let's be honest, if you must live behind ten-foot-thick walls, it's probably a sign there's something wrong with the surrounding society, so once England and other countries became more stable, with fewer wars, windows were the order of the day. So please remember that any time there is a feast set in a castle, with people wearing armor (no) and eating roast turkey (which is American, so no medieval feast would have them) under the light of a stained-glass window, it's all wrong.

THE LAST DUEL (2021)

Ridley Scott has already been mentioned twice in this chapter, but in 2021, he was at it again. This time it's 1386 France and the very full-blooded *The Last Duel* that deals with the last judicial duel permitted by the Parlement [*sic*] of Paris. This is one of the rare movies set around the era of the Hundred Years' War that isn't Henry V and the Battle of Agincourt. And it was a fascinating anachronism even for the people of the time.

Trial by combat was far more common around 1000 AD than in the late fourteenth century. The idea was simple: God would decide, so various trials by ordeal or combat were commonplace. People swear oaths on relics, and in the absence of a strong, centralized authority, people let the greatest authority, the Lord God Almighty, dispense justice. Consequently, as monarchies spread their power, influence, and, perhaps most importantly, their courts throughout the land, the need for such trials faded away. In *The Last Duel*, Sir Jacques Le Gris is accused by Marguerite de Carrouges, the wife of his rival Sir Jean de Carrouges, of raping her. Jean demands trial by combat and Jacques obliges. Now even in the Middle Ages people knew that big guys always seemed to have God on their side when they fought little guys, but in this instance, both men had martial backgrounds, and so the outcome was not foreseeable.

By the 1380s, full-plate armor was standard equipment for a knight; that much is accurate, but at one point they are battering each other with swords, and that is not. It doesn't take a medieval warfare expert to work out that a sword will do nothing to somebody covered in steel plates of armor. The reality was that while the sword was the symbol of chivalric prowess, on the battlefields of Europe at this time, bludgeoning weapons were far more common. Warhammers, maces, even battle-axes were the order of the day.

There is another point worth raising concerning the portrayal of women: When aristocratic ladies and women of the court are shown in public, most of them are not covering their hair. This would not have happened. We've all seen the images of women wearing white cloth cowls and conical hats, and that really was the fashion.[3] A woman revealing her hair was too provocative for the time. Only peasant women and sex workers showed off their hair.

A final point: In the movie the French king is Charles VI, known as Charles the Mad. His incompetence led to further gains by the English crown at the time. How mad was he? He once spent months in bed because he thought he was made of glass and was worried that if he got up he would shatter. His daughter married Henry V, and their son, Henry VI, clearly shared that same mental illness with his grandfather.

HIGHLANDER (1986)

If there's one area that gets a lot of love in the Middle Ages, it's Scotland. It was the location for the shooting of *Monty Python and the Holy Grail*, it is basically the title of *Highlander*, and while shot in Ireland, it runs through the very veins of *Braveheart* like porridge through real Scots.

Highlander is a fantasy movie about immortals who can only die by having their heads removed. The story is based around Connor Macleod, who realizes he is one of the immortals when he's not quite killed by the Kurgan and is taught the ways of the immortals by Ramirez. The story continues down the centuries to 1986 New York. The film producers had the French actor Christopher Lambert and the oh-so Scottish Sean Connery for the two main roles. So, of course, they had the Frenchman (who could barely speak English) play Connor, and Connery got to be the Spaniard Ramirez. It was an interesting decision by Connery to play Ramirez as Scottish.

Bizarrely, the Kurgan were a real central Asian people from the Iron Age, roughly the third century BC. They are known for their distinctive burial mounds scattered on the Asiatic Steppe and are not known for wearing 1980s-style goth armor as epitomized by Clancy Brown in a deliciously evil role. This is, however, the only reference to this obscure people in a Hollywood film.

Highlander is dumb in so many ways, but for action and adventure, it passes the time. It was a disappointment at the box office, but home rentals and sales of the video/DVD were strong enough to lead to more films and a

TV show. Despite its many, many flaws there is no doubt that the other great character in the film is the Scottish Highlands. They are beautifully shot, memorably so when a helicopter films Connery and Lambert training on a cliff edge. You want to go there immediately.

Scotland has always had the image of a wild frontier. When I was working at Visit Britain (the tourist board), there was always tension between Visit England and Visit Scotland. To be blunt, Scotland, as a country on its own, has the most recognizable branding in the world with the Highlands, Edinburgh Castle, Loch Ness (with or without a monster), the thistle, haggis, Balmoral, whisky, tartan, porridge, bagpipes—it's a long list. After that, think of things that are distinctively English: Stonehenge, Big Ben, fish and chips . . . um . . . warm beer . . . the list isn't as good. *Braveheart* takes that sentiment and ramps it up.

BRAVEHEART (1995)

The story of William Wallace is a contentious one. The basic facts aren't disputed, but most of the color around the tale was created by a minstrel called Blind Harry about 170 years later. Here's a tip for being a good historian: If your source is called "Blind Harry," it's probably not the most accurate. To be fair to Harry, his goal was to entertain. Wallace was given a wife (this came even later) to link one of the clans to this legendary freedom fighter. The reality is that little is known about the real man, but Mel Gibson knew a good story when he saw one and didn't care about historical accuracy or English sensibilities.

Like many of the movies already discussed, *Braveheart*'s goal was not to be a documentary but an entertaining film. However, unlike the harmless silliness of *The Adventures of Robin Hood* or the hyperstylized imagery of *300*, *Braveheart* goes out of its way to give the impression it has done its homework and stuck to the facts. Its bias and cartoony take on the realities of the era have echoes today, with Scottish politicians declaring they watch it every year and referring to it in speeches. This is where Hollywood turning whole cultures into good guys and bad guys has real-world implications.

The film's screenwriter, Randall Wallace, has gone on the record that he didn't want to worry about dates and numbers, but instead, to make the kind of movie that moved him as a kid. That's fine, but don't then start putting up dates and breaking your own movie's logic in the process.

For some idea of how much contempt this movie has for the facts, let's look at the opening date. It declares that it is 1280, and the voiceover tells us the Scottish king (presumably Alexander III) is dead. Okay . . . but . . . Alexander died in 1286. Why get that wrong? It doesn't change the story or the narrative, but in the opening moments we already know nobody behind the movie cares about facts. And here's the important thing: Most moviegoers don't know that Alexander III ruled Scotland from 1249 to 1286, so the moviemakers get away with it.

The next big issue is the implication that the English have been ruling Scotland for a long time, let's say a decade. But in 1280, the English weren't even in Scotland, and fast-forwarding to 1286, English aggression against Scotland was only just starting. These are important motivators in a movie: the downtrodden revolt against an evil overlord, and against all the odds, a ragtag bunch of rebels defeat the bad guys. It's the basic plot of *Star Wars*, only this isn't in a galaxy far, far away, it's a real place, with real people being depicted on screen.

English villainy is laid on thickly when we see an act of *prima nocta* (first night). This is a Victorian myth about the Middle Ages and how the local lord got to sleep with the bride on the first night of marriage. It was designed to show just how barbarous our ancestors were. Except that if you know anything about the Middle Ages, it's that they took their religion seriously, so the idea that local lords had such a right, by law, doesn't sound like it would fit into that kind of society . . . because it doesn't and it didn't and that's because it is made up.

An interesting omission is that of one Andrew Moray. I don't blame *Braveheart* for this because he's quite obscure, but he is also fascinating. Moray was one of the lords who, by the 1290s, was fighting against the English. He was doing well and merged his forces with those of William Wallace. Contrary to the movie, Scotland was not some kind of egalitarian Hobbiton (the houses are complete nonsense, too); it was a feudal society, just like England or France. As such, title meant a lot, and Moray was more senior in the pecking order than Wallace; therefore, he had to be the man in charge at the Battle of Stirling in 1297. So, why is the film and the story by Blind Harry not about Andrew Moray? The answer is he died in the battle. Now there is a great victory, but who gets to take credit? The second-in-command, William Wallace. It's quite telling that a year later, at the next major pitched battle Wallace fights against the English at Falkirk, he loses. Could this be because he's missing the real mastermind? Who can say?

That it's never good when a movie breaks its own internal logic can be seen at the two (expertly shot and directed) battle scenes. The first one is of the great victory at Stirling Bridge, but the battle portrayed went down nothing like the real one. The genius of the battle from the Scottish perspective was that it was the perfect ambush. The English had more of everything: infantry, equipment, cavalry; in a pitched battle, the Scots stood little chance. So, they waited for the English army to start crossing the very narrow bridge at Stirling, and they waited until about a third of the army was over the bridge before they attacked. The English were out of formation, with most of their troops on the wrong side of the river. It was tactical genius. That's what really happened, but according to the film, there was a lot of rude shoving and pushing in a muddy field, and the Scots won because they "wanted it more." Pretty unedifying. Further, the film portrays the front rank of the English filled with Irish mercenaries. They are seen to charge into battle, only to stop and slap the backs of their spiritual brothers, the Scots, before turning on their paymasters to fight for "freedom." So, switching sides is a good thing, according to the film.

In the other battle, the Scottish nobles refuse to join battle and leave the site of the clash, having been paid off by Edward I. This is bad; these wicked traitors have turned their backs on "freedom." But it's the same tactic. If both sides use it (and coincidentally, both sides win), why is it not the same rule for all? The film's message is that it's okay for Wallace but underhanded and deceitful for the English to do the same thing.

Then there's the look of the film. Mel Gibson does the icons of Scottishness in spades. There are lots of shots of beautiful countryside (some Irish, some Scottish), but it certainly looks like the Hollywood-required amount of mist and lichen, dappled light and granite cliffs. Then there are the tartan kilts. They're about as Scottish as it gets, right? Well, no. The description of a kilt is first recorded in the sixteenth century. The "nit" is referred to as the great kilt, which was a full-length garment whose upper half could be worn as a cloak. The kilt we think of as the traditional kilt emerged in the eighteenth century and is essentially the bottom half of the great kilt.[4] So, what they are wearing is at least two hundred years too early (and that's being generous). Then there's the blue war paint called woad; this was worn by both the Celtic and Pictish tribes of Britain during the Iron Age.[5] This had died out as a ritualistic war paint by the end of the Roman era, so no army in Scottish history would ever have looked like the one shown in *Braveheart*. And as for them not wearing underpants under their kilts, that wouldn't have been a big deal at the time. Does anyone think the English were wearing tighty whities under their trousers? No, the history of the undergarment begins much later than this era.

Perhaps the greatest insult this movie dishes out is the way it treats real people to fit a pleasing Hollywood formula. After his wife dies, Wallace catches the eye of Princess Isabella, who is due to be married to Prince Edward (later Edward II). It's implied that Isabella is with Wallace's child, meaning he had the last laugh and the son (who we know will be the very successful Edward III) is half Scottish. This is nonsense. Isabella was nine years old and living in France at the time of Wallace's death; therefore, this could never have happened.

Then there is the terrible trope in Hollywood around the "dead gay." Over the years, more and more characters of different sexual orientations are represented, but their death rate compared to their straight colleagues on screen is shocking. Here we see Prince Edward fawning over a young man, possibly Piers Gaveston, who was highly likely to have been Edward's real gay lover. Gaveston would eventually be executed but not for more than another decade when Prince Edward was now King Edward II. However, in *Braveheart*, this young man is thrown out of a window on the orders of Edward I, and it's all done for a cheap laugh.

King Edward I was a remarkable monarch. As a prince he went on crusade and nearly died at the hands of an assassin in the Middle East (he beat his assailant to death with the only thing he had nearby, a wooden stool). His father was captured during a civil war, and Edward kept on fighting, eventually besting his father's captor and winning the war. He conquered Wales, creating the title of the Prince of Wales (Edward II was the first to have the honor). He built the best castles in Europe, but this cost so much he exiled all the Jews in England (who he owed money to). He was referred to in his own lifetime as both "the flower of chivalry" and "the hammer of the Scots." When Alexander III died, it was suggested that the only remaining member of the Scottish family tree, a young girl in Norway (referred to as the Maid of the North), should be brought back to Scotland so she could marry his son Edward, who was also a young boy at the time. The marriage would unite both crowns, make Scotland an equal partner, and everyone would be happy. But sadly, the Maid of the North died crossing the North Sea, and then Edward, spotting weakness in his northerly neighbor, began turning up the heat, which led to war and the events depicted in *Braveheart*. Edward was a complex man with a lot to like about him; therefore, to portray him as little more than a cackling villain is not doing him justice.

RAPA NUI (1994)

Then we come to *Rapa Nui*, a film you are unlikely to have heard of, and when I tell you it's about Easter Island, you are likely thinking, this is in the wrong chapter. What its inclusion here highlights is how "The Middle Ages" is a very Eurocentric view of history, and all eras are artificial constructs that reveal an inherent bias. While the term is useful in describing European history, it is meaningless in describing the history of places like India, North America, or China. I have heard the carved stone heads on Easter Island (the island called "rapa nui" in the local language) described as "Stonehenge on a tropical island." But Easter Island is not tropical, and the moai (carved heads) were constructed from around 1250 AD to roughly 1500 AD. So, in theory, William Wallace could have sailed there and seen them being carved. By contrast, Stonehenge is Neolithic and the famous stones were erected roughly around 2500 BC. Apart from that it's a great description.

Rapa Nui the film is an extremely ambitious Hollywood attempt to reconstruct a piece of forgotten history about an ethnic group that has shrunk over the centuries. It was also a colossal financial flop. The modest budget of $20 million saw a return of only about one-third of a million at the box office. Amazingly, I saw the film when it first came out (I was doing my degree in archaeology at the time, so I was the apparent target market of one). The director (Kevin Reynolds, hot off *Robin Hood: Prince of Thieves*) made sure that most of the cast were of Pacific Island and Polynesian ancestry.

The film concentrates on the antipathy between two groups, the long ears and the short ears. It also shows the worship of the moai fading to a new religion known as the birdman cult. While this is all ethnographically accurate, it's been taken too literally as, to this day, there is ongoing debate about what "long ears" and "short ears" mean. Another reading is that the terms represent the aristocrats versus the peasantry, but the reality is we will never know for sure. Also, while moai worship did fade and the birdman culture did rise, there is no evidence of animosity. The change could have been gradual (like the spread of Christianity in the Roman Empire), but to make an interesting film, the director had to make guesses based on the little that is known. In any case, it was nice to see this important Pacific culture getting representation on the big screen.

NOTES

1. Anonymous, *The Anglo Saxon Chronicle* (Whitefish, MT: Kessinger, 2012), 50.

2. Jem Duducu, *Deus Vult: A Concise History of the Crusades* (Gloucestershire, UK: Amberley Publishing, 2014).

3. Rose Eveleth, "The History of Cone-Shaped Medieval Princess Hats," *Smithsonian*, December 30, 2013.

4. Matthew Newsome, *The Early History of the Kilt* (exhibition), Franklin, NC, Scottish Tartans Museum, 2015.

5. Julius Caesar, *Commentaries on the Gallic Wars*, Roscoe Mongan, trans. (London: Hardpress, 2018), 12.

Chapter 3

The Bloody Tudors

The Tudors ruled England for just over a century, from Henry Tudor's victory at the Battle of Bosworth in 1485 to the death of his granddaughter Queen Elizabeth I in 1603. It was a period of tremendous cultural change in Britain. The previous ruling dynasty of England, the Plantagenets, had ruled for about 350 years, but it was in the Tudor era that we saw the rise of the printing press and the endless cycle of religious violence as Protestants and Catholics gained or lost favor, depending on the monarch at the time.

This period is unusually well defined, and the following Stuart era also genuinely changed the social and political landscape not just of England, but of Scotland as well. This eventually led to the Acts of Union in 1707 under Queen Anne, the last Stuart monarch.

As a teenager Edward III had to escape the clutches of his mother and her lover to become fully independent. Once he was free, he had his mother barred from the court and her lover executed. Then he started a campaign of warfare against the French (known as the Hundred Years' War). His first major clash took place in a naval battle at Sluys in 1340, where he took a crossbow bolt in the thigh but still managed to pull off a victory so decisive that through the next century France did not even dare to attempt an invasion of England. In 1346 he crushed the French at Crecy and founded the Order of the Garter. Two years later, Black Death swept across Europe, killing between a third and half the population. In 1356, Edward was busy, but his son, known as the Black Prince, was so victorious against the French at Poitiers that their king was captured and put in the same castle with the Scottish king, who Edward had also beaten.[1]

All of this was more than a century before the Tudors, so why mention it? Because many of us don't know this part of history. Edward III is a great story, with everything anyone could want, but it very rarely gets told. I have never understood who gets to pick the bits of history we remember. I get why nobody talks about Henry III, he wasn't particularly interesting, but I would argue that the story of Edward III is a lot more interesting than that of Henry

VIII or, indeed, Elizabeth I. While I agree that we need more stories about women in history, it's not like Elizabeth I doesn't get her chance to shine. She is hardly obscure. What is it about the bloody Tudors that leads to the same old stories being trotted out ad nauseum?

People tell me I don't give Henry VIII enough credit, that his break from Rome was a cultural event that would shape the religion and politics of the whole of Britain and Ireland for centuries to come. This is true, but that's not what all the films are about, are they? Most focus on the bloody wives: divorced, beheaded, died, divorced, beheaded, survived. People like a good story with a bit of sex and violence. Well, Edward III has that, and unlike Henry VIII, he actually achieved his ambitions on the continent and had a male heir and then a grandson to inherit the throne. In the era just before the Tudors, Edward IV and Richard III are both very interesting monarchs, but unless Shakespeare is involved, they rarely get a mention. Same for the monarchs just after the Tudors: James I/VI with the gunpowder plot and the unification of the English and Scottish crowns, which was a huge deal. And that's before we get to his son Charles I, who was embroiled in two rounds of civil war and was eventually beheaded. These are big moments in British history, but there aren't many films out there on them.

However, when it comes to films about, say, Queen Elizabeth I, the material is endless (although she's sometimes shown through the lens of her captive cousin Mary, Queen of Scots): 1936's *Mary of Scotland*, 1937's *Fire Over England*, 1939's *The Private Lives of Elizabeth and Essex*, 1940's *The Sea Hawk*, 1955's *The Virgin Queen* (Bette Davis gets to be Elizabeth in both this and the previous one), 1971's *Mary, Queen of Scots*, 1992's *Orlando*, 1998's *Shakespeare in Love*, Shekhar Kapur's two films with Cate Blanchett, 1998's *Elizabeth* and 2007's *Elizabeth: The Golden Age*, and 2018's *Mary Queen of Scots*. And that's just the movies; I'm not including the large quantity of TV shows out there. By comparison, Edward III appears in one film in the whole of the twentieth century: He has a supporting role in 1955's *The Dark Avenger*, which is about his son, the Black Prince. Seen it, heard anyone ever talk about it? No, neither have I.

I'm not saying this because I'm some weird fanboy of Edward III or because I don't like Cate Blanchett; she's amazing and I would happily listen to her read the London phone book from 1987. What I'm saying is that there are loads of really interesting stories in history that just never get told because we get the same moments regurgitated by Hollywood over and over again. Why? Who was clamoring for another telling of the Mary, Queen of Scots, story in 2018? Unsurprisingly, it hardly set the box office on fire.

The problem with history is that we look at it the wrong way around. This idea first came to me in a history class when I was a kid. I'm of the generation that grew up with all the World War II movies on TV on Sunday afternoons.

I was steeped in the war, so when we studied Hitler in school, part of me thought, what was the point—he was always going to lose. But of course, it didn't look that way in 1939, or 1940, or even 1941. It's only in hindsight that we start making those sorts of comments, but I was young. What did I know? The point is that whether we're discussing World War II or the Tudors, the stories have become so familiar, the facts so well-trodden, that they sap the suspense and crush the drama.

When *Game of Thrones* was shown on TV, viewers' reactions reached fever pitch when the series went past the books because . . . well . . . now everyone was in the dark. What would happen to Tyrion? Would Daenerys and John hook up? Nobody knew. It was described as fantasy but was inspired more by the War of the Roses or Tudor politics than *Lord of the Rings*, and the thrills came from seeing events unfold without the advantage of hindsight, just as Henry couldn't have known as he married his brother's widow that she would be the first of six wives (technically five, as his first marriage was annulled so they were never married, but that's being pedantic—which is kind of the job description for a historian).

If drama is all about the mystery of the resolution of the story and we've known what happens in Henry VIII's life for nearly five hundred years, there is an unhelpful disconnect which sometimes leads to woeful overcompensation in Tudor stories. On more than one occasion I have watched a Tudor drama show Henry making profound statements of love to Catherine of Aragon. If this was a normal drama where we don't know what will happen next, we would call that (with hindsight) clever foreshadowing, but the fact is that we do know they will separate, and the overemphasis on the permanency of the relationship in the hands of some writers just makes Henry look like a fool.

My best guess as to why the Tudors endure is that, for a change, it's about the women. We have three queens: Mary of England, Mary of Scotland, and Elizabeth, all sole rulers. Then with Henry it's the fascination of his marital affairs, often seen from the perspective of his wives. This is taken to its logical extreme in the musical *Six* (which at the time of writing is still on stage but is in discussions to be made into a movie). The musical stars the six wives and Henry isn't in it at all. It's a vibrant feminist retort to the monarch, which in its own way rewrites history and not necessarily in a helpful way. So, according to *Six*, the Tudors are all about "girl power" . . . . c'mon, really?

A MAN FOR ALL SEASONS (1966)

Now let's tear down almost everything I've just said as we start with an amazing film, the pinnacle of Tudor historical drama, *A Man for All Seasons*.

This isn't a salacious, poorly acted drama about Henry and his wives; instead, the movie is based on a play about one of the key players in Henry's court, Sir Thomas More, who was Henry's lord chancellor. So this story is largely about the men.

More was utterly loyal to Henry, but when Henry broke from the Church (which took years, it wasn't an impetuous overnight act), things began to sour between them. Crucially, More refused to sign a letter asking Pope Clement VII to annul Henry VIII's marriage to Catherine of Aragon. Furthermore, he also refused to take an Oath of Supremacy, declaring Henry VIII Supreme Head of what will be a Protestant Church of England.

Both movie and play move from the court, where Henry is furious with his lord chancellor, to a trial where More's very life is on the line. More will not countenance his actions as anything other than noble. He eventually goes to the Tower and before his beheading utters the words, "I die his Majesty's good servant, but God's first." These are the genuine last words of Sir Thomas More.

What we have is about six years distilled into two hours, which will always make things more dramatic, but the film is serious, intelligent, and while condensed, perfectly summarizes the events around Henry's break from Rome and the impact it had on English society and people's loyalties as so eloquently stated in More's last words. It was a huge critical and commercial success. Paul Scofield played More and won the Best Actor Oscar for his performance; the film also won Best Director for Fred Zinnemann and Best Picture, along with three Oscars in other categories.

However, like some of the other films mentioned, *A Man for All Seasons* does its best to make our protagonist as blameless as possible and the antagonist as blameworthy. The film shows that before his execution, More retired and stayed out of politics, so a principled man who tried to stay out of the turmoil. In reality, he didn't; he poked the hornets' nest from time to time, which was never a good idea where Henry VIII was concerned. Likewise, the prosecutor in his trial, Richard Rich (his real name) wasn't quite as conniving and aggressive as is shown. He was only doing his job, one the rightful King of England had given him. As crimes against history in Hollywood movies go, this is minor stuff, but it shows again that even in the most accurate portrayals on screen, even in those with very noble intentions, 100 percent accuracy is impossible.

When it comes to sensitive historical drama interested in the wholeness of its characters (a lot of which is invariably guesswork), this is one of the best ever made. It's the gold standard to which all other Tudor dramas should aspire and copy but don't.

THE PRIVATE LIFE OF HENRY VIII (1933)

One of the earliest depictions of Henry VIII was *The Private Life of Henry VIII*, starring Charles Laughton as Henry. Laughton was a British stage actor who would go on to star in many films, but in 1955, he directed *Night of the Hunter*, a film that today is seen as one of the great movies of the 1950s. However, Laughton found studio interference exasperating and that, along with the fact that it didn't promote the film, meant it was a big flop at the box office; so after his directorial debut, Laughton never directed again. But all that came much later, after *The Private Life of Henry VIII* was a huge international hit and made Laughton's name as a top rank movie actor. Indeed, at the 1933 Oscars, Laughton won Best Actor and the film was the first British production to be nominated for Best Picture.

Does the film cover the complexities of the Reformation or the impact on English society after the Dissolution of the Monasteries? No. That boring stuff is for academics. This can only be described as a romp involving Henry and his wives. There is almost no history in this historical story.

The film is of its time in that I could spend the rest of the book talking about what it got wrong. It's a 1930s production like *The Adventures of Robin Hood*. Its goal was to entertain rather than be a documentary—and it was designed to be a vehicle for Laughton and his wife Elsa Lanchester. The film picks up after the execution of Anne Boleyn and takes the viewer through the relationship Henry had with each of the other wives. The closest they got to historical accuracy was getting the names right. What is bizarre is that of all the remaining wives, you would think Elsa would have chosen to play Jane Seymour, the one Henry genuinely loved and who tragically died in childbirth. But no, she went for wife number four, Anne of Cleves.

The story goes that Henry VIII was so wowed by the dress in her portrait that he didn't pay much attention to her face. When they met, he didn't like her, and they divorced because neither party found the other attractive. Why Elsa went for "the ugly one" is something of a mystery, but the film completely changes the narrative. Now we have Anne deliberately making herself unattractive so she can return to Germany to marry her sweetheart, which is the opposite of what happened. This is made even more ridiculous when they play a game of cards on the wedding night and agree that if she wins, they can divorce and she can go home. Elsa performs wearing the most outrageously fake blonde wig ever to have graced the silver screen. Playing cards did exist at the time of Henry VIII but not the laminated fifty-two-card deck of the modern world. Not only did this scene never happen, it couldn't have happened. It is yet another reminder that the further back you go in cinema history, the less people care about historical accuracy and is a reminder of how recent that concern (or paying lip service to it) is.

But the film is fun and very 1930s. There are glimmers here of female empowerment that play quite well to a modern audience. Henry is rarely in control and the women each have a scene to steal. And, of course, there are just four wives to focus on. What does not stand the test of time is the last line uttered as a dying Henry looks into the camera and says, "Six wives, and the best of them's the worst." In fact, we do know Henry VIII's last words were, "Monks, monks, monks" and not a gag about his wives. Of course, as they are his last words, we do not know if the reference to a Catholic form of cleric is a sign of regret over the split from the Roman Catholic Church, whether he felt harassed by them, or if these were just the random thoughts of a dying man.

THE OTHER BOLEYN GIRL (2008)

Then there's *The Other Boleyn Girl*. Based on Philippa Gregory's novel of the same name, it raises the valid point that Anne Boleyn was never meant to catch Henry VIII's eye; that was meant to be her sister Mary. To this day I can't work out if the title is clever, playing off expectation, or if it's simply uninspired; it's your choice.

This film featured three of Hollywood's brightest stars: Henry VIII is Eric Bana (seemingly having learned nothing from *Troy*), Scarlett Johansson is Mary, and Anne is played by Natalie Portman. With all due respect to Paul Scofield and the rest of the cast in *A Man for All Seasons*, now we have some real sex appeal. Regardless of your personal preferences, these three are hot, and it's nothing to do with the locations or large crowd scenes; these three can't help themselves as they look lustily at each other, or you, in the audience. This is going to get steamy.

Except, to keep a 12A (UK) or PG-13 (US) rating, it doesn't. This film could have been made in the early 1960s for all the boundaries it pushes. The real Mary Boleyn went to France and had an affair with King François I. He liked her so much he nicknamed her "my hackney" because she was a fun ride (a comment preserved for the ages).[2] When the French queen (Claude) grew tired of the affair, she had Mary sent back to England, where she went out of her way to bag a second king and, for a time, did so. I think we can all agree that to sleep with the King of France and the King of England is an impressive accomplishment, so to portray her in the film as shy and nervous in her dealings with Henry is the opposite of what we know about the real woman.

In Mary's seduction scene with Henry, he says quite touchingly that he knows what it's like to be the second born. For Henry this is true, but Mary was the older sister. There is, however, a real tragedy that links the two that is never mentioned. Before the nineteenth century illness was generally poorly described. For example, there is still debate about exactly which pathogen caused the Black Death in the 1300s, and reports of other strange illnesses were probably some kind of virus, but we have no hard information.

From 1485 to the mid-1500s, Europe was swept several times by something called the sweating sickness.[3] It's generally not that well known, particularly when compared to bigger killers like the plague, or smallpox, or even good old-fashioned cholera. The disease began very suddenly with a sense of apprehension, followed by cold, violent shivers and headaches, with severe pains in the neck, shoulders, and limbs, all of this accompanied by overwhelming exhaustion. I am aware that this could sound like a hangover or a bad cold, but the malady got far worse. After the cold stage, which might last anywhere from thirty minutes to three hours, the hot and sweating stage followed. The characteristic sweat broke out suddenly and without any obvious cause. Accompanying the sweat was a sense of heat, headache, delirium, rapid pulse, and intense thirst. Palpitation and pain in the heart were also frequent symptoms. In the final stages (the mortality rate was up to 50 percent in some places), there was either general exhaustion and collapse or an irresistible urge to sleep.[4] One attack did not offer immunity, and some people suffered several bouts before dying. What caused the sickness was never discovered, and why it faded away is also unknown, but it was never seen again in England after 1578.

This illness changed the course of history. Arthur, Prince of Wales, elder brother of Henry VIII, contracted it and died in 1502, while his widow, Catherine of Aragon, recovered. So, Henry had seen the effects of the illness firsthand; so too had Mary, who lost her first husband to the disease. I think this is a genuinely interesting point, which Hollywood thought best to discard.

If I'm going to critique Mary's onscreen persona, then there's also Henry who is written as oddly gullible. The image of Henry VIII as a fat, angry monarch is partially true, and then there are the fun facts that in later life he kept a battle-axe by his bed and that he was the first British monarch on record to have eaten turkey (Henry gorging himself on a turkey leg is a popular image). But he was so much more than that, particularly in his early years. This was a monarch who so elegantly defended Catholicism against the rising Protestant movement in a long treatise that the Pope gave him the title Defender of the Faith. Henry kept this title after the split with Rome, and it was even more appropriate when the King or Queen of England became the head of the Anglican Church. It is a title still in use today.

Then there's Anne Boleyn. She has a huge number of defenders because this was a woman who was executed on false charges and whose daughter grew up to be the legendary Queen Elizabeth I. My point is this: An unjust end to your life and your daughter's awesomeness do not automatically make you awesome. Anne was not an exceptional queen; she made powerful enemies in her fight to marry the king, and she paid for it with her life. I have always rated Natalie Portman's acting talent highly, and when she breaks down, I believe it, whether talking about her first role in *Léon* (known as *The Professional* in the United States) or *V for Vendetta* or here, as she awaits the swordsman and her execution (it is true that Henry paid for the best French swordsman to execute her, a strange kindness, to be sure). Indeed, if her hair looks a little strange in the film it's because it was still growing back after she shaved it for *V for Vendetta*.

Among the blatantly false charges against Anne was that she was having an incestuous relationship with her brother George. This was not taken seriously at the time, but it is given credence in the movie as, after Anne has a stillbirth, she begs George to impregnate her, but he refuses. Is it a great bit of drama? Not really, it's unsavory, made worse because the film is reinforcing a five-hundred-year-old lie.

THE TWISTED TALE OF BLOODY MARY (2008)

Also coming out in 2008 was *The Twisted Tale of Bloody Mary*. Starring Miranda French, it never got a theatrical release (that I can find) but is one of those docudramas that have become ever more popular. It is the only movie I know of that is exclusively about Mary I of England.

The docudrama is the bastard child of the documentary and the historical drama. That this genre sits between two stools usually means it is inferior to both. That is certainly the case here. Getting academics to advise about a period may ensure historical accuracy and stop scenes of Henry VIII playing cards with Anne of Cleves, but the historian is not in charge of the edit, and moviemakers are not obliged to show everything. For example, I once watched a docudrama about the uncovering of a significant find of carnivorous dinosaurs in America. I realized about halfway through that the term T. rex was only ever used during the re-creation scenes and that the paleontologists on site mentioned only "apex predators and carnivores." The filmmakers wanted to talk about "T. rex" because they sell, but the experts were never going to say something factually inaccurate (at least not deliberately), so the filmmakers edited around the problem.

This is the problem with *The Twisted Tale of Bloody Mary*; there's not enough budget to do the topic justice, and the title alone tells you all you need to know about the balanced view of Mary. The film is trying to be a psycho-thriller about a woman who was dubbed "Bloody Mary" by her Protestant enemies. Even the children's nursery rhyme "Mary, Mary" doesn't put her in a good light as the "silver bells and cockle shells," etc., are an oblique reference to implements of torture and execution.

At the very start of Mary's reign there was another woman who was a claimant to the throne, and I'm not talking about Elizabeth. It was Lady Jane Grey. She was never formally crowned but had technically ruled for a grand total of nine days. Jane was a great-granddaughter of Henry VII and was a first cousin once removed of Edward VI. But she was a Protestant and would uphold the Church of England as Henry VIII and Edward VI (briefly) did, whereas everyone knew Mary was a staunch Catholic and would tear it down and perhaps start executing high-profile Protestants (which she did). As such, Jane was the long shot but also the best option as a Protestant replacement to Mary in 1553.

With such a short reign, it's impossible to discuss Jane's accomplishments; she is a minnow, a footnote, and totally irrelevant in history. But a young woman doomed to be executed on the order of another woman, Queen Mary, who was bearing down on her with all the inevitability of a storm on the horizon, makes for perfect dramatic material. Jane knew she was completely out of her depth, a pawn in the schemes of various powerful men. She became so stressed her hair began to fall out and her skin and fingernails to peel. By the time she was removed to face a formal trial, she was a shadow of her former youthful self. Her execution in 1554 was immortalized in a frank and shockingly evocative (and historically inaccurate because it shows the events indoors and her outfit doesn't look very Tudor and she positively glows in the scene, let's put all of this down to "artistic license") painting by the French artist Paul Delaroche in 1833. Any filmmaker seeing this painting would feel a light bulb go off in his head and think, what a great tragedy to tell.

We even know what went down on the day of her execution. Normally the condemned forgives and pays the executioner. This time around, the axman explicitly asked her forgiveness, which she granted him. Then she made a statement and asked a question, "I pray you dispatch me quickly. Will you take it off before I lay me down?" (a reference to her decapitation). The executioner answered, "No, madam." She put on a blindfold but couldn't find the block to rest her head, so a witness came to her aid. With her head on the block, she said her last words from Saint Luke's Gospel, "Lord, into thy hands I commend my spirit." The axman cut off her head with one swing. She was just seventeen.

These events have been turned into two feature films and a silent short (so even Jane gets more screen time than Edward III). The silent short, which was part of a series called *Wonder Women of the World*, was called simply *Lady Jane Grey. The Court of Intrigue* came out in 1923 and made little impact. Today I can find no prints online.

TUDOR ROSE (1936)

In 1936 there was *Tudor Rose* (known less poetically as *Nine Days a Queen* in America). If you remember my comments about the difference between "based on" and "inspired by," this film is very much "inspired by" events in the life of Lady Jane Grey. It was a modest hit and people liked it, but the critics took it to task for ignoring the most basic of facts. Even the crown she wears seems to have been inspired by the contemporary crown jewels of the 1930s rather than something worn by a monarch four hundred years earlier. The acting by modern standards is wooden, while the script and received pronunciation of *everyone* make it virtually unwatchable. There is one inadvertently funny moment at the worst possible time: Rather than showing her execution (which apart from the axman asking for forgiveness is totally wrong), you see the ranks of onlookers watching and then pigeons perched on the ramparts flying off as the sound of the axe comes down. I say the "sound of the axe," but presumably, to make it more dramatic, it sounds like they blow her up with dynamite or shoot her out of a cannon. You have been warned.

LADY JANE (1986)

So, after *Tudor Rose* there was definitely room for improvement; any average filmmaker could do something better. So, in the 1980s we had the far superior (which wasn't hard) *Lady Jane*, directed by legendary theater director Trevor Nunn and starring Helena Bonham Carter (who even at age twenty is technically too old to play the role). Interestingly Cary Elwes, who plays Guilford Dudley, is directly related both to the real Dudley and Lady Jane Grey. Once again, we have a movie playing fast and loose with history. In the film Dudley and Grey are imprisoned together, which makes it seem like the imprisonment happened because they were married. In reality, the marriage took place only about six weeks before Edward died, and Jane became a pawn in the games against Mary. In fact, at this point, the two barely knew each other and were imprisoned separately.[5] Indeed, you can find the name "Jane" scratched into the wall of the cell where Dudley was imprisoned in the Tower of London. This time the politics take a back seat to the love story between Dudley and Grey. It is a kind of Romeo and Juliet, two doomed teenage lovers, the victims of circumstance. It fits the history quite well. Comparing the Delaroche painting to the two movies and the historical facts is interesting: who knew that the same woman could die four completely different ways. Bonham Carter is excellent in the film, and her execution scene is heartbreaking as she reaches out, blindfolded, to find the block and is helped by one of the witnesses. However, this time her last words are not of faith but a whispered, "Guilford," showing that even in death she thinks of her love. Oh, how the poets applaud, but we know that's not how it went down.

What is telling is that two Tudors, Henry VII and Mary (yes, okay, and Edward but he ruled for such a short time he doesn't count), who get very little love are the grandparents of them all (literally, in some cases). Henry VII had to win a war to become king (he was a usurper, and the first Welsh King of England, which helps to explain why Henry VIII and Elizabeth I were ginger. Joke!) He's a great story, ultimately with a happy ending, and played right, there's a sequel about his son and another one about his granddaughters.

Similarly, if *The Twisted Tale of Bloody Mary* had had a budget and was a properly scripted movie, the idea of a psychological study of Mary I would be brilliant. We get flashes of it in *Elizabeth*, but a whole film that leans into the Hammer Horror of her reign would do well; and then, by including Henry and Elizabeth, box office success would be guaranteed. If a Hollywood producer reads this, let's talk.

MARY QUEEN OF SCOTS (2018)

Mary Queen of Scots is an interesting film that opens up a few topics of conversation. The phrase "they don't make them like they used to" is true. Digital cameras and CGI are a world away from the practical effects of *Ben-Hur*, but sometimes CGI sets and stunts don't have that "weight" that live action by real people conveys. Then there's acting itself: It is assumed that acting has gotten better, and I think it's fair to say that when you compare the average modern film to the average film from the 1930s, this is true. It's also great to see more ethnicities and women getting more roles both in front of and behind the cameras. All of these are positive improvements in the industry.

So far, so good, but to assume that care for history has increased over the last century is demonstrably not true. Filmmakers now feel obliged to project that the film has done its homework before we discover ten years later in a retrospective documentary that scenes from the script were being written the night before shooting. The screenwriter was having a nervous breakdown and the producer wanted to do a sci-fi version in the first place, so no historical research was done apart from a quick look on Wikipedia. But this barely contained mess is carefully stifled before the film comes out. People were flawed one hundred years ago, and they are still flawed today, and Hollywood always wants to make money. There's a good reason why it's called "show business."

Mary Queen of Scots was a modest success, but its marketing and costume choices did it no favors. The trailer uses this line from the film: "You murder me, you murder your sister." To be kind, I think it meant "sister" in the sense of the sisterhood, two women trying to survive in a man's world. It was, however, an unfortunate choice of words as this Mary and Elizabeth were real-life cousins, so it already looks like they haven't done any research. Also, the men in Elizabeth's court seem to be dressed in black at all times, which is historically inaccurate but does show off the amazing dresses Margot Robbie wears while playing Elizabeth. It's a choice but not a historically accurate one.

Perhaps the biggest crime the film commits is a crime that Hollywood has perpetrated a thousand times. It makes up a bit of history to heighten the tension. The problem on this occasion is that the fans of the Tudors are savvier now than they have ever been, and we now have social media to broadcast our outrage. As such, the movie got some strong pushback from possibly its most crucial scene where Mary and Elizabeth meet surreptitiously in a stable. The two women exchange barbed comments the way two boxers exchange punches. Saoirse Ronan and Margot Robbie are in top form in an exhilarating clash of wits and ideology. There's just one problem: The two queens never met face-to-face. This is not up for debate and is an example of how those pesky facts can damage a damn fine script. By including this, it alienated the fans of the Tudors, the key demographic.

One thing this movie does get right that so many historical films get wrong is lighting. This will be discussed in another chapter, but the thing about castles and many other locations in the past is they were dark and gloomy, and candles just don't throw out nearly enough light. Again, if you're going to spend a fortune on a big and highly ornate set, you want to show it off and get that budget on the screen. Think *Cleopatra* or a typical Bollywood film. But the lighting in this film is muted (sometimes helped by all those men in their dark clothes). The atmosphere feels genuine and is a credit to the cinematographer.

Let's look at some of the real history, and hopefully you'll see that a story going on in the background about Mary, Queen of Scots, could be a great movie in its own right (or at least a tense, low-budget B-movie).

Mary has become something of a political figure. Scots use her as an example of English interference, and while they have a point, she wasn't exactly a haggis-eating, tartan-wearing innocent herself. Her mother was French, and her grandmother was Margaret Tudor . . . of those Tudors south of the border. She was also a Catholic and there was a lot of plotting around using her as a substitute for the Protestant Queen Elizabeth of England. We obviously have no recording of her voice, but if she had an accent, it would have been French; it certainly wouldn't have been the broad Scottish brogue Saoirse Ronan went for in the film. She's not the only one, but the device is used to ramp up the Scottish/English rivalry.

Mary is often regarded as a kind of female "Braveheart," where Scotland = good and England = bad. But the politics of the time were far more complex than that. In summary, Mary had already been imprisoned in Scotland and even fought in a battle for the rights of her infant son James. The Battle of Langside in 1568 was a small affair between her forces and those of the Regent Moray. When Mary lost, she was forced to flee south of the border, where she hoped to get a warmer reception than that of her enemies in Scotland. She miscalculated and was imprisoned in England for about twenty years before her eventual execution.

But even in her imprisonment Mary still constituted a threat to Elizabeth . . . but there was a problem. There was no way the English queen could execute Mary on a whim; hard evidence of threat and danger was needed, otherwise it would set a dangerous precedent. Foreign powers were communicating with Mary, and while defenders say she was a pawn in bigger games, she did answer the letters and they weren't exactly "stop it, I'm very loyal to Elizabeth. Shoo now, I have no interest in your plotting." Intercepting her communications was hard but cracking the code they were written in was harder.

In the end it took every connection Sir Francis Walsingham (Elizabeth's trusted adviser and spymaster) had to intercept a coded letter and pass it to Dutch cryptographer Philip van Marnix. A queen's life hung in the balance while Marnix worked on the fiendishly difficult code. When he cracked it, the letter revealed that Mary would indeed go along with a Catholic invasion of England. The letter signed her death warrant. Despite the hard evidence, Elizabeth vacillated due either to feelings for a blood relative or worries that the plan could backfire or both.[6]

Mary was executed on February 7, 1587. The first blow missed her neck and struck the back of her head with the flat of the blade. The second blow killed her, but part of the neck remained attached. The axeman had to cut that off with a knife before the head of a queen could be displayed. Nobody would defend her execution, but it was an occupational hazard at the time. Under Mary I of England's rule there were times when it looked like Elizabeth could have met the same fate as her mother. It was a more brutal time. During her reign Elizabeth faced the dual threats of being a woman and a Protestant in a religiously divided Europe. In 1570, Pope Pius V issued the Papal Bull referred to as *Regnans in Excelsis*. In it he calls Queen Elizabeth I of England a heretic and excommunicates her, adding that anyone who would overthrow her (by killing her) would be given the same indulgences as if they had gone on crusade to the Holy Land, meaning all sins would be wiped away and a place in heaven guaranteed.[7]

ELIZABETH (1998)

Now we come to perhaps the most complete vision of a Tudor monarch in Shekhar Kapur's two films with Cate Blanchett: *Elizabeth* and *Elizabeth: The Golden Age*. There have been discussions about a third film at the end of Elizabeth's life as Blanchett ages. It is an ingenious plan and if there was ever a woman born to play Elizabeth Tudor, it is the awesome Blanchett.

One problem with Tudor history, compared to say the times of Richard the Lionheart or Cleopatra, is that we are now in an age where more and more people are literate. The printing press had been invented, and as such, there are more documents to fill in the blanks and give us a more rounded picture of people and events at the time. We are also at a point when art has become more naturalistic compared to the medieval era, and Hans Holbein's depictions of Henry VIII and his court (my favorite painting of all time is *The Ambassadors* by Holbein) bring to life long-dead people. It makes lying or altering the facts harder to do. Shekhar Kapur wants to have the history as a backdrop to a character study of a very interesting woman in a very turbulent time. That's fair, but those pesky facts keep getting in the way, at which point a writer has to make a decision: make the facts fit the story or make the story fit the facts. With his two Elizabeth films Kapur has clearly gone with the first option even to the point where some of Elizabeth's costumes are noticeably historically inaccurate but enable the visualization of her feelings.

Some filmmakers make the argument that they are aware they are changing history, but they are doing it to make the story interesting so people will be drawn in and inspired to learn more. It's a wonderful "get out of jail free" card. If this makes those writers and directors sleep soundly, then the notion serves some purpose, but often historically accurate films are just as interesting—and that's not what happens in real life. People go to a film: if they like it, great. What's next? Few people walk out of a multiplex and think, the first thing I must do is buy a book about what I just saw . . . and I'm saying that as the guy who loves both movies and history.

Stories stick in people's minds much longer than bare facts, and we like them. From the time we are children, listening to the stories read to us, to adulthood when we enjoy blockbuster films, more people will simply accept the story as told than will question its authenticity. There may be more people who think Kapur's films are historically correct than there will be people who have read a good biography about this Tudor queen and know otherwise.

Now let's take a look at that trickiest of historical subjects, historical love lives. *Elizabeth* leans heavily on a romantic angle. Elizabeth never married or had children, but as well as being a queen, she was also a normal woman who must have needed love in her life, so what's the deal? A historian will say, we don't know; a film director will say, that's not good enough, and so the required romantic relationship in *Elizabeth* revolves around Robert Dudley, Earl of Leicester. There is evidence that he was an early favorite of Elizabeth's at a time when they were both young and might have become lovers, but while we don't know that for certain, the film leaves us in no doubt that they loved each other even though it remains a little coy about a physical/long-term relationship.

Then there's Sir Francis Walsingham, head of the spy network to keep Elizabeth safe (we have already seen him crop up as the man responsible for intercepting Mary, Queen of Scots's coded messages). In this film he is introduced lolling around with a young man, and it is strongly implied that they are lovers (Walsingham subsequently murders him with complete indifference). Do we know if Walsingham was gay? No, and there is zero evidence of it. We know he was a spymaster, but did he himself ever actually kill anyone? There is no evidence of that, but with his first scene and the subsequent chilling murder, we get the idea that Walsingham is not to be crossed. This is a clever ploy to demonstrate the spy's character, but at the same time, we have made all kinds of other, inaccurate conclusions about him.

(There's a "blink and you miss it" role for the future James Bond as Daniel Craig plays a Catholic spy who is captured, tortured, and killed. So even James Bond can meet a grisly end if he crosses Sir Francis Walsingham.) Sometimes age is an issue. Who wouldn't want Sir Richard Attenborough in their film? But here, he is an old man playing Sir William Cecil, a man in his late thirties. Cecil advised Elizabeth until his death in 1598; however, that time frame in Attenborough's case would make him over one hundred by 1598.

Elizabeth features quite a few scenes of torture and a fair bit of nudity too. Don't forget this is 1998, well before TV shows like *Spartacus, Rome*, or *Game of Thrones*, so it could be said that *Elizabeth* showed that historical dramas can be portrayed with sex and violence and still be taken seriously. The film went on to win one Oscar and five BAFTAs.

ELIZABETH: THE GOLDEN AGE (2007)

Then there's the sequel *Elizabeth: The Golden Age*. Interestingly, in order to get the widest possible audience, the film has no nudity and very little blood and so achieves a more family-friendly rating (12A in the UK or PG-13 in the United States). But on to the main event, the Spanish Armada. It's 1588, and this is a pivotal moment in history for England and for Elizabeth. Had the Spanish Armada succeeded in linking up with the troops in the Spanish Netherlands, England did not have the army to beat an experienced and well-equipped Spanish force. It wouldn't necessarily have been game over, but the armada was certainly the biggest threat to England since William the Conqueror in 1066. So, Elizabeth set out to rouse her troops at Tilbury, where she delivers a barnstorming speech, the most famous lines being: "I know I have the body of a weak and feeble woman; but I have the heart and stomach of a king, and of a king of England too, and think foul scorn that Parma or Spain, or any prince of Europe, should dare to invade the borders of my realm: to which rather than any dishonour shall grow by me, I myself will take up arms, I myself will be your general, judge, and rewarder of every one of your virtues in the field."[8]

The film inexplicably fumbles this most open of goals. For starters they don't use the famous line about heart and stomach, and secondly, presumably because of Blanchett's success in *Lord of the Rings*, we see Elizabeth clad in armor. She looks amazing, but there's just one problem: She never wore it, and there are no pictures of her wearing it. There are some conflicting reports of her wearing some military paraphernalia but nothing like plate armor; she was never in a battle so never needed it (there is some evidence she may have worn a few items that resembled armor, but nothing like what is shown in the film). For all the historical liberties taken, what we see in this scene might as well be Galadriel talking to the men of Gondor, and from here, the list of historic nonsense goes on and on.

Clive Owen as Sir Walter Raleigh could hold his own against Errol Flynn himself in the swashbuckling stakes; however, almost everything he does is wrong or never happened, including that he was not in overall command of the English forces: That was Robert Dudley. The budget was not the size of *Lord of the Rings*, and as a result, only one ship was built for filming. To save money, one side was modeled on English ships of the time and the other was made to be Spanish, but they had to lay down smoke so you couldn't see the differences in the background. *Elizabeth: The Golden Years* is certainly one of the better Tudor movies, but there's no getting around the fact that it isn't as good as its predecessor. Saying that, if the band gets back together for a third movie about Elizabeth's last years, I would love to see it.

In my discussions about this era, there has been one obvious omission, a black hole in both history and the movies that I have apparently forgotten. Fear not, Shakespeare is so important to both our understanding of the Tudors, Stuarts, British culture, and even screenplays that he gets a whole chapter to himself.

NOTES

1. Jem Duducu, *The Busy Person's Guide to British History* (Seattle: KDP, 2013), 166–79.

2. Alex von Tunzelmann, "The Other Boleyn Girl: Hollyoaks in Fancy Dress," *The Guardian*, August 6, 2008.

3. Jem Duducu, *Forgotten History: Unbelievable Moments from the Past* (Gloucestershire, UK: Amberley Publishing, 2016), 125.

4. Duducu, *Forgotten History*, 126.

5. Nicola Tallis, *Crown of Blood: The Deadly Inheritance of Lady Jane Grey* (London: Pegasus Books, 2016), 322.

6. Jem Duducu, *Slinkys and Snake Bombs: Weird but True Historical Facts* (Gloucestershire, UK: Amberley Publishing, 2021), 168.

7. Jem Duducu, *Deus Vult: A Concise History of the Crusades* (Gloucestershire, UK: Amberley Publishing, 2014), 219.

8. Anonymous, *Cabala, Mysteries of State* (London: British Library, 1694, 2011 online).

Chapter 4

To Bard or Not to Bard

Born in 1564, the most important writer in British history came from humble beginnings in a small town in the Midlands called Stratford-upon-Avon. He is said to have died on his birthday in 1616, which is also St. George's Day, named for the patron saint of England. This is a little too neat, and history is rarely this satisfying. His baptism date is not the same as his day of death, so it's a clever story that could be true but will never be proven definitively.

IMDb (Internet Movie Database) is a valuable resource. For example, when you see someone in a film or TV show and think, where have I seen them before, the IMDb website has the answer as searches can be conducted either by the title of a film or by the name of the performer. If you search by the name of a film (or TV show), you can pull up a full list of cast and crew, actors, directors, writers, and so on. Someone like Katharine Hepburn, with a long and impressive career, has a substantial 191 credits. But someone like Danny Trejo, who says yes to anything, often doesn't know the name of the project he is working on, and constantly pours out work of varying quality (for example, in 2021 and despite COVID-19 restrictions that greatly limited movie/TV production, he appeared in fifteen different shows and movies) has more than 606 credits to his name at the time of writing (it will be more by the time you look).[1]

But there is an outlier, a person with more credits than anyone else on the entire website, a man who died not only before the internet was invented, but before the invention of film or even the electric motor, and that person is the glovemaker from the Midlands, William Shakespeare. At the time of writing, he has nearly 1,644 writing credits and a total of around 1,732 total credits. By the time this book gets into your hands, it will have gone up. Putting it simply, he is the single greatest inspiration to Hollywood there has ever been: That's why there has to be a chapter on him. Shakespeare is right there at the very dawn of cinema. One of IMDb's earliest entries is 1898's *Macbeth*, followed by *King John* in 1899 and *Hamlet's Duel* in 1900. This was at a time when films were silent and lasted for minutes and, as such, are not filmed versions of the plays, but a few choice scenes recorded for posterity.

Every nation has their great writers, whether it's Goethe in Germany or Luo Guanzhong in China or Chinua Achebe in Nigeria, but for better or worse, it's impossible for any of them to match the quantity and quality of Shakespeare. His plays have been translated into every language in the world (including Klingon), and he goes so far back in time that there are literary arguments about exactly how many of his attributed works are his and his alone. Speaking as a writer, I don't think most people have any idea how many others it takes to deliver the end product. This book may have my name on the front cover, but it would be very different without my copy editor whose contributions are invaluable but invisible. And that's before we get to those at the publishing house who ensure that my work meets their standards and requirements, so perhaps five others will have tweaked my manuscript before publication—and I'm hardly Shakespeare. So, let's give Shakespeare a break: Just because he had some help and others contributed, it's still his work, and I say thirty-eight plays (others say thirty-seven) and 154 sonnets (plus two long narrative poems as well as other, shorter poems) amount to a staggering body of work. So, how many Shakespeare plays can you name? I'm going to guess you can come up with five without breaking a sweat, and I've already mentioned three.

William Shakespeare is a giant of literature and theater; nobody in all of history can withstand a comparison to the man. Find his plays boring? I bet you use phrases from his body of work. Ever had "too much of a good thing"? That's from *As You Like It*. Are you "my own flesh and blood"? Have you ever been "cruel to be kind" and do you believe "the clothes make the man"? Those are all from *Hamlet*. And if you believe "the world is my oyster," that's from *The Merry Wives of Windsor*. The list is a very long one.

Other writers have mastered a language—Shakespeare invented it. He is responsible for the modern English language, but I will argue to the grave that he did not coin the word *elbow*. The phrase "elbows him" is in *King Lear*, so Shakespeare probably did invent the word's verb form, and we all know what "elbowing" means. But I cannot believe that prior to the late sixteenth century, no one in Britain had found a name for the bend in the arm. It really hurts when you bang it, and I cannot believe someone would complain about the pain in their "as of yet unnamed" body part.

English is a strange mongrel language: It has bits of Latin, some French, a dash of Norse, and a sprinkle of German in it. It breaks all its own grammatical rules and is not purely phonetic. Think of cough and plough—why do they sound so very different? It's a mess. Maybe Shakespeare didn't come up with *elbow*, but he did genuinely come up with new words, including *caked* and *cold-blooded*. My favorite is what we call man's best friend. Prior to the Tudor era, a canine was called a hound, from the German *hund*, but by the 1600s the word had changed to dog. No one can say for sure why, and although we know Shakespeare did not coin it, he did use it. Words pass in and out of fashion; for example, the medieval word for bumblebee is dumbledore—and yes, the word inspired J. K. Rowling.

What shouldn't be forgotten is Shakespeare was never writing exclusively for the elite. A Tudor-era play was a chaotic affair. Actors would not only speak lines to each other but to the audience to get a bit of crowd participation. During fight scenes men were encouraged to come up from the crowd and bulk out the numbers as they playfully dueled with each other (injuries had to have occurred). There were jokes with lavatorial references and sexual innuendo (included to entertain those in "the pit"), and violence, assassinations, battles, poisonings, torture, suicide, and cannibalism all feature in Shakespeare's plays. So, the next time a director is accused of dumbing things down, his response could be, I took my inspiration from Shakespeare.

Nods to the pit notwithstanding, over the centuries Shakespeare's plays became the intellectual property of the elite so that by the nineteenth century, the contemporary language of his works became the famous RP, Received Pronunciation, the voice of the elite and highly educated. Now the plays no longer spoke to the masses; now children were forced to study his plays in school. They became "worthy" and took on a reputation for being less than exciting—boring, in fact. The words were dissected, the iambic pentameter alien to common speech was a mystery to be calculated. Shakespeare was put on a pedestal and in the process became about as much fun as extra math lessons on a Friday afternoon.

The sonnets get regular mentions in movies (a character quoting Shakespeare shows the film/character to be cultured), but it is the plays that are the meat in Shakespeare's intimidating list of writing credits. Not all are five-star works, but many are. Have a look to see not only how many you have heard of, but how many about which you know at least vague plot details. The following list has been compiled in the order the plays were written; it's from the website of the Royal Shakespeare Company (based in the bard's hometown of Stratford-upon-Avon) that has a page dedicated to summarizing his works, so I will say this is definitive:

The Taming of the Shrew
Henry VI Part II
Henry VI Part III
The Two Gentlemen of Verona
Titus Andronicus

Henry VI Part I
Richard III
The Comedy of Errors
Love's Labour's Lost
A Midsummer Night's Dream
Romeo and Juliet
Richard II
King John
The Merchant of Venice
Henry IV Part I
Henry IV Part II
Much Ado About Nothing
Henry V
As You Like It
Julius Caesar
Hamlet
The Merry Wives of Windsor
Twelfth Night
Troilus and Cressida
Othello
Measure for Measure
All's Well That Ends Well
Timon of Athens
King Lear
Macbeth
Antony and Cleopatra
Coriolanus
Pericles
Cymbeline
The Winter's Tale
The Tempest
Henry VIII
The Two Noble Kinsmen[2]

Some of these are better known than others, but all of them have been put on film. A look at the list shows that Shakespeare did some real deep dives into history. Take for example Coriolanus. He was a real Roman general given that name after conducting the successful siege and capture of the town of Corioli (in modern-day Italy). This was all happening in the fifth century BC (at roughly the same time as the Greco-Persian Wars), when Rome was little more than a city-state, and centuries before the Punic Wars, which resulted in the Roman domination of the Mediterranean. Like virtually everyone else, I came to this obscure general through Shakespeare. The play has been made into a film multiple times, most recently in 2011, directed by and starring Ralph Fiennes, who changed the setting to the modern day, turning Coriolanus into a gun for hire, a mercenary warlord. So, if a play like *Coriolanus* can get multiple movies, imagine the list for better-known works like *Macbeth, Hamlet, Julius Caesar,* and *Romeo and Juliet.*

Shakespeare was not the first to turn history into a story, but he certainly established the benchmark for the genre. There is little written information about Coriolanus; any compilation of the historical and archaeological records would make for a short article, a very short article. That is not going to work for a play, so Shakespeare takes the bare bones of what is known and layers on the story he wants to tell in the same way that the film *Lady Jane* uses real history as a framework to tell a doomed love story.

Shakespeare's works are jigsaws of history: He is making history, but he is also a reflection of his times, and further, he is playing fast and loose with the known facts. If we complain about the likes of *Braveheart* changing things to make a more compelling story, then we must lay the same charge at Shakespeare's feet. Because his works have been around for more than four hundred years, his "rewrites" have seeped into the popular subconscious. While his plays are generally split between histories, tragedies, and comedies (those bloody unfunny comedies: Shakespeare is credited with inventing the term *bloody* as a curse rather than a description), the histories form the largest body of his work and, as such, will take up most of this chapter.

Julius Caesar is one of the few people from the past who has virtually global recognition. He was already well known to the people of Europe before Shakespeare's play, but as usual, the bard takes a person from the past and preserves them in amber for future generations to marvel at . . . sort of.

If I were to ask you what Julius Caesar's last words were, you are likely to say, "*Et tu Brute*" (well done on the Latin by the way). These are the words from the play, but we have plenty of historical evidence about the events on the Ides of March in 44 BC, so we know that last sentence was a bit of a trick. We know Caesar was killed on the Ides of March, and it is commented on as a prophecy of his demise as early as Plutarch. So that has to be contemporary, right? No. One of the dangers about ancient chroniclers is that just because it's an "old dead dude" (to quote from *Bill & Ted*) doesn't mean they were contemporary to the events they are describing. Plutarch was writing one hundred years after Caesar's death so he could well be embellishing the story. Shakespeare took the writings of Plutarch in apparent good faith, and he included the same idea of the Ides of March being a portent of death in the play. Is this Shakespeare deliberately fiddling with history? No, but what comes next is. Caesar's famous last words, said as he bled out surrounded by the knife-wielding senators, is a Shakespearean invention. Contemporary or near contemporary sources are conflicting, but that line isn't once mentioned. Only one record reports that he did say something along the lines of "you too child," which is similar but not the same. But let's face it, if he had been stabbed nearly two dozen times, it is unlikely he was going to have the time or the blood to the brain to say something memorable, and most sources indicate he went down silently or with a groan. Either way, no one-liner. So, this is an unambiguous example of how Shakespeare's decision to put on a good show has changed the perception of popular history for centuries.

CESARE DEVE MORIRE (2012)

There are endless examples of Shakespeare's international appeal, such as *Zulfiqar* in 2016: a Bollywood crime drama inspired by the plots of both *Julius Caesar* and *Antony and Cleopatra.* But perhaps one of the most exciting recent versions of the play as a film is *Cesare Deve Morire.* What makes this Italian film so special is it follows the rehearsals for and then shows scenes from a prison performance of the piece. All the prisoners are genuine prisoners, and it was filmed in Rebibbia Prison in Rome. It won the Golden Bear at the Berlin International Film Festival and is one of the many examples of how Shakespeare is used as a means of rehabilitation. While the story may be set in Ancient Rome, Shakespeare was so good at writing rounded, three-dimensional characters and putting them in compelling and believable situations that he can speak to a prisoner in the twenty-first century in a country that doesn't even speak English. That is powerful writing.

Julius Caesar is so important to European history we would know about him with or without Shakespeare. However, Henry V is not such a big name, and while he is hugely important in English (and French) history, he is just one of many warrior kings from the Middle Ages 1,500 years after Julius Caesar's life. Henry only gets the respect he is due because of one of the most patriotic plays ever produced by anyone anywhere. Indeed, even more so than Julius Caesar, Henry V as a historical figure is seen almost exclusively through the lens of the play, at least by the general public.

Henry V knew what propaganda was. The famous side-on portrait shows him with a severe haircut, a deliberate decision by the king to look like a monk so that ambassadors to the court commented on his simple clothes and thought he looked like a priest rather than a king. So, a monarch outwardly showing his rejection of worldly things. A cynic would say it was good PR; a fan would say these were a sign of his humility.

Although side-on portraits were popular at the time, there is another reason why Henry chose the pose, and that was because he had a livid wound on the other side of his face. As Prince Hal he had been putting down a rebellion in Wales when he was struck in the face by an arrow from a Welsh longbow. So, the handsome portrait of Henry V is really that of a battle-scarred warrior with a bowl haircut.[3]

The rough events of *Henry V* fit real history. In Act II, before heading to France, there's a plot by the Earl of Cambridge and two accomplices to assassinate Henry at Southampton. This is based on real events. Henry's father, Henry IV, had usurped the throne, so Henry V was still vulnerable to a dynastic challenge. Indeed, it would be his victories in 1415 that would finally ensure his claim to be the legitimate King of England, for surely those successes meant he was blessed by God. And while Henry did carefully plan for the siege of Harfleur and successfully storm it, he never said, "Once more unto the breach, dear friends, once more," or "Close the wall up with our English dead." But the problem for the real Henry V was that while Harfleur had been a success, it had taken too long, and as such, all the money spent on the campaign would result in a solid performance but nothing earth shattering. Putting it simply, the effort didn't match the reward. After a long siege an army is always in a worse state than at the start, as poor weather and disease creep into physical well-being and morale. It was October, a time when the campaigning season for war was normally over. There was no logical reason to look for battle: It was the wrong time of the year, the army was sick and denuded, and the French had now had time to gather a much larger and better equipped force. But Henry knew he needed something else to make 1415 his year. The two armies famously met on Saint Crispin's Day, the 25th of October 1415. The English were clearly outnumbered, but Shakespeare, being Shakespeare, exaggerated the numbers (which to be fair, almost all historical chronicles do). We know that Henry did speak and walk among the men before a battle no one else wanted to fight.[4] All logic dictated that this was a battle best avoided. From Shakespeare we get these famous lines:

We few, we happy few, we band of brothers;

For he to-day that sheds his blood with me

Shall be my brother; be he ne'er so vile,

This day shall gentle his condition.[5]

We don't know exactly what Henry said, but we do know it gave the troops the resolve they needed. The Battle of Agincourt was another disaster for the French, who had already tasted the vicious sting of English and Welsh longbow volleys. The mud from the nearby River Somme (yes, the same river floodplain that the World War I battles would be fought on) meant the French knights in their full-plate armor became slow-moving targets for English archers with armor-piercing arrows. Modern estimates put the English forces at around seven thousand (where 85 percent of the army was archers) and the French at around twenty thousand. The English seemed to be outnumbered three to one, but by the end of the day, about six hundred English had died to the French six thousand, with another one thousand captured. In the play the numbers are markedly different: According to Shakespeare the French suffered ten thousand casualties, the English, fewer than thirty.[6] So the bard turned a great victory in real life into a legendary one. Of course, the physical limitations of theater mean things like battles have to be described. The four lines quoted from the Saint Crispin's Day Speech is from a longer speech of fifty lines, but modern audiences don't need narration during scenes of four-hour-long movies, so it's abridged versions that make it to the big screen.

HENRY V (1944)

Perhaps the two most famous versions committed to film highlight the flexibility of the play. First there is 1944's *Henry V*, directed by and starring Laurence Olivier. It starts as an actual onstage play before broadening out into a cinematic experience in a bit of visual trickery akin to Dorothy in *The Wizard of Oz* opening the door in a black and white house to reveal the colorful world of Oz outside.

This *Henry V* was made during World War II and filmed before D-Day. It may be about the English fighting in France five hundred years earlier, but it was clearly referencing a new fight about to happen in France, where, according to the film, it was all clear blue skies and a very clean Agincourt battlefield. Because they were all off fighting, there weren't enough young men in Britain to pad out the battle scenes, so it was filmed in neutral Ireland. Budgeted at £2 million, it was the most expensive British movie ever made at the time. But Olivier had problems with rationing and a lack of materials. He also had no stunt coordinator, so he had to teach the Irish extras how to do their stunts himself; he did his own, too, and fractured his shoulder in the process. Most of the cuts from the source material are to do with negative comments about Henry as king (these were allegedly imposed by Churchill himself). So, the usual three-hour run time was cut down to two hours and fifteen minutes. This made it a little more viewer friendly, but this also made it unambiguous: The English were the good guys and knew how to win battles in France, important messages for audiences in 1944.

HENRY V (1989)

Then there's Kenneth Branagh's version of *Henry V*, and like Laurence Oliver, he too both directed and starred in his film. Branagh's version is very different but nods to the one made forty-five years earlier, and as they are also exactly the same length, Branagh makes a connection to film history. His performance is impressive, and for the first time, we get to see a real Battle of Agincourt, authentically portrayed, with mud everywhere. So after the connections to Shakespeare, Olivier, and film history, we see a further connection with the Somme's mud, integral to the events of 1415 as well as to those of 1916.

In Branagh's film, the same events happen in the same way, but rather than showing the glories of war as Olivier was obliged to do in 1944, the emphasis now was on the horrendous cost of war. Same story, same playwright, but very different interpretations. Branagh's budget was over four times that of Olivier's, but forty-five years later, that had no meaning in terms of what it could buy. Ironically, despite all the hardships suffered in the production of Olivier's film, it has the look and feel of a Hollywood sword-and-sandals epic, whereas Branagh's feels like a low-budget indie film. The battle scenes may have utterly different tones, but they are both exhilarating, and to the modern eye, Branagh's version probably feels more honest.

Henry V is a great subject for both play and film, but the man himself is relatively obscure. Had Shakespeare decided to do a play about Edward III rather than Henry V, we might well have some clever quotes from the Battle of Crecy and the founding of the Order of the Garter. Henry V is absolutely an example of a historical figure made famous by the ultimate kingmaker, Shakespeare.

"Now is the winter of our discontent" are the opening words of *Richard III*. It's with this play that we get to see Shakespeare's real-world concerns and his motivation for changing history. Many historians say that Richard III was the last Plantagenet king, the first being Henry II in the 1100s. I've never bought that Henry II is from a dynasty separate to that of his mother. The very intimidating Empress Matilda (a daughter of England's King Henry I) fought a twenty-year civil war with the usurper King Stephen to get her son on the throne. But the point is that for (at least) three hundred years, members of the same family ruled England until Richard III was killed at the Battle of Bosworth in 1485. The victor of the battle was Henry Tudor, who became Henry VII and the founder of the Tudor dynasty. So, if Richard III needed to be killed by the founder of the next dynasty Henry VII, and the playwright is writing at the time when Henry VII's granddaughter was ruling the land, then Richard has to be the kind of evil villain who deserved that sort of death.

Anything else might make the Tudors look like usurpers, and Elizabeth was the kind of ruler who would have the head of anyone with even a whiff of treason or sedition about them.

While it is true that Shakespeare's characters are timeless and explore the flaws and virtues of human nature, it's important not to update it to the point of silliness. Take for example the 2003 National Theatre production of *Henry V* in which Adrian Lester played the titular king. This caused a stir among certain groups because Lester is Black, but that is not what I found troubling (after all, no actor plays Henry as he really looked, with his terrible haircut and massive scar). No, it's the fact that it was set in the modern day, so instead of wearing armor, he wore camouflage with a bulletproof vest and brandished an automatic pistol. During the main event at the Battle of Agincourt, they had a genuine armored personnel carrier on stage (the National Theatre made a big point about how hard this was to do and how proud they were that they had pulled it off).[7] Excuse me? I get that they were updating it, but how is there any threat to the "band of brothers" if they sit behind an APC firing off its heavy machine guns? It was a cool idea that didn't work the moment anyone thought about the source material.

Richard III is Tudor propaganda and should be read with emergency access to a more factual and favorable biography about the man. However, the debate that raged for more than four hundred years was whether Richard III was a hunchback. Ableist bias is common in many cultures, where disabled individuals are thought to be punished for past deeds in another life or their bodies' ailments are an outer sign of inner evil. It's all very nasty and all too common. So, at the time of writing, making Richard ugly on the outside showed the audience his inner ugliness too. But then Philippa Langley did something amazing in 2012.

As part of my university studies, I participated in and/or read up on hundreds of archaeological digs. There are some fundamental rules that apply no matter what the age of the site or where it is in the world. Little ceremony was given to the king of the previous and now defunct dynasty, and we know Richard III was hastily buried in Leicester. Under the circumstances, it was a small miracle his body was given a proper burial. A couple of generations later, the grand churches and monasteries of England were looted and sometimes torn down during the Dissolution of the Monasteries as Henry VIII created the Church of England. At the time, Richard's tomb was highly likely to be a target for destruction, but it was never identified, and the site of his burial eventually became a parking lot in Leicester, where any remains would most likely have been destroyed. Then Philippa Langley turned up in September of 2012 and started excavating. Simon Franaby (of *Horrible Histories* fame) was on hand, making a documentary about the project. Langley was intense (to be polite) about her work and the whole dig had an air of the absurd about it.[8]

But then the very first pit revealed a full skeleton with prominent scoliosis (curvature of the spine). Never in the history of archaeology has the first pit come up with exactly what they were looking for. The chances of there being remains in the first place were ludicrously small, but finding them on the first attempt was just incredible. Langley demanded the remains be put in a coffin with Richard's flag draped over it. Again, never in the history of archaeology have human remains been treated this way. Although it was (astoundingly) likely to be Richard, no tests had been carried out yet, so to pretend that the remains were conclusively Richard's broke all the protocols. Langley got what she wanted. A makeshift coffin and flag were produced, and a funeral procession carried out. DNA tests later revealed that Langley was right, and the remains were indeed those of King Richard III. A king who died a traitor had been hastily buried without shroud or coffin in the grounds of a friary destroyed in the Dissolution. After much controversy he was reburied in Leicester Cathedral (this whole surreal story was turned into its own film, 2022's *The Lost King*).

While Shakespeare's *Richard III* is a highly biased piece of propaganda, he wasn't wrong about Richard's deformity. Some have queried how someone with a hunchback could fight wearing full-plate armor. This is to misunderstand how armies were equipped. In more recent times, the government provides all the equipment needed, but back then everyone brought their own. This explains why peasants invariably had little or no protection (although the training to pull the bowstring of a longbow put such pressure on the body it is easy to identify the remains of archers on medieval battlefields as, invariably, some of their vertebrae are fused together after years of practice), and the lords had their suits of armor tailor-made. Richard had a curved spine, so they made armor to fit his contours; it's not a mystery.

Events in the play unfold largely as they did in real life, but it's the motivations that are utterly different and define Richard III as a chillingly evil despot. For instance, the story around Lady Anne is just slanderous. In the play Richard boasts that he will manipulate Lady Anne into marrying him even though he killed her father and husband. While it is true that both were dead, they are known to have died in battle, and no one knows who killed them. Anne is seen grieving over the corpse of her husband and cursing the one who killed him. This never happened and, in reality, there is the much sweeter story that Anne and Richard were childhood sweethearts who were brought up together at Middleham Castle.[9]

Then there are the two princes; their story could be a whole book on its own (and has been). Cutting a long story short, while it doesn't look good for

Richard (he seems to have benefited most from their deaths), there is no evidence he ordered their deaths, and all the scenes of plotting are pure fantasy.

Next up for examination is the Battle of Bosworth, where Richard III sees that all is lost and needs to get away, famously saying, "A horse, a horse, my kingdom for a horse." This is the exact opposite of what happened. Richard should never have engaged in battle with Henry Tudor, because he had everything to lose and nothing to gain. Henry Tudor's claim to the throne was paper thin, and there was no sign of a popular uprising to support him against Richard. When Richard saw that Henry was relatively isolated from his retinue in the battle, he and his own bodyguards charged them. This was not the action of a coward but of an aggressive leader, and it nearly worked. How do we know that? Because Henry's standard bearer, the man mounted next to Henry, was killed in the attack.

RICHARD III (1955)

Laurence Olivier once again gave his all as an English king, but Richard was a very different figure to Henry V. This king was grotesque, with an elongated nose as well as a hunched back. This was a very literal retelling of Shakespeare's version of events, and it's obvious Olivier was depicting a man of pure evil. Olivier's interpretation was bold and easy to parody, perhaps most memorably by Peter Sellers doing a perfect impersonation of Olivier as Richard III reciting the Beatles' song, "A Hard Day's Night."

RICHARD III (1995)

Forty years later, Sir Ian McKellen cowrote and starred in a very pared-down version of the play (under two hours) but still called *Richard III*. The clever thing here is that the story was moved to the 1930s, and Richard's (genuine) boar standard was repurposed as a fascist symbol (a stand-in for the swastika). The message of the play has been changed from the evils of the old regime to the evils of fascism. This one is my personal favorite, and the scene where Robert Downey Jr. is killed by a dagger that comes up through his bed and into his abdomen is a wonderful example of great practical special effects.

THE MERCHANT OF VENICE (2004)

After one problematic portrayal, let's look at another, not from the histories but from the tragedies, *The Merchant of Venice*. Filmed as early as 1911, it has been a cinema staple for more than a century. There is, however, a very big problem with this play's anti-Semitism.

In today's social media world, someone is always ready to be offended by something. It's impossible to please everyone all the time, but we should all be able to agree that anti-Semitism is evil. John Mann wrote *Antisemitism: The Oldest Hatred*. The Ancient Egyptians, the Romans, the medieval Spanish, and the Nazis don't have much in common except they all hated the Jews.

Nowadays, a showing of *Gone with the Wind* comes with an introductory warning that its racial portrayals are "of its time," and I will have more to say about this film in the chapter on the US Civil War. Shakespeare's plays also have their problems. Even defenders of *The Merchant of Venice* call it "a problematic play" (personally, I'd call *Richard III* a "problematic play"), but *The Merchant of Venice* is more than that, it's anti-Semitic. However, using that warning from *Gone with the Wind*, it is true that it is also "of its time." So, am I suggesting that we cancel Shakespeare or take this play off the list? No, but context needs to be added for today's audiences.

As I briefly mentioned earlier, in the late thirteenth century King Edward I exiled all the Jews of England. This was a cold, calculated move to erase the huge debts he had accrued. He was neither the most rabid antisemite of the time nor the first European monarch to do this: The French had done it a generation earlier. Further, it was greeted with widespread approval in England, showing everyone at the time to be fundamentally anti-Semitic. The story of the Jews in Europe is long and sad. To give just one example, in the 1090s, when the First Crusade was being preached and knights were being encouraged to travel to the Holy Land to fight the infidels, not everyone could go. It was expensive and dangerous and not everyone could be a knight. So, what could the locals do to help this divine effort? Why not attack local communities of non-Christians as an act of solidarity? So yes, the Jewish populations of Europe were attacked and murdered (particularly in areas that are now modern Germany).[10] That was five hundred years before Shakespeare wrote this play and 850 years before the Holocaust. So, there were no Jews in England when Shakespeare was writing. Jews were allowed back into the country when England briefly became a republic in the mid-1600s under the lord protector Oliver Cromwell, at least a generation after the death of Shakespeare.

Defenders of the play also say that compared to other Christian depictions of Jews at the time, Shakespeare's is fairly nuanced. This is a terrible argument. The Jews of Venice were grouped together in ghettos (this is where the term comes from) that were locked at night, kind of like an open prison. Meanwhile, in other parts of Europe, the myth of blood libel, in which Jews were falsely accused of murdering Christian children in order to use their blood in the performance of religious ceremonies, took hold and spread.

There are child saints from the Middle Ages, still revered today, who are said to have been victims of this blood libel. My personal view is that the chapels, statues, and icons reflecting these odious lies should be dismantled. They were wrong five hundred years ago and they are still wrong today. So yes, stacked up against that level of superstition and hatred, Shylock doesn't look so bad, but to a modern audience, to call him sympathetic is taking things too far.

In the 2004 version of *The Merchant of Venice*, Al Pacino brilliantly channels Michael Corleone as his Shylock. It is a sumptuous production, and while Shylock is not the good guy, they do fix the other problem with the play by showing Venice's canals. It's a minor issue compared to Shylock, but Shakespeare managed to write an entire play set in Venice and never once mention the canals . . . which is kind of what Venice is famous for.

Quite simply, *The Merchant of Venice* preserves sixteenth-century attitudes toward a people who have for so long and continue to be the victims of hatred.

In the sea of gems the bard has given us, perhaps the most precious jewel is *Romeo and Juliet*, but the story is not original to Shakespeare. The basic plot and even the names of the star-crossed lovers had been kicking around for some time. There were Italian versions and French versions, and in 1562, there was the narrative poem *The Tragical History of Romeus and Juliet* by Arthur Brooke. Shakespeare took this English poem and fleshed it out into a broader story and added his own magic with the prose (although, very specifically, made Juliet younger, from about sixteen to thirteen which is . . . well . . . I'll just leave you with that thought). The story may be a timeless classic about teenage sex, gang violence, and suicide pacts, but it doesn't really have a lot to say about history except for two screen versions which take this sixteenth-century story and jump it into the twentieth century. One works magnificently, the other is nonsense.

ROMEO + JULIET (1996)

But back to our two young lovers, with a look at *Romeo + Juliet* (they took out the *and* and replaced it with +, so it's already super edgy and modern, isn't it?) Directed by Baz ("I've got a short attention span") Luhrmann, it stars a very young and beautiful Claire Danes and an equally young and beautiful Leonardo DiCaprio. If you were a teen or in your early twenties in the 1990s, this was the coolest film ever. Every young woman circa 1996/1997 had, by law, the CD of the soundtrack. I know this to be true because it followed me around, everywhere I went. If, however you're just coming to the film now, you are likely to find it a frenetic mess, with some decent performances swamped by every visual and editing tic Luhrmann could devise. It's like watching a performance of the play while somebody throws glitter in your eyes and occasionally sings a karaoke version of a song they heard in the car that gave them "feels."

Just as *Henry V* doesn't work with armored personnel carriers, so relocating this story from 1500s Italy to 1990s LA creates problems. Oh, so very cleverly, when someone asks for their sword or rapier, there is a closeup of a gun showing that "sword" or "rapier" is the maker's name, but crucially, when Romeo kills Tybalt, he is exiled (the same way it happens in the play)—but that's not how the US justice system works. Oh, you murdered someone? Right, we will send you to live in a trailer park in Nevada. It's total nonsense. Also, while it is true that the street violence depicted in the play could be turned into the gang violence on the streets of Los Angeles, I would argue that Luhrmann's version does it in such an elaborate and crazy way it wouldn't be believable in any age.

WEST SIDE STORY (1961, 2021)

A far better update that takes the bard into the twentieth century is a film so brave that it ditches the title. I am talking about *West Side Story*, made into film in 1961 and remade sixty years later in 2021.

I have been on quite a journey with this musical and its undeniably outstanding soundtrack. My mother had an original record from the 1960s, complete with a sleeve and booklet that described the production's efforts to portray as authentically as possible the white and Puerto Rican gangs in the postwar era in New York. I loved how the fighting was choreographed (it was the same for *Hero*). As I grew up, I still loved everything about the film except that I began to see the whole fight/dancing thing as silly. This has been spoofed many times, but perhaps best on *SNL* with Robert Downey Jr. and Will Ferrell as members of the Cobras waiting to fight the Panthers.

There is the same level of emotion in both the play and the musical, except that in the latter, there is a message about the need for communities to get along with each other and the dangers of gang violence (unlike the 1961 film, which has multiple casting issues, genuine Puerto Rican and Latino cast members are used in the 2021 version). The genius of Spielberg is he took a perfect movie (of the 1960s) and remade it even more perfect for the 2020s. This is how to bring the four-hundred-year-old story of Romeo and Juliet up to date.

A final point about some considerations when updating Shakespeare: The only person to commit the whole of *Hamlet* to the big screen is Kenneth Branagh, who again both directs and stars in the movie. He set his version of the play in the early 1800s, explaining that it is the most recent period in which modern viewers think people spoke anything like the language of Shakespeare. I would agree, so if *Romeo and Juliet* is going to be set in the 1990s, why not modernize everything around it and the words too? It happens all the time: take for instance the rom-com *10 Things I Hate About You*, which is a modern retelling of *The Taming of the Shrew*.

RAN (1985)

Sometimes there is a metaphor inside a period version of a Shakespeare-inspired film as in *Ran*, Akira Kurosawa's final samurai masterpiece. It is based on *King Lear* and is staggeringly epic. It's almost as if he takes cinema from everyone else, creates this, and then hands it back saying, okay, now beat this. The story is set in feudal Japan, but after all the bloodshed and stupendous set pieces, we are left with a lone blind figure on the top of a cliff, searching around for the way ahead. In this instance, we've had all the moral messages delivered about Lear and his choices, but Kurosawa went on to say that the blind man is the world right now, searching for a future that doesn't involve nuclear war (a concern during the Cold War) but which could just as easily be read as climate change today.

MACBETH (2015, 1971)

My final choice of play (I could, of course, go on for much longer) is *Macbeth*. This is traditionally included with his tragedies, but Macbeth was a real eleventh-century king of Scotland. Macbeth could be described as another problematic play as it breaks Shakespeare's own rules. While the bard has always played fast and loose with his histories by never allowing the facts to get in the way of a good story, overall, there is usually a fair correlation between his play and historic events. This was not the case with *Macbeth;* here, he took the name of an obscure monarch and made up a story that bears no resemblance to known events or the people involved.

Much has been made of the supernatural elements in the play and the fact it's based in Scotland. And who should become King of England after Elizabeth died? James, the son of Mary, Queen of Scots. James was crazy about the supernatural world, so much so that even before he became King of England, he wrote a book (the first British monarch to do so) called *Daemonologie*. It was about necromancy, witches, and anything that goes bump in the night (Shakespeare is credited with inventing the word *bump*), and it was a huge hit.[11] So, if Shakespeare wanted to impress the new monarch, what could be better than a play about what he likes based in the place he comes from? Macbeth was so ancient a king he had no relation to James and, conveniently, could be turned into anything Shakespeare wanted.

There are moments in the play that have a basis in fact. The previous king was Duncan, but Macbeth had nothing to do with his death. It's suggested in the play that Macbeth ruled for months before there was an uprising against him. But no, he ruled from 1040 to 1057 and his successor was his stepson Lulach. None of this is really sounding much like the play, is it?

What's worse is when we get to Lady Macbeth, who is portrayed as one of the wickedest women in fiction (history?). This is outright slander. Gruoch ingen Boite (her real name) had already been married once before she married Macbeth, and it was in that marriage that she had her one and only son Lulach. Hardly anything is known about her except her name appears in two grants: one is made for the church of St Serf; the other is for the Culdee monastery at Loch Leven. The only thing we can reasonably extrapolate from this is that she was a religious woman who took her spiritual duties seriously. So, the chances of her ever saying something like, "Come you spirits, that tend on mortal thoughts, unsex me here," are unlikely to zero. Neither is she likely to be a person plotting assassinations and goading her husband into regicide.

The 2015 retelling of the tale, starring Michael Fassbender and Marion Cotillard, is a full-blooded affair set in the Middle Ages. Like so many of the play's interpretations, historical realism is not what they are going for, but it looks magnificent, and the two leads are exceptional, with a special nod to the use of war paint to make Macbeth look particularly feral in the battle scenes. This movie, like *The Green Knight*, feels real, earthy and visceral. Can you learn any Scottish history from watching? Absolutely none. But it is an amazing film.

Orson Welles starred and directed a version of *Macbeth* in 1948 to solid if not gushing reviews. Then there's the 1971 version directed by Roman Polanski. This was his first film after *Rosemary's Baby* and the murder of his pregnant girlfriend Sharon Tate and seems to be catharsis on film. While it is a respectful retelling of the play, it is not an exaggeration to say this film is dripping in blood. All versions true to the source material will be dark and murderous, but this iteration feels very raw.

Going back to where I started on Shakespeare, no matter where life takes us, we are always tethered to our past. Shakespeare has gifted us and countless generations with his works of genius, but he never forgot where he came from. Before going to London and achieving fame as a playwright, he worked as a glovemaker in the family business in Stratford-upon-Avon, and it amuses me to think that while he wrote about kings, battles, gods, and fairies, he also managed to insert about seventy references to glovemaking in his works. His dad would be proud.

NOTES

1. Brett Harvey, *Inmate #1: The Rise of Danny Trejo* (documentary), 2019.

2. www.rsc.org.uk/shakespeares-plays.

3. Edith Pargeter, *A Bloody Field by Shrewsbury* (London: Headline, 2016), 288.

4. Juliet Barker, *Agincourt: The King, the Campaign, the Battle*, new ed. (London: Abacus, 2006).

5. William Shakespeare, *Henry V*, Act IV, Scene 3.

6. Barker, *Agincourt*, 474.

7. Michael Billington, "Henry V" (review), *The Guardian*, June 14, 2003.

8. Louise Osmond, *Richard III: The King in the Car Park* (documentary), 2013.

9. Annette Carson, *Richard III: The Maligned King*, reprint ed. (London: History Press, 2009), 21.

10. Jem Duducu, *Deus Vult: A Concise History of the Crusades* (Gloucestershire, UK: Amberley Publishing, 2014), 38.

11[1] Timo Ryynanen, *James VI: The Demonologist King: Demonic Descriptions and Their Context in James VI's Daemonologie*, dissertation, Univ. of Eastern Finland, 2010.

Chapter 5

Eastern Promise

This chapter will not get a historical introduction as there is no way that a couple of paragraphs can do justice to the thousands of years of history of these great "eastern" nations which have contributed so much to world history. It is, however, worth including a chapter on how other countries retell the events from their past to show that Hollywood storytelling isn't the only way to do it, and at times it isn't just Hollywood that gets it wrong.

When you see the word *Bollywood*, what does it conjure in your mind? I'm going to make a guess and say vivid colors, intricate dance choreography, beautiful women catching the eye of an impossibly macho guy. All of those are iconic Bollywood elements, but that's not how it started.

First, a word on technical terms. India would prefer the term *Indian film industry* because the term *Bollywood* refers specifically to Hindi language films being made (or at least financed) in the media capital of India, Mumbai (formally Bombay).[1] In a country with over twenty official languages, the largest population in the world, and multiple religions, Bollywood is the best known and the largest sector of film production in India, but it is by no means the only one. There's a Jollywood, the remarkably named Chhollywood (after Chhattisgarh state and language), and two completely different Tollywoods, to name just a few. They have different filmic styles, languages, and cultural imperatives. However, the rest of the world has embraced the term *Bollywood* to include any film of Indian origin, and as such, this is the term I will use for Indian movie productions.

RAJA HARISHCHANDRA (1913)

The very first Indian film is *Raja Harishchandra*. Obviously, it was not in color nor did it have sound. It was directed by Dadasaheb Phalke, who is often referred to (quite rightly) as the Father of Indian Cinema. The film is a fairy tale portraying a divine ruler who becomes the perfect benign ruler. The narrative shadows the story of a holy figure, obviously inspired by Jesus (a sign of the colonial influence at the time), but it also makes a huge political point: This just and moral ruler is Indian, not British.

Basically, it didn't matter what the topic of the movie was in India for the first thirty-plus years of film production, a time when it was under British colonial rule. The rise in the popularity of homegrown films was rapid, but when the British woke up to the trend, they sought to limit what could be portrayed. By 1920 they had put various restrictions on the content not to censor sex and violence (which weren't likely to be portrayed in India any more than in Ipswich), but to limit freedom of speech and to stop the spread of dangerous talk about Indian independence. Of course, the Indian filmmakers found plenty of ways to get around this, which brings us to the music.

India (which to be clear, also then included modern-day Pakistan and Bangladesh) under the British had a literacy rate of less than 20 percent, and the country had at least twenty different languages.[2] So how to get a common message across to people? Well, how do advertisers on the radio get their products to stick in your mind? The answer is with a catchy tune. As soon as sound became part of the technology of movies, the Bollywood musical was born. Any potentially political song had carefully arranged lyrics that never overtly criticized the British but, instead, talked metaphorically about the joys of being free.

Looked at this way, Indian cinema pre-1947 could be said to be a vital part of the history of the times regardless of the genre being depicted. The importance of music and lyrics spreading an anti-colonial or antiauthoritarian message may be an indicator of how everyday people in the past dealt with occupation, whether they were the indigenous peoples of Mexico under the Spanish or the Celts in Britain under Roman rule. The behaviors of the average worker in the fields were never documented by the imperial overlords.

It is interesting that a classic Hollywood film, contemporary to this era, also shows defiance to the occupier with song. I am, of course, referring to 1942's *Casablanca*. Music is dripping through the pores of this film. The song "As Time Goes By" was not written for that movie; it was a popular song years earlier, but it perfectly fitted the mood of nostalgia for an earlier, happier time for both the characters in the story and for the moviegoers themselves. Then there is the famous scene where the Germans start to sing triumphantly, and the locals strike up with "La Marseillaise" and drown them out. They have done nothing wrong; no harm was done to the Germans, but a defiant point is made through song. The scene is made even more poignant as some of the cast were either Jewish or immigrants from countries that at the time of filming were under Nazi occupation. It's as if *Casablanca* had taken notes from Bollywood.

MOTHER INDIA (1957)

The *Citizen Kane* of Indian cinema is *Mother India*, not because it redefined cinema, but because it became a blueprint for Indian films moving forward. It's the story of a poor woman in a tiny village who tries to raise her sons (the husband is absent) despite many hardships. It is a metaphor for India itself, the catharsis the nation needed after independence from the British Empire, and was so popular it was still in cinemas in 1990.

After India's independence post–World War II, the country was finding its place in the world. Artists could now write about anything they wanted to, and as color came in, the musical numbers got bigger and became ever more extravagant. Because Indian moral codes were very similar to many cultures in the Middle East and Asia, the films exported well. The industry was already set up to put subtitles on every film in their own country, so adding Arabic or Mandarin was easy.

What Bollywood offered was something impossibly exotic, and it came to the attention of officials in the oddest of places, the Soviet Union. The USSR was certainly not going to bring in all those capitalist movies from America, but strangely, a family in Moscow in 1960 would think nothing of going to a Bollywood film on a Saturday night. By the 1990s, Bollywood, not Hollywood, was the world's number one producer of feature films.

I spoke to a young up-and-coming actor in Mumbai (during my time at Visit Britain) who complained that Western actors had it easy. They had only to act and look good, whereas he had to do those things plus be able to sing and dance. Those were the minimum requirements in Mumbai, but in the West, they are seen as separate skills, and we are often surprised when we see actors who can also sing and dance. I lost touch with that young actor, but as I haven't seen his name at the top of a Bollywood poster, I guess he never quite cracked it. India's Bollywood is a tough and ruthless industry—and a difficult one to get into.

However, all this history and nationalist (and religious) pride comes at a cost. Many of the films are, to a Western audience today, problematic—and that's being kind. I have read and heard Professor Sunny Singh describe how the racial stereotypes are linked to colonialism.[3] This is indisputable, but colonial rule ended seventy-five years ago. The idea of the downtrodden punching up against the overlords is a very old idea and not unique to India, but at what point does that sentiment turn into outright racism?

THUGS OF HINDOSTAN (2018)

Thugs of Hindostan is a Bollywood action-adventure film in the style of *Pirates of the Caribbean*. To put this into context, this was the same year *Black Panther* came out in America, a film lauded for its inclusiveness and racial sensitivity. *Thugs of Hindostan* did not do well at the box office nor did it get particularly positive reviews. The criticisms were about the sluggish plot and other issues we see every day in Western films. However, nobody talked about some deeply troubling stereotypes. Unfortunately, this film is just one of *many* examples. At one point the heroine is captured by a bunch of British soldiers. She is then forced to dance for them as the crowd of Caucasian men look on lasciviously. She is clearly in danger of sexual assault. Then, dressed as a British officer and wearing whiteface to blend in with the British redcoats, one of the Indian heroes jumps in and dances lecherously with her.

If you are white, how does it feel to be portrayed as a potential rapist? Did acts of violence and rape happen under British rule? Yes, but was that standard practice? Did every British officer and soldier carry out such acts? Absolutely not. Events such as the Amritsar Massacre in 1919 where more than four hundred unarmed civilians were killed were crimes against humanity, but it should be remembered that events like this were not commonplace, were carried out by Gurkha and Sikh soldiers, and shocked the British establishment as well.[4] In other words, there is a nuanced and complex conversation to be had, but there's no time or desire for that in the middle of an adventure movie. I accept that India had to push against white power in the 1930s, but by 2018, everyone on screen was born at least a generation later than that, so is this an acceptable stereotype?

LAGAAN (2001)

Perhaps the most Indian of Indian historical movies (and a monster box-office smash) is *Lagaan*. The hero is Bollywood legend Aamir Khan. It is loosely based on real events during British rule when a dispute between a poor town and the (invariably evil) British local lord will be sorted out not on a field of battle, but on a cricket green. It has everything you could want from a film: songs and dances, training montages, gripping sports action, brave heroes, and evil villains. Cricket has been wholly embraced by India; it's one of the consequences of British rule that everyone can agree was a good thing, but having the Indians beat the British at their own game is super sweet.

There is a strange exception to this rule of the evil British. In the 1990s, Bollywood wanted its own taste of the exotic, so the stories began to go to places like Paris or Rome, or again, those beautiful highlands of Scotland (to make that happen, deals were done with Visit Scotland). These created a new trope in the historical dramas of Bollywood. The scenario now becomes one where the British army does something unspeakable to the locals, but a reticent Scottish officer, who goes along with the orders, eventually sees the light and joins the Indians. So, the Scottish and the Indians have always known that the real enemy is the English.

A final point to be made about these Technicolor spectacles, where melodrama is king, is that they are not the place to look for historical realism. In the past, music was used as a means of keeping traditions alive and of signaling defiance of the occupation. The films served a purpose, but one thing we know for sure is that a crowd of people spontaneously bursting into song and carrying out intricately choreographed dances isn't real life. But gritty historic authenticity isn't Bollywood's goal. Their historical dramas have more in common with the sword-and-sandals epics of the 1950s and 1960s than something like *Saving Private Ryan*. And in a way, this is a sign of the strength of Western films, where countries can show the good and bad of their past. Being able to criticize yourself is a sign of self-confidence. Think for a moment about how many Hollywood films show America's flaws, everything from *All the President's Men* to *Milk* or *The Trial of the Chicago 7*. In fact, in America, if there's a film about political history, it is far more likely to be negative than positive. This is important because if all the culture does is show your fellow citizens as flawless good guys and all foreigners as evil bad guys, it leads to some dangerous conclusions.

And that is a familiar trait with Chinese cinema too. The period from the mid-1800s to 1949 is referred to in China as the "century of humiliation." Today China, like India, has never been stronger, and yet both nations like to put out a contradictory message, one of national strength but also one of victimhood.

In the 2015 Chinese film *Wolf Warrior*, a modern-day action film, there is a scene where the leader of the elite military squad declares, "Those who desecrate our nation shall be hunted to the ends of the earth." The tone of the movie is very much something like a Michael Bay film (think *The Rock*), but whereas Bay's jingoism leans on literal flag waving and American exceptionalism, it doesn't make explicit threats to other nations.

So again, as with India, the central message of virtually all Chinese media is China=good, foreign=bad. This is complicated by the messages of Chinese superiority mixed with the fear that the foreign makes things messier. The vast majority of Chinese films are set pre-1912. They may take place in the century of humiliation or in a fantasy world, but they are more likely to be set in the age of the emperors, from the first, that of the legendary Qin Shi Huang (who got the terra-cotta warriors as a grave gift), to the Qing Dynasty before its collapse in 1912.

HERO (2002)

Jet Li portrayed characters at both ends of China's dynastic period in two movies released just four years apart. First is *Hero*, set somewhere around 220 BC at the time of the first emperor Qin Shi Huang. In this story Jet Li is literally a nameless hero who, along with his accomplices, plans to assassinate the great man with a weaponized lute. This story, despite its ridiculous conceit, is real, but (spoiler alert for an assassination attempt from more than two thousand years ago) . . . the plan failed.

Classifying this film as just wuxia, a martial arts film, is not doing it justice. Every shot is a painting, every fight is a choreographed dance of such exquisite intricacy and beauty it is literally poetry in motion. In one scene in a forest, the bright yellow leaves match the bright yellow robes of the combatants, and in another, everything is red, including all the leaves on the trees; another set piece is all in vivid blues. Color is vital to the film as other scenes are played out from different points of view, and they are all visually stunning. It is easily one of the most beautiful movies ever made. The impossibility of the martial arts style matches the impossible beauty of the sets and costumes as the artists leap incredible heights, cartwheel infinitely in the air, and cut arrows out of the sky (one of the few examples of arrows being just arrows, the film is so gorgeous there is, for a change, no need to add fire to them).

This is a movie that is clearly inspired by history and nothing more. Director Yimou Zhang was aiming for a feeling of awe, not trying to accurately re-create third century BC China. The assassination attempt failed because the assassin was stopped before he could land his fatal blow. In the movie, the emperor convinces Jet Li that China needs his (the emperor's) wisdom and strength and only a country as great as China could be managed by such a strong, centralized force (and is of course a metaphor for the ruling Communist Party).

FEARLESS (2006)

Then there is *Fearless*. Here Li plays Huo Yuanjia, a real person in history, but now the time is the early twentieth century, just a couple of years before the fall of the Qing Dynasty. Yuanjia is a reluctant fighter, having killed a man in the past with his kung fu expertise. He sets up the Jingwu Sport Federation, the first attempt in China to turn a brutal form of combat into a competitive sport. But those evil foreigners don't like it and set up a tournament where he must beat a British boxer, a Spanish swordsman, a Belgian soldier, and a Japanese martial artist. All of this because the blatant xenophobia is not just against Westerners, but also against the Japanese. (For decades in the first half of the twentieth century the Japanese carried out multiple atrocities in China. One of the worst was the so-called Rape of Nanjing, where up to 300,000 civilians were killed in December 1937 and January 1938.)[5]

Will the reluctant Yuanjia heed the call and represent China in this tournament? Can Yuanjia beat these embodiments of foreign interference in China? I am not mocking the outcome. It's the same setup for a Western hero like James Bond: You know he's going to win because that's what the paying public wants to see. Except James Bond is fictional, whereas Huo Yuanjia was a real man who, around 1909, really did set up a sporting version of martial arts, although it is better translated as the Chin Woo Athletic Association. And there really was an international fight between Yuanjia's protégé Liu Zhensheng and a Japanese judo expert. The result was disputed, which led to a brawl between the groups, and a number of Japanese fighters were injured. Yuanjia didn't fight as he had tuberculosis and died in 1910.

So, has the film successfully depicted the real history? No. Was it trying to? Again, no. We are back to the intent of the film director, and in this instance, we again have a piece of history being turned into a modern-day parable. It would be pointless to pick it to pieces in terms of historical content, although its message of sticking it to the foreigner isn't very palatable to anyone outside of China. If the story had been told in the West, there would invariably have been a relatable foreign character to take the edge off things and not make everything so black and white.

For a long time, China and Hong Kong were known for their exciting martial arts movies. And if there is one epicenter of martial arts in China, it is the Shaolin Temple in Henan. The monastery was founded in the late fifth century AD, about the same time as the collapse of the Roman Empire in the West. Roughly a century later, under the Sui Dynasty, we get the first records of the monks starting to learn kung fu (which literally means hard work) as a martial art. The reason was one of practicality: This was a time of instability and lawlessness and monks had to take a vow of poverty. As such they could not arm themselves with expensive swords. So, when they traveled through the bandit-infested countryside and needed to protect themselves, they used the techniques of unarmed combat or fought using a staff. A thousand years later, and in the 1500s, the monks were being drafted in to fight piracy (the coast is a very long way from the landlocked Henan region of China).

So even before the invention of cinema the Shaolin warrior monks were a legend in their own country. Just putting the word Shaolin into the title of a martial arts movie shows they are a genre in their own right, whether it's 1974's *Five Shaolin Masters*, 1983's *Shaolin vs Lama* (not the animal) or 2001's (surreal comedy) *Shaolin Soccer*. These films have no historical value, but they do have a huge cultural one. Many of these films feel obliged to deliver Buddhist philosophy amongst the kicks. They are, after all, warrior monks and not just some sort of Chinese ninja. Many countries have martial arts, but China is (rightly) seen as the epicenter and, as a result, produces the finest martial artists and martial arts films ever seen on screen. And they are not one-note films, ranging as they do from the impossible dream-like fights of *Hero* or *Crouching Tiger, Hidden Dragon* to something more brutal and realistic like the films of the legendary Bruce Lee.

In the film *Jackie Chan: My Stunts* (1999), Chan is critical of the surreal martial arts seen in wuxia films like *Hero* and shows how unsatisfying it is that a hero simply points his sword and flies up. Instead, he shows how it is much more fun to see the hero carry out acrobatic skills to get up to the roof of a building. Jackie Chan may be best known for his contemporary films such as *Police Story* or *Rush Hour*, but he has done plenty of period pieces too, such as *Drunken Master* (1978). Chan, like the Shaolin movies, is not interested in getting the right cloth for the outfits or whether the architecture is accurate for the era; he spends his time working out the blindingly fast and inventive fight choreography. The fight scenes in *Drunken Master* are based on a technique called drunken boxing (Zui Quan), where the stances aren't as rigid as other forms, so the fighters look drunk. Chan takes this literally and he fights better when drunk. Authentic as they seem, please remember that Jackie Chan, a martial arts legend, was sober when filming these.

While Chinese box office, post–COVID-19, has never been better, its critics have never been louder. Modern Chinese cinema is constantly looking at Hollywood for inspiration. The problem is an imitation is never as good as the original. Ironically, back in the 1990s and early 2000s, Chinese cinema was the darling of the international circuit, and many films were received to acclaim: 1991's *Raise the Red Lantern* (a thoughtful drama about a woman who becomes the fourth wife to a warlord in that era after 1912, a time of civil unrest), 2001's *Beijing Bicycle* (a modern drama about a boy's stolen bicycle and his need to get it back to do his job), and 2007's *Lust Caution* (about a woman who becomes the mistress of a powerful official during the Japanese occupation of Shanghai). All these films have something to say and all are set after the imperial era. Going back to *Wolf Warrior*, if the biggest influence for your film is Michael Bay, then you really have nothing to say.

THE GREAT HERO YI SUN-SIN (1962)

South Korea in the twenty-first century is remarkably vibrant in terms of exporting its culture overseas. K-pop bands like BTS are known throughout the world. For a time Psy's "Gangnam Style" was the most viewed song on YouTube and, with over four billion views, is still one of the biggest. 2019's *Parasite* won Bong Joon Ho Best Director and Best Picture Oscars, and in 2021, *Squid Games* ruled Netflix. In the same year, (actually ethnically Chinese) stuntman/actor Simu Liu graduated from *Kim's Convenience*, a TV sitcom about Korean immigrants in Canada, to full-blown Marvel superhero in *Shang-Chi and the Legend of the Ten Rings*. These are all as achingly modern as it gets. What people don't associate with Korea is history, and Korea has a long and fascinating one. Invaded by China, the Mongols, and Japan, it has carved out its own unique culture against its larger and sometimes very aggressive neighbors. Indeed, today it is a nation still torn in two by a war that happened seventy years ago.

Perhaps the greatest hero in Korean history is Yi Sun-sin. He has been turned into multiple movies and two have the same title, *The Great Hero Yi Sun-sin*. Then there's 2005's *Heaven's Soldiers*. And let's not forget the 105-episode TV drama *Immortal Admiral Yi Sun-sin*. I think you can guess by now that Admiral Yi is a big deal in Korea . . . and you've probably never heard of him. So here's a brief history of a remarkable man.

Yi was an admiral in the Korean navy, but his career started in the army. After passing his military examinations in 1576, he became an officer and, later, a general in the army. During this time the Jurchen people (from Manchuria) were regularly invading Korea. Yi's successes in his battles with them meant that by 1583 he had crushed them and captured their chief, putting an end to the Jurchen incursions. Yi was the man of the hour. His acclaim was so great that he was imprisoned by a rival, General Yi Il, so as not to garner too much power and admiration. Counterintuitively, the undefeated general ended up being a prisoner.

Although his incarceration was relatively brief, it was an appalling way to treat a successful general. After a few years of being either imprisoned or lying low, Yi thought he had made amends even as the political landscape in Korea was changing. This allowed him, once again, to climb up the ranks. and by 1591, rather than being a general in the army, he was now in charge of the navy. His promotion came just in time because between 1592 and 1598 the Japanese repeatedly attempted to invade Korea as a springboard into China. Yi understood the situation and the potential danger if Japan had greater resources than Korea. Knowing that he had less of everything, he ensured the navy's logistics were up to scratch to keep his navy fighting fit, because even after a naval victory, damage would have been inflicted on the fleet and would have to be rectified.

His plan worked like a dream because, while he couldn't stop the invasion, for the next six years he fought a total of twenty-three naval battles against the Japanese. Each one might not have been a stunning victory, but he more than succeeded in terrorizing the Japanese vessels.

The Koreans had decided to build stouter ships than those of the Japanese. Their design meant that the Korean ships could support more cannons and soak up more damage, but even so Yi was often outnumbered in his battles. An example of this can be seen in the key Battle of Myeongnyang (this battle is the centerpiece of the 2014 movie *The Admiral: Roaring Currents*) in the autumn of 1597. In this engagement, Yi had thirteen ships against 133 (the numbers are contested by historians, but this is the scenario in the film). This battle resulted in a major naval defeat for the Koreans, so it was seen as a last stand, and Yi anchored his "turtle ships" in the Myeongnyang Strait. The current initially brought the Japanese in, and the heavier Korean ships soaked up the damage as they pounded and sunk numerous oncoming Japanese vessels. Then the current changed, leading the Japanese vessels away from the battle, and their sheer number became a hindrance as Japanese vessels collided and got in each other's way, allowing Yi and the Koreans to pour on cannon fire. Thirty-one Japanese vessels were severely damaged or sunk, with no losses for the Koreans.

Yi was so effective that the Japanese used a double agent to discredit him. Amazingly, this worked, and he was once again imprisoned and tortured. Korea's useless King Seonjo wanted to have him executed; however once calmer heads prevailed, Yi was released and allowed to return to his post. Yi was obviously a remarkable man who resumed his duties as if nothing had happened.

In the winter of 1598, Yi was again winning against the Japanese at the Battle of Noryang, when he was struck under the armpit with a bullet. He knew he was dying but did not want to let something as minor as his own death jeopardize another victory. At his request, Yi's nephew wore his armor and the battle was won. The Japanese invasion faltered, and Korea was saved. When the news came out that Yi had died, the entire navy wailed in grief and shrines were erected in his honor.[6] With all of this in mind, it is unsurprising that Yi Sun-Sin is a national hero in Korea and is the reason why there are so many Korean films about him. None of them are going for 100 percent historical accuracy. He's a national legend, so that is the way he is always going to be portrayed.

TAE GUK GI (2004)

Another Korean film that was a big hit domestically but also made an impact internationally is 2004's *Tae Guk Gi*, known in English as *Brotherhood*. It's *Saving Private Ryan* meets a Korean melodrama. Two brothers are conscripted during the Korean War and end up in the same unit. The older tries to protect the younger by doing the dangerous missions. It has the gritty look of *Saving Private Ryan*, but the body count and heroics are more like something from *Where Eagles Dare*.

MY WAY (2011)

Finally, there is *My Way*. This is the story of a Korean man called Jun-shik Kim who, just before World War II, was conscripted into the Japanese imperial army which was occupying Korea at the time. In the summer of 1939, as a soldier in the Japanese army, Kim fights against the Soviets in central Asia (this clash in Mongolia is known as the Battle of Khalkhin Gol and Japan's defeat explains why, in 1941, they attacked Pearl Harbor but not the USSR).

In the film, Jun-shik Kim is captured and taken to Russia, where he is now a POW. Then in 1941, Germany invades the USSR, and he is conscripted again, this time into the Red Army as Stalin desperately struggled to slow the onslaught of Hitler's war machine. Now Jun-shik Kim is fighting on the front line only to be captured by the Germans and put in a Wehrmacht uniform before being stationed in Normandy, where he was on D-Day . . . and where he is captured by the Americans! He is now a POW for the rest of the war in Britain. It all seems totally unbelievable, and in the movie there is even a secondary plot about him being a runner in competition with a Japanese rival, but apart from that, all of his story seems, quite astonishingly, to be true. There is even a photo of him in a German uniform with American soldiers on D-Day. The man's real name was Yang Kyoungjong. All we have is the photo and his personal testimony, so his story cannot be verified, but at the same time, it's the only plausible explanation for a Korean fighting for Germany in Normandy in 1944.

And so we come to that other giant of Asian cinema, Japan. As soon as I write Japan and history, I know what comes to mind: It's one word, *samurai*. After that we might get geisha, kimono, cherry blossom, and something like Himeji Castle. These are all legitimate images of Japanese culture, but as with most things in life, it's more complicated than that.

Here's a bold statement: The samurai were invented in 1900. You are likely thinking I haven't done my research. However, the way the West (and in some ways, Japan too) thinks about samurai can be traced directly back to the 1900 publication of *Bushido: The Soul of Japan* by Inazo Nitobe.

Nitobe wrote the book in English in America, and it was his book that brought the mythologized idea of the samurai into popular culture. The real samurai began around 1000 AD and continued until the 1860s. While their bravery was already legendary in Japan, the almost supernatural view of their nobility and skill came with Nitobe's interpretation.

A fair comparison is with the knights in medieval Europe: They were respected at the time, but their reputation grew after their era as tales were embroidered and facts ballooned into legends. The knights and the samurai were both feudal servants who used their martial skills to serve their lord. But the knightly era in Europe lasted a maximum of five hundred years, whereas that of the samurai lasted for more than eight hundred, so of course they changed over the centuries.

The book was a smash hit and suddenly the samurai, the katana (sword), and Bushido (moral code) became far better known and greatly admired in the West, all this around the same time Russia was to go to war with Japan and lose. Japan became the first Asian power to defeat a Western one, which only enhanced the image of Japan's martial prowess.

Ironically, it was only years later that this book was translated into Japanese and was once again a publishing sensation. It's still in print, still with historically inaccurate but suitably cool images of samurai on the cover. So, while it can be concluded that the image of the samurai in the West starts with this book, samurai history, of course, goes back much further.

All the movies I am about to discuss have been influenced by Nitobe's book. Some of the events described did happen, but were the samurai that cool? Highly unlikely. Their eight-hundred-year-long heritage is portrayed by three different filmmakers and their samurai visions:

NICHIREN TO MŌKO DAISHŪRAI (1958)

First, there is *Nichiren to Mōko Daishūrai*, a historical drama by Kunio Watanabe. The hero is not a samurai but Nichiren, a real and highly revered Buddhist monk from the Kamakura period in Japan. He taught Buddhist philosophy, and multiple monasteries were founded by him and his followers. Many of these institutions still exist today, more than seven hundred years later.

In the film, Nichiren is the spiritual leader at a time of genuine existential threat to Japan as Kublai Khan had sent a Sino-Mongol fleet to invade and conquer the country in the late thirteenth century. We do see samurai, but they are background players to the central role of Nichiren. This is all going on at roughly the same time as the events in *Braveheart*. The Mongols had conquered everywhere from Russia to China to central Asia and the Middle East through to Korea. If all those great powers had crumbled, what could Japan possibly do to stop them? The answer came when a huge tropical typhoon blew up and smashed their fleet to pieces as the Mongols were landing. This was not a time for Bushido, but a time for Buddhist prayer. A divine protection had been given to the blessed islands of Japan. The year was 1274. Then, after rebuilding the entire fleet and training a vast new army, the Mongols came again in 1281, when, incredibly, a second typhoon destroyed this armada as well. Japan had been blessed by a divine wind that protected the archipelago from foreign invasion. The name for divine wind in Japanese is "kamikaze."

The film is not great by modern standards. Nichiren is full of hope, stoicism, and philosophy, and it does seem at times as if *everyone* (except Nichiren) is crying into their sleeves. This film could be the world's greatest example of teary speeches. Let's leave it with the phrase "it hasn't aged well." But the point of its inclusion is it does show the samurai were an established fighting force by the 1200s. The film costars Takashi Shimura, who was a lot better in a film that came out four years earlier and which comes up for discussion next.

SEVEN SAMURAI (1954)

Of all the films mentioned in this chapter there is one that is not only a stone cold classic, with one of the highest Metacritic scores of any film ever (with a 98/100), but also has the rare distinction of snaring the attention of Hollywood. If imitation is the greatest form of flattery, then Akira Kurosawa's *Seven Samurai* will be smiling for all of eternity. Obviously remade into *The Magnificent Seven* (which had multiple sequels and remakes itself), it has influenced many other genres, getting official recognition in the *Star Wars* animated show *Clone Wars* and, unofficially, in every single scenario when a bunch of poor people need a group of hired guns to help them out, whether it's *Battle Beyond the Stars* (starring George Peppard) or *The A-Team* (starring George Peppard).

The story of *Seven Samurai* is completely fictional. It is set in the Sengoku era in Japan (the 1500s, so we are now in the Tudor era in England) when the country was constantly in the throes of civil war. It was a lawless time and villages like the one depicted in the film must have grown tired of either bandits or armies marching through their farms, taking what they wanted. But this particular village decides to do something about it and promises to feed seven down-on-their-luck samurai if they defend the village. The residents start off by hiring the ageing but wise Kambei (played by Takashi Shimura, who gives one of the most charismatic performances ever committed to film). However, even Shimura is overshadowed by the manic performance of Toshiro Mifune as Kikuchiyo.

This film had praise heaped on it on release, but does it hold up in the twenty-first century? After all it's nearly three and a half hours long, in black and white, made less than ten years after World War II, and is in Japanese with subtitles. I first saw it on TV as a kid. I had missed what I now know to be the first twenty minutes, but I was mesmerized for the rest of the film. I have subsequently seen it many times, and I have shown it to both of my boys when they were about ten/eleven years old; they loved it too, particularly the antics of Kikuchiyo. I conclude I have raised them well as they (correctly) see it as superior to *The Magnificent Seven*, which has the notable advantages of being in color, in English, and substantially shorter.

The attention to detail is intimidating. The village was built from scratch using traditional methods. Kurosawa wrote out the names and family trees of all the one-hundred-plus residents of the village so the actors and extras could immerse themselves in village life. Each of the samurai are (loosely) based on real samurai from the Sengoku era. Production was halted twice due to overrunning the budget. At the time, the film was the most expensive ever made in Japan although Toho (the production company) was to have two massive hits in 1954: this and *Gojira* (*Godzilla*), both of which attracted international attention, so it all worked out in the end.

There is an important historical fact to consider: The feudal age in Japan was hierarchical, and everyone knew their place. A samurai was a warrior who fought for a lord; if the lord died, it meant tough times because the samurai were not allowed to do any other job (this is explained in the film). A samurai without a lord is in a shameful situation, and as such, they have a different name, ronin, in essence a sword for hire, a mercenary. As all the samurai in this film are masterless (and Kikuchiyo is pretending to be a samurai but was once a farmer), a more appropriate title would be *The Seven Ronin* as nobody in the story is technically a samurai.

A number of film critics have said that *Seven Samurai* is the first action movie (which most people would assume must have been created in Hollywood). There is a difference between a movie with action in it and an action movie. For example, more people die in *Spartacus* than in *John Wick*, but you know which one of those films you'd call an action movie.

One of the ways it is seen as the first action film is that the action tells us something about the person's character. Early on in the film we see the samurai Kambei take control of the situation when there is a kidnapping by a madman. To get near the kidnapper he takes decisive action and cuts off the topknot of his chonmage hair style. The topknot is as much a part of the samurai image as the katana sword. A samurai would never cut it off, but by doing so, Kambei has the perfect disguise and now looks like a monk, not a warrior. It's this attention to the culture of the Sengoku period that adds flavor and a feeling of realism to the film. It also shows Kambei to be practical and single-minded in achieving his goals, and we see that he's willing to make a personal sacrifice to help someone else.

Other elements brought together for the first time in a film have since become standard action tropes, for instance, slow motion. The duel where Kyuzo proves he is a sword master shows the single blow and the collapse of the enemy duellist in slow motion to highlight the awe and precision of the man (it also helped cover up the fact that the actor playing Kyuzo had never before held a sword). That plus the idea of the reluctant hero and the feeling that while outnumbered, they were never outgunned, were innovative concepts. The list goes on and on.

Kurosawa had already done the spellbinding *Ikiru* in 1952, again with Takashi Shimura. This was a contemporary story of an office-bound bureaucrat who finds out he has terminal cancer and tries to find meaning in his life by building a children's playground. It is haunting, poignant, and incredibly touching. But despite it being one of Kurosawa's best, there is no action and no samurai, so nobody talks about it.

RASHOMON (1950)

However, it's with Toshiro Mifune that Kurosawa is consistently excellent and, most often, dealing with feudal Japan. The film that brought Kurosawa to the world's attention was *Rashomon*, which has both Mifune and Shimura in it. The story is centered around the death of a samurai; what happens before and after the assault are shown from four different perspectives and these do not match. The viewer is left to piece together the story that is most likely the truth. In this, Kurosawa created an entirely new storytelling structure that, like so many of his other greats, has been endlessly copied . . . sorry, I mean that it inspired other films, including *The Last Duel* (mentioned in the chapter on the Middle Ages), made seventy-one years later. This is a testament to Kurosawa's genius, stretching across generations of filmmakers.

YOJIMBO (1961), *SANJURO* (1962)

Seven Samurai and *Rashomon* became indie film darlings, the sort of movies shown in local independent cinemas, where the audience drinks white wine

spritzers and popcorn is banned. But Mifune and Kurosawa made more main-
stream action films too. *Yojimbo* (bodyguard) and its sequel *Sanjuro* are just
plain fun. This time rather than the hyperactive Kikuchiyo, Mifune plays the
supercool and very calm ronin Sanjuro.

It's easy to assume that *Yojimbo* is set a few years after *Seven Samurai*,
but no, it's set in 1860. The only clue that time has really progressed is that
while Sanjuro has no problem dispatching dozens of thugs with his sword, he
eventually faces somebody with a pistol, a weapon that simply didn't exist
in Japan in the Sengoku era. But if you're not Japanese you're not going to
know that. Same too with *Sanjuro*, when you might wonder why a woman has
blacked-out teeth. Is this poor prosthetics to portray her as a toothless hag?
No, it was the fashion at the time for married women to do this; it's called
"ohaguro" and conveyed high status. Kurosawa had done his homework, and
so will you to get all the nuances.[7]

Yojimbo was famously remade as yet another western, this time *A Fistful
of Dollars*. Interestingly, the sequel, *A Few Dollars More*, wasn't based
on *Sanjuro* but has its own place in cinema history. Coming up in the next
paragraph there's a big spoiler alert for a film you've had more than sixty
years to see.

In the last scene of *Sanjuro*, Mifune faces off against a noble but deadly
samurai when they agree to fight even though Mifune doesn't want to, seeing
it as a pointless waste of life. When the duel takes place, Mifune, in one blow,
slashes open his opponent's neck and out explodes the biggest, most pressurized fountain of blood ever seen in cinema up to that point. Fortunately, it's
in black and white or American censors would have cut the whole scene. The
effect was created using carbonated water that rather than slow releasing to
produce a steady flow (of a chocolate syrup mixed with carbonated water), it
all went off at once. This became the standard samurai slash gash (my own
term) and appears everywhere in samurai movies of the 1960s and 1970s. It's
even referenced in *Kill Bill: Volume One*.

KAGEMUSHA (1980)

Then there's Kurosawa's full-color and hugely epic *Kagemusha*. Most of
Kurosawa's earlier films set in feudal Japan were about the lower rungs
of society. If there were any samurai, they were invariably brought low.
Kagemusha tells the story of a real warlord from the Sengoku period called
Takeda Shingen, known as the "Tiger of Kai." This man fought in more than
twenty battles and sieges, more than most generals in world history. He was
one of the most powerful daimyos (feudal lords) of the era but was killed in
1573. The film shows us the grand strategies of the age when we see Japanese

society from the top down and not from the point of view of a villager or a bandit. We see the diplomatic wranglings between kingmakers, and we see a battle of epic proportions at the end. I said *Hero* is one of the most beautiful films ever made, but *Kagemusha* is also in the conversation.

RUROUNI KENSHIN (2012)

If there is a halfway point between anime (Japanese animation) and Kurosawa, *Rurouni Kenshin* and its multiple sequels is it, directed with constant ingenuity by Keishi Ohtomo and starring Takeru Satoh (so gorgeous it's like he's just stepped out of a J-Pop band and strapped on a katana). Kenshin is a young samurai/assassin (so already historically inaccurate) in the Boshin War. The background to the war began with the constant civil strife of the Sengoku period and came to an end with the decisive victory by a daimyo called Iyasu Tokugawa at the Battle of Sekigahara in 1600. He and his successors set up the Tokugawa shogunate and closed the doors of Japan to any outside interference, calcifying the culture for over 250 years. Then, in the 1860s, there was an attempt to modernize, to try to catch up with the West after an American mission arrived in Japan and alerted the shogunate to its stagnation. The subsequent Boshin War was not just a civil war but an argument about tradition and modernity between the shogun and the emperor. It is hugely important in understanding how feudal Japan became modern Japan and the country's inherent militarism from the 1870s to 1940s.

This is all discussed as an auburn-ponytailed Kenshin (no traditional chonmage hairstyle for him), bearing an X-shaped scar on his cheek, fights for justice. After the Boshin War, Kenshin (who has multiple names) declares he will kill no more. To facilitate this vow, he uses a katana with a back blade. (A katana blade is slightly curved, which allows it to cut deeper than a straight-bladed European weapon.) Kenshin modifies his katana so that the outer curve is blunt, but the inner curve facing him is razor sharp. As such, he can still fight and, most importantly, protect the weak from injustice, but he can't kill with a back blade. The idea for such a sword is absurd (with no historic precedent). Why not just have a totally blunt katana or use a bokken (wooden training sword), like the awesome (but real) swordsman Miyamoto Musashi? But the sword is a metaphor. The sword still has a lethal edge, but it is facing the man who used to be a killer; every time he draws it, it is a reminder of his past and what he promised never to do again.

We are now in the world of color, and as the opening scene in a snowy battlefield is something Kurosawa could have directed, we quickly get into cartoon territory. We are also starting to see modern clothes, and in the second film in the series, the bad guy has a battleship complete with naval gun turrets as a base of operation. This would be ridiculous in *Nichiren to Mōko Daishūrai,* set as it is in the thirteenth century during the Kamakura period, but it is more easily explainable in the Victorian era when *Rurouni Kenshin* is set and is a visual reminder of how long the era of the samurai truly was.

THE LAST SAMURAI (2003)

This era rarely gets a mention in Hollywood, but there is one big-budget exception, *The Last Samurai.* It was one of the films greenlit because of the success of *Gladiator,* so that, plus Tom Cruise, plus filming in New Zealand, which was raking in the cash at the time with the *Lord of the Rings* movies, were all guaranteed to make it a hit . . . which it was, but one with a very muddy history. The plot is basically *Dances with Wolves* (many reviewers described it as Dances with Samurai). All Japanese tropes are present and correct: Ninjas! Honor! Samurai! Swords! Tea ceremonies! But it does do a good job of showing the huge culture clash with the West when an American coming from the US Civil War arrives in a Japan still living the same way it had when America first interacted with Europeans.

Apart from those points, everything else in *The Last Samurai* is historically inaccurate. Two points to highlight this: The local daimyo appears to be living in a tiny village rather than a castle suitable for a man of his standing, and secondly the rebels do not want to use firearms (in reality they did, because they had existed three hundred years earlier at the peak of samurai martial culture). It very much falls into the golden era of Hollywood's reading of history and shares more of its DNA with *The Adventures of Robin Hood* than *Seven Samurai.*

A final point on the katana: In all these films there is huge reverence for the primary weapon of the samurai. Prestigious museums around the world display them with the same sense of awe and admiration shown to crown jewels. The very finest katanas are right up there with the greatest weapons ever made, but not every sword could be master crafted when equipping an army of thousands. Reading comments by real samurai from the past, we quickly get the impression that for them the katana was just a tool. It is often forgotten that they spent long hours practicing archery (one of the samurai uses a bow in *Seven Samurai*), something that is rarely mentioned in the films because everyone wants to see a sword fight. There are lots of references in historical records to samurai using several katanas in a battle because some would invariably break during the fighting, hardly the superpowered image we have of them today.

Pole arms, spears, bows, double-handed swords, all were used by samurai through the eight-hundred-plus years they existed. We occasionally see these other weapons, but they are invariably wielded by a bad guy. Heroes use katanas; it's a fact . . . according to the movies.

Of course, when dealing with the artistic output of an entire continent, with dozens of languages, this chapter can only offer sample snapshots. One of the joys of Asian cinema, particularly from Japan, is their storytelling traditions are completely different from those of Europe. Because of this, their stories feel fresh and unique to the average jaded Western cinemagoer. Consider this chapter an introduction to the genre, and if it sparks an interest, there are hundreds of great movies to explore.

NOTES

1. www.nfi.edu/what-is-bollywood.

2. Jayant Pandurang Nayaka and Syed Nurullah, *A Students' History of Education in India (1800–1973)*, 6th ed. (New Delhi: Macmillan, 1974).

3. Professor Sunny Singh, Hist Fest conference, 2018.

4. Vanessa Holburn, *The Amritsar Massacre: The British Empire's Worst Atrocity* (London: Pen & Sword, 2019).

5. Iris Chang, *The Rape of Nanking: The Forgotten Holocaust of World War II* (New York: Basic Books, 1997).

6. Jem Duducu, *Forgotten History: Unbelievable Moments from the Past* (Gloucestershire, UK: Amberley Publishing, 2016), 140–42.

7. Donald Richie, *The Films of Akira Kurosawa*, 3rd ed. (Oakland: University of California Press, 1996).

Chapter 6

Little Wuthering Prejudice

The period from the 1770s to the 1880s saw the biggest changes in global society ever. It started with the American colonies successfully rising up against their colonial masters to create a brand-new state, free of a monarchical system, and was followed only a few years later by France rising up and literally cutting off the head of its own royal regime. The French Revolution morphed into France militarily threatening all of Europe, and after twenty-five years of conflict, Europe was sick of war.

The early to mid-1800s was a time of tumultuous change across the world. Within the space of just two years, Moscow and Washington, DC were in flames, thanks to invading armies. Napoleon, one of the greatest generals in world history, terrorized three different continents with his armies. And in the cities of Britain, colossal, world-altering change was literally building a head of steam as the Industrial Revolution took hold and shifted society and the global environment forever. At the start of the 1800s, most people in Britain lived in agrarian villages, but by the end of the century, the majority of the population lived in industrialized cities, connected by railways, with access to a revolutionary means of communication, the telegraph.

So, given these turbulent times, it is surprising and somewhat odd that a lot of the 1800s is shown through small scenes of family life, written largely by women. There are dozens of film adaptations of novels by the Brontë sisters and Jane Austen, and the number jumps up dramatically when TV adaptations are included. By contrast, English-language films about Napoleon are few and far between, with only 1970's *Waterloo* showing him in all his glory. Oddly he appears in somewhat comedic roles in sci-fi films such as *Time Bandits*, *Bill & Ted's Excellent Adventure*, and *Night at the Museum: Battle of the Smithsonian*. But all things considered, this era in literature is where women, for a change, beat the guys hands down.

Why is it that *Wuthering Heights* and not *Waterloo* gets the attention and the remakes? I have a theory: Social history is more relevant to us than great leaders or historic battles. Think how much society changed when we stopped being hunter-gatherers and, instead, settled into small villages and farms. Imagine how, in the space of one person's lifetime in Britain, the balance of work moved from agricultural to industrial, and small medieval towns like Liverpool and Manchester turned into giant cities full of factories. These are the events that affected everyday lives, then and now. But there is no neat narrative to hang them on; there's no single person who led the charge and challenged the system. Because there's no useful story to tell, it's left to the historians to try to keep children awake as they discuss subjects like the Industrial Revolution. Similarly, industrialization led to all kinds of significant changes in political philosophy, but Karl Marx working in the British Museum Reading Room to come up with *The Communist Manifesto* and *Das Kapital* is never going to be a blockbuster movie (I'm not sure he would approve anyway).

That's the social history side, but then there's Napoleon. He is a genuinely great story, but he's also an expensive story to tell. He appears in 1956's *War and Peace*, but he is not a main character, and this is not a satisfactory retelling of Tolstoy's classic book. The making of the film was an epic undertaking which did not reap the right level of financial reward. Then there's *Waterloo*, with Rod Steiger as an excellent Napoleon. It was enormously expensive to make but didn't set the box office on fire and ended up making a loss. Napoleon made costly mistakes in his career, and it seems the same happens when the man is put on screen.

BARRY LYNDON (1975)

Stanley Kubrick had wanted to return to the historical epic in the 1970s, and there's an entire library of the prep work for his planned movie on Napoleon. However, due to prohibitive costs and the fact that *Waterloo* flopped, the highly ambitious project was shelved. Some of it was retooled into *Barry Lyndon*, a story based on a forgotten but important war of the mid-1700s called the Seven Years' War. Like many of Kubrick's later films, every frame is an oil painting, particularly when set in this era. He also created the most realistic lighting in any Hollywood movie ever made, but it wasn't easy. Kubrick wanted to make the audience feel like they were in a room in 1759, so there was no light except from the candles. Everything would be too dark to film with standard lenses, but Kubrick used a Carl Zeiss Planar 50mm lens, which was incredibly rare and expensive as the lenses had been developed for use by NASA in the Apollo moon landings.

Barry Lyndon may look great, but most people find it a slog. Kubrick is often accused of being cold, a watchmaker of a director. As such, it is technically perfect, but in terms of wit, dialogue, and characterizations, Jane Austen beats him hands down. Before the era of digital effects, a battle scene with thousands of men needed thousands of extras. And that wasn't cheap. To keep costs down to a manageable level, *Waterloo* was shot in the Soviet Union where thousands of soldiers in the Red Army were used as extras. But that had problems of its own, particularly with the cavalry charges as they looked so real the soldiers tended to scatter despite assurances that the cavalry would slow down before they reached them.

What about now? In the twenty-first century, digital effects must have brought costs down, right? This is true but men standing in long lines firing smoky muskets two or three times a minute is not what modern audiences are looking for in epic action movies. At the time of writing there is a plan for Ridley Scott to do a film about the rise of Napoleon, with Joaquin Phoenix in the starring role. But Scott has yet to start shooting, and Phoenix is now about as old as Napoleon was at the end of his career at Waterloo. Remarkably, Napoleon was only twenty-seven when he came to Europe's attention when he conquered Italy in the late 1790s.

So, audiences like the frocks and the ballroom dances and even the uniforms of the era, but battle scenes are expensive to film, and nobody wants to see lines of men blindly firing at each other through smoke. Therefore, it's better to go for the stories that delve deep into the soul and, unlike almost any other historical topic so far mentioned, are sometimes laugh-out-loud funny.

Behind the books written by the famous women of the era is the tragic reality that none of the three Brontë sisters lived to forty; Jane Austen died at forty-one and Louisa May Alcott did only a little better, making it to fifty-six. It was still too soon. In a way their books are a cynical reminder of how Hollywood works: The good news about long dead people is they are a recognizable brand, with no copyright. A movie about Henry VIII guarantees there will be enough base-level interest and recognition to ensure the film will at least break even, and it's even better news that no royalties will have to be paid to the royal family. However, if you are adapting, say, *The Other Boleyn Girl* by Philippa Gregory, even though it's about Henry VIII and the scenes are fictional, the living author is going to get a payday. But once the author is dead and a few decades have passed, no copyright laws apply, so whether it's Shakespeare or Jane Austen, there is all the name recognition and potential fan base with none of the costs. What could possibly go wrong?

PRIDE & PREJUDICE (2005)

Let's take Jane Austen. While she has six novels to her name, the four published during her lifetime, *Sense and Sensibility*, *Pride and Prejudice*, *Mansfield Park*, and *Emma*, have all been remade multiple times over a century of cinema. Sometimes they are made under another name, like 2001's *Bridget Jones' Diary*. Updated to modern London, it was based on a best-selling book by Helen Fielding. She may have updated the setting and added some great gags about female sexuality, but the plot structure and even Mr. Darcy (played in the film by Colin Firth, who only a few years earlier had played Mr. Darcy in a TV adaptation of *Pride and Prejudice* to huge acclaim) were there. I am not a fan of rom-coms because, generally speaking, they exist in a sea of mediocrity, but this is a great film, with some genuinely funny gags. However, it's telling that the subsequent books/films aren't as good as the first because . . . well, they aren't based on a classic Jane Austen novel.

The original story is about the sacrifices women must make in Georgian society in Britain. The protagonist is Elizabeth Bennet, a young woman with her own mind. Unfortunately, the family is in a precarious financial situation because Mr. Bennet (her father) has five daughters and no son, and his property can only be passed to a male heir. Mrs. Bennet (the mother) also lacks an inheritance, so the family will be destitute upon his death. Therefore, it is vital that at least one of the daughters marries well to support the others. The novel revolves around the importance of marrying for love rather than money or social position despite the pressure to make the "correct" match. One of the daughters is going to have to do the right thing for the sake of the family but faces a potentially loveless marriage in return.

This plot had never before appeared in any book, and yet it has been a consideration in every culture and society. Today we talk about arranged marriages as a novelty or as coming from cultures not European, but even a passing familiarity with feudal politics shows that daughters were traded like prizes or peace treaties in the past. This tension between marrying for love or alliance is one of the plot points of *The Last Duel*. Of course, none of these women (in some cases preteen girls) would have a say in the matter. But now we see that situation from the point of view of a fictional character so well written that it could be describing the dilemma of millions of real women throughout history.

Can the average person in the street relate to being locked in gladiatorial combat? No. Or how about withstanding a cavalry charge of knights in shining armor? Not really. But can we all relate to the complexities of romantic relationships and family commitments? Absolutely. I will put my hand up and say that I don't love these books and films, but I admire them. I want to go to the movies for escapism, whether through complex plots, action adventure, or sheer spectacle (and occasionally all three—I'm looking at you, *Inception*). So, while I understand the appeal of these very human elements and the relatability of their stories, they are not my idea of a great Saturday night out.

That is my personal view, but the genre is extremely important for Hollywood and movie audiences. These stories are those of women in a male-dominated world talking about the most human of experiences: love, marriage, friendship, and family relationships. By doing so they avoid some of the usual pitfalls and clichés that Hollywood (and TV land) fall into. The two-hundred-year-old story told in *Pride and Prejudice* is so often revisited because it remains fresher than anything a modern screenwriter can come up with. The 2005 version starring Keira Knightley is a historically accurate costume drama in that everything looks roughly era appropriate. Is it the greatest version ever? No, but if you want to watch a film adaptation rather than a TV series, this is a great introduction to the genre.

This brings us to the strange word choices used to describe the genre. If a film is set in the past and is serious as opposed to being funny, it's historical drama, right? And yet there are different phrases used to convey slightly arbitrary differences. The main ones are "historical drama," "costume drama," "war movie," and "period piece." If it's a drama set in the past, everything could be described as "historical drama," but what the term usually means is anything before the 1800s. (Why? I can find no satisfactory reason.) So, *The Other Boleyn Girl* is "historical drama" then, right? Well, yes, but it might also be called a "costume drama" because this phrase tends to describe a female-oriented drama set in the olden days, so on that basis, *The Other Boleyn Girl* and *Pride and Prejudice* would fall in the same genre. A "period piece" tends to mean "within living memory," so *The Godfather*, which was made in the 1970s but set in the 1940s, is a period piece. A "war movie" could, in theory, be anything from *Troy* to *Braveheart* to *Dunkirk*, but the term tends to mean wars of the twentieth century even if some of them are within living memory (so we could say they are "period pieces" as well). Of course, some films have a bit of everything: is *The English Patient* a war film or a period piece or a costume drama? It's the same issue with *Atonement*. The terms are pretty arbitrary when we start looking for the logic, but because most of the books/movies discussed in this chapter are written by women, about women, for probably a largely female audience, they all tend to be called "costume dramas," which seems to imply a film less worthy than those otherwise classified. I suspect that "costume drama" and "chick flick" are film equivalents, and that neither term is meant as a compliment which is not fair.

Many of these source works are so complex and layered that they are more often adapted into a TV miniseries than films, and because their stories are so timeless, they have been transported to different cultures around the world, for instance 2004's Anglo-Indian production *Bride and Prejudice*. Of course, there is also the truly bizarre 2016 film *Pride + Prejudice + Zombies*. If you missed this one, you will not be surprised to hear that the combination of a zombie movie and the plot of *Pride and Prejudice* is a better idea than its actual realization.

SENSE AND SENSIBILITY (1995)

Pride and Prejudice is probably Jane Austen's best-known book, but *Sense and Sensibility* was her first novel. It's a coming-of-age story (possibly the first of this genre) involving the Dashwood sisters (there are three, but this is mainly about the two older ones, Elinor and Marianne) who must move with their widowed mother from the estate on which they grew up to a modest home on the property of a distant relative, Sir John Middleton. Of course, being a coming-of-age story (where we get three for the price of one), there's love and heartbreak and many other of the teenage emotional tribulations, and yet this was written before Napoleon invaded Russia.

Austen's work is nothing if not about the human experience, but she, like many writers over the years, has been attacked for her portrayal of women coping with dominating male characters and putting up with it. This is a charge raised mainly by feminists, and as a man, I feel ill-equipped to rebut. What I can say is the books and movies accurately portray the issues women in the late eighteenth and early nineteenth centuries faced, and virtually every woman I know (all of whom would describe themselves as feminists and they certainly have no problem with giving me their opinions) loves the movies/books. I leave it to you to decide if these are feminist works.

One of the most successful screen versions of *Sense and Sensibility* stars Emma Thompson as Elinor and Kate Winslet as Marianne, with Hugh Grant looking suitably dashing as Edward Ferrars. It's a standard version that could be shown to anyone studying the text, and it's like the sword-and-sandals films in that everything is scrubbed up and clean. Apparently, these people lived in a world where there was no mud or dirt, everything was in an excellent state of repair, and everyone had exceptional dental care.

EMMA (1996, 2020)

Moving quickly on to *Emma*, another story that just gets remade all the time. Gwyneth Paltrow's version from 1996 handled the story very well. Job done for the next thirty years, but no. In 2020 we had *Emma.* (the period is important apparently). This one is a little more hyperstylized but still sets the story in the early 1800s (with everyone wearing vivid colors that would never have existed at the time). Anya Taylor-Joy is excellent as Emma, but apart from some nice costumes, what did it have to say that was noticeably different from the 1996 version?

You may find it strange that I should mention the color of the clothes, but the story of color in textiles is an interesting one that stretches back thousands of years. Prior to the invention of modern industrial dyeing techniques, cloth would be dipped into a vat of a dye made from colors found in nature. Dip a piece of cream-colored cloth in a blue dye and the result would be a light pastel blue. To obtain a richer, darker blue, the process would have to be repeated multiple times until the desired shade was achieved. It was a time-consuming process, which meant that a richly colored shirt would cost five or six times more than a standard pastel one. So, rich colors were associated with rich people because only they could afford them.

Peasants wore the most basic of clothing made of cotton or wool, with no coloring at all. The original cream color of the cloth became, over time, covered in the dirt and grime of everyday life, turning their clothing brown. The nursery rhyme "Baa, Baa Black Sheep" has sometimes been banned because people assumed it was a racist metaphor. It isn't. It was a song that sprung up in the late thirteenth century about the onerous wool taxes imposed by Edward I. In the textile industry black wool was worth far less than white for the very practical reason that black wool could not be dyed.[1]

The Europeans have long associated purple with luxury. This is because prior to the invention of artificial dyes, producing purple was a staggeringly expensive process. The only natural source of the color comes from maritime snail shells found in the Mediterranean. The color comes from crushing them, and it took a huge amount of effort to get enough dye to color a cloak, which had to go through the process multiple times, so it soon becomes apparent that only a king or emperor could ever afford such an item. Indeed, in the late Roman era (and later, in the Eastern Roman Empire) children of the emperor born during his reign were known as Porphyrogenitus: literally, "born in the purple," because there was a purple room in the palace in Constantinople. These children were thought to have a more valid claim to the throne than older children not "born in the purple" (this did lead to civil wars, but that's another story).[2]

The Chinese had the same problems producing yellow cloth, so that became the imperial color. Anyone else caught wearing yellow would be sentenced to death, but this was hardly a worry as it was so wildly expensive that no one apart from the emperor was likely to afford it. This also explains why the Forbidden City is covered in yellow tiles as it's a way of saying, look what I've got that you can't have.

The first artificial pigment was Prussian blue, created at the very start of the 1700s. It took a while for it be upscaled from a color in the painter's palette to a fabric dye, but from the mid-1700s onward, Prussian blue was the color of the Prussian Army, basically declaring, look what we can make, and you know which army this is. So, there's a lot going on with the use of color in history, but Hollywood so often gets it wrong.

WUTHERING HEIGHTS (1992, 2011)

In any discussion of British literature written by women, the Brontë sisters come after Jane Austen. To keep things manageable, I won't be discussing Anne, who is probably better thought of as a poet, so I will start with Emily and her 1847 masterpiece *Wuthering Heights*. Interestingly, it was originally published in three volumes which included Anne's *Agnes Grey*.

Unlike Austen's witty and almost sunny novels, *Wuthering Heights* is a very different piece of writing in the style of Gothic fiction. The book takes us through the life of Heathcliff, from childhood (spoiler alert for a nearly two-hundred-year-old book) to his death in his late thirties. He was abandoned by his family in Liverpool, but he is taken in by Mr. Earnshaw, the patriarch of the house called, surprise, surprise, Wuthering Heights. Heathcliff develops close relationships with members of his adoptive family, especially the daughter Catherine (Cathy), but things do not go well, and he ends up becoming a servant. He runs away when Catherine decides to marry another. He returns years later, rich and educated, and sets about gaining his psychological revenge on the two families that he believed ruined his life. It is a dark and twisted tale, and by the end everyone is dead, mad, or unhappy. This is not a feel-good story. Some have described it as *Romeo and Juliet* set on the Yorkshire moors, but I think the more apt Shakespearean comparison would be with *Macbeth*.

Wuthering Heights had some very strong contemporary reviews, my favorite being from *Graham's Lady Magazine* published in Philadelphia: "How a human being could have attempted such a book as the present without committing suicide before he had finished a dozen chapters, is a mystery."[3] Mary Shelley's *Frankenstein* had come out in 1818, so these two books are a sign of the growing literary confidence of women in Britain in the nineteenth century. Emily and Mary would be damned if they were going to write soppy romances; instead, they wrote about reanimating corpses and psychological torment. They were way ahead of their time.

There was a silent film version of *Wuthering Heights* in 1920, and Laurence Olivier played Heathcliff in the 1939 version. In 1970 it was time for a young Timothy Dalton to be Heathcliff. All of these movies are of their time and tell us little about the history of the era. The concern was for drama and things to look "old" rather than fastidiously drop in context of the period's politics or era-appropriate belt buckles. In 1992 Juliette Binoche was Cathy and Ralph Fiennes was Heathcliff, and it was a formidable production that still works today. However, it's 2011's version directed by Andrea Arnold and starring Kaya Scodelario as Cathy and James Howson as Heathcliff that is arguably the best. This time around, casting a mixed-race actor to play Heathcliff adds to his portrayal as isolated and alienated. The movie itself seems to have been filmed in bleak-o-vision, where everything is earth, mist, and gales. The tumult of the emotions in the book were always mirrored by the wild and untamed Yorkshire moors, but they had never been so vividly portrayed as they are in this film. But enough! Timeless as it is, do we really need a retelling of the story every twenty years, with at least one TV adaptation in the middle?

JANE EYRE (1943, 1996)

Moving on, we come to Charlotte Brontë and *Jane Eyre* (as a teen I used to get confused about whether Jane Eyre was the author or the book's title). Charlotte was the first of the sisters to gain recognition as a writer, and *Jane Eyre* is another complex novel with telling social commentary.

The novel is unusual in that it is written in the first person. It is set not in Charlotte's time, but in the generation before, during the Napoleonic Wars. It has five distinct sections: Jane's childhood, her education at Lowood School, her time as the governess at Thornfield Hall, where she meets Edward Rochester, her time in the Moor House where she is proposed to by a clergyman (she declines) and, finally, her reunion with and marriage to Rochester.

As with others discussed, the book is morally complex and full of insights into attitudes of the time as reflected most notably in the character of Bertha, a woman of Creole heritage and Rochester's wife, someone described as being violently insane. The general assumption in the book and at the time (and most troubling for the modern reader/audience) is the darker the skin the more likely mental instability will manifest. It's a completely unacceptable and inaccurate racist view. But as the saying goes, one hundred years ago everyone was a racist (which has some truth in it). What this means is that more modern adaptations have had to make revisions or simply be unwatchable.

Much like the works of Austen, *Jane Eyre* highlights issues around marriage and is so frank in its depiction of women's choices and men's advances that it was condemned at the time by some in the press as anti-Christian, about as negative an assessment as could be had in 1847. To a modern audience it may seem quaint, but once again we have something fictional that feels real because it is an honest reflection of the time in which it was written.

The book has been a perennial classic on the silver screen with the first silent short made in 1910; two more versions came out in quick succession in 1914 and 1915. In 1943 Joan Fontaine was Jane Eyre playing opposite Orson Welles as Edward Rochester. This is a film Welles didn't direct, so he is basically just taking a paycheck. A very young Elizabeth Taylor also appears in it.

The film certainly does not seem to be set in the early nineteenth century, and it is interesting to reflect that in the roughly 130 years since the time of the book and the time of the film, options for women hadn't changed that much.

1996 seems to have been a peak year for book adaptations of classic women's literature. This time we have Franco Zeffirelli, probably best known for his versions of Shakespeare plays (in particular 1968's *Romeo and Juliet* and 1990's *Hamlet,* starring Mel Gibson), directing Charlotte Gainsbourg as Jane and William Hurt as Rochester. There's also a very young Anna Paquin as Jane Eyre when she was a child. Unlike the 1943 version, this one is set in the correct era although the halls at times look more like castle dungeons.

We get yet another adaptation in 2011 (the frequency with which the years push out remakes of the giants of women's literature is proof of the lack of originality in Hollywood). Mia Wasikowska is Jane Eyre and Michael Fassbender is in fine form as Rochester. Did it need a remake? No, the 1996 version is a very strong one. Is it a good remake? Yes, it's perfectly service-able. The issue with any remake (or cover song) is if you're not going to do anything different with the original why bother? So is this as distinctive as 2011's *Wuthering Heights*? Not even close.

LITTLE WOMEN (1949, 1994, 2019)

And now we come to Louisa May Alcott's *Little Women,* originally published in two parts under two separate names. Unlike the other writers mentioned, Alcott was shrewd enough to cash in on the success of the original book and wrote two sequels: *Little Men* and *Jo's Boys*. Barely two years separate the original two-part story and *Little Men*, but readers had to wait fifteen years for the third and final installment.

The original is about a house of . . . well . . . women, four sisters and a mother. The story is set during the US Civil War, and their father is a chap-lain in the Union army. Like *Sense and Sensibility* (written some sixty years earlier), this is a coming-of-age story. The age differences among the sisters allows Alcott to show the complexities of growing up at different stages, everything made more poignant against the background of the bloodiest war in American history. Putting it simply, there aren't as many men around as there used to be. So, we follow Meg, Jo, Beth, and Amy as they come to terms with the realities of their poverty and a world upended by war as they gradu-ally mature into young women.

This view of life from a female perspective was new and refreshing. While it's clearly written to depict the time of civil war and its aftermath, it could just as easily be about women during the Hundred Years' War in France. And while the women are fictional, they are based on real-world observations and their experiences feel real too.

Filming it is almost a cottage industry in and of itself. The first version was a silent movie short in 1917. At this point in time, people working on the film could have, theoretically, met Louisa May Alcott, who died in 1888, just twenty-nine years earlier. Indeed, many older people knew what that era looked like because they, too, had lived through it. The Battle of Gettysburg was then barely fifty years old, and veterans could still be seen on the streets of American towns. Making it look authentic was relatively easy as clothing of that era was still being worn.

The first serious full-length movie with sound was 1933's version which has Katharine Hepburn as Jo. It's fine but was superseded by the 1949 film, which did it all again, with a few more scenes, but this time in color. Starring June Allyson as Jo, Margaret O'Brien as Beth, Elizabeth Taylor as Amy, and Janet (yes, I was in *Psycho* but I did so much more than that) Leigh as Meg. The scene where Amy puts a clothespin on her nose in an attempt to make sure she has a lovely nose is still funny and touching. Like all color movies of the time, it was filmed in super vivid colors; nothing is subtle and greens (for example) are *green*. Once again, the sets are spotless and the costumes are in rich hues. You just don't get the feeling that these "little women" are actually poor, which does take away from the drama. Poverty has meant different things in different periods and places. In the nineteenth century in America, poor meant not necessarily guaranteeing three meals a day, but none of these women look like they've missed lunch. Clothes would have been mended and handed down. Rooms wouldn't have been freshly painted. And while actresses for the camera wear makeup to look their best, poor women in the 1800s would never have been able to afford such luxuries. The cost of distressing clothes and sets is extra money to make everything . . . look worse so it's understandable why this wasn't done. It's an honest attempt to re-create the book in period style, but there are better versions out there.

In the mid to late twentieth century, *Little Women* was regularly revived on the small screen, but then it was as if Hollywood suddenly woke up and remembered that this was a beloved story with no royalties to be paid, and what followed was a flurry of productions at the end of the twentieth century into the twenty-first. In 1994's version Susan Sarandon played the mother, with Winona Ryder as Jo, Kirsten Dunst as Amy (when she's younger), Claire Danes as Beth, and Trini Alvarado as Meg. And with this film a pattern emerged: Whether it was *Sense and Sensibility* or *Little Women*, the cream of the young actresses of the time were selected for the roles. A few were already famous, but most would go on to become bigger stars, some winning Oscar glory. It's almost like these films were a rite of passage for an actress in her late teens or early twenties. There isn't a male equivalent to this. Obviously, young men get to be in all kinds of films and usually get paid more than women, but there is no standard group of stories of young men that keep getting made over and over again. But in this 1994 version there is a young actor who goes on to bigger things: one Christian Bale, who many forget started off as a child actor in *Empire of the Sun*.

The 1994 version of *Little Women* is curious. Released around Christmas, the moviemakers seemed to have anticipated the timing and lean heavily into the winter theme so that the story sometimes feels rather like *A Christmas Carol*. It also suffers from the "everything is spotless, the clothing is made of vivid colors, and the lighting is perfect" syndrome which shows a lack of authenticity. It is strangely anachronistic in its choices to show the past, apparently taking the sword-and-sandals movies as a point of reference, rather than anything resembling real poverty in the mid-nineteenth century. But in one piece of good news, the movie has that rarest of rare touches (for its time), a female director, Gillian Armstrong. Hollywood was finally allowing women to tell stories about women.

Then in 2018, just in time for the 150th anniversary of the book, a new version came out, one that lazily decided to do it all in modern times. You've probably never seen it; nobody talks about it and that's all I'm going to say about it. However, just one year later we had the most recent film adaptation starring Saoirse Ronan as Jo, Emma Watson as Meg, Florence Pugh as Amy, and Eliza Scanlen as Beth. This one was also directed by a woman, Greta Gerwig, and even won an Oscar for Best Costume Design.

Most of these classic books have multiple excellent film versions, so people watch the one that speaks to them. But it seems each version of *Little Women* doesn't quite hit the nail on the head . . . until we get to this one. It's taken 102 years, but finally, there is one that has the acting—yes, that was always a given—but now it actually looks like it's about a struggling family of women in the mid-nineteenth century. Natural light is used, colors are a little more muted, plus there is Meryl Streep as Aunt March, so you know it's going to be good. And a brief shout-out to Timothée Chalamet, who gets to have even more tousled hair than Christian Bale in the role of Laurie.

While the majority of this chapter has been on the women who have shaped our interpretation of the nineteenth century and focused it on the very micro level of the nuclear family (usually from the female perspective), there is one man who takes a similar perspective, who wrote in the same century, and who also has a cottage industry of productions around his work: the journalist from Portsmouth called Charles Dickens.

Perhaps only second to Shakespeare, he produced quantity as well as quality. The main works (and there are more) that keep getting made into films (and TV) are *The Pickwick Papers*, *Oliver Twist*, *Nicholas Nickleby*,

David Copperfield, Bleak House, Little Dorrit, A Tale of Two Cities, Great Expectations, and, perhaps the biggest one of them all, *A Christmas Carol*.

Most of these were serialized in newspapers before they were collected into books, and this explains why there are so many cliffhangers: Readers felt compelled to rush out and buy the next edition so they could find out what happened. Dickens was a master of his craft, but he paid dearly to get there. His early childhood was idyllic, but when his father was forced by his creditors into the Marshalsea debtors' prison in Southwark, his wife and youngest children joined him there, as was the practice at the time. Charles, then twelve years old, boarded with Elizabeth Roylance, a family friend, and visited his imprisoned family every weekend. To pay for his board and to help his family, Dickens was forced to leave school and work ten-hour days earning six shillings a week pasting labels on pots of boot polish. Everything eventually worked out and Dickens became a journalist, but unsurprisingly, this experience left a scar that not only influenced his writing, but led to his becoming an advocate for the reform of socioeconomic and labor conditions as well.

Like Shakespeare I will have to choose a few select examples because he has (at time of writing) 446 writers' credits on IMDb. Again, like the women writers (particularly Austen), war is often in the background, but Dickens was never interested in writing about war as such. He wanted to highlight the struggles of the poor, and it is arguable that he did more for the working class than Karl Marx.

OLIVER TWIST (1948, 2005)

Oliver Twist was originally serialized in a newspaper but came out as a complete work in 1838. It is the tale of an orphaned boy in the poorhouse who is sold into an apprenticeship with an undertaker. He meets the Artful Dodger, a member of a gang of child pickpockets, run by the elderly criminal Fagin (who some see as an outdated anti-Semitic stereotype, but who others see as a loveable rogue). It is not hard to find where the influences for this story came from in Dickens's life. It is a powerful condemnation of poverty in Britain during the era of industrialization and empire and has been translated into virtually every language on the planet. Sometimes the names and even the title are changed. Oliver Twist is a completely alien name to someone who speaks Mandarin, so in China it's *The Orphan Boy from the Foggy City* and remains popular to this day.

What's especially interesting about *Oliver Twist* is that it is an example of a story that is never updated (although Disney did turn him into a cat in *Oliver & Company*). The original story is set in Victorian times, and the movies all portray it in that era. It was first put on film in 1912, and adaptations have been made regularly since then, but it wasn't until 1933 that there was a full-length feature film. It was a perfunctory adaptation, which in 1948, was improved upon in every possible way by David Lean's version, with a young Alec Guinness as Fagin. In 2005 another great director had a go with Roman Polanski's interpretation, the first feature-length version in color (that wasn't animated . . . or the other one, which I will be coming to). It was an instant classic and one that has an air of authenticity, with grimy streets, candles struggling to illuminate rooms, and everyone but the rich looking sweaty and dirty. This is what poverty looks like. But it is not unrelentingly bleak; it has wit and humor while making a powerful point about destitution, child labor, and social inequality.

OLIVER! (1968)

There is one Hollywood genre that hasn't had much of a mention so far and that is the musical. Oddly enough, this grim story about domestic violence, criminal gangs, and poverty was turned into a hit stage musical under the subtly different title of *Oliver!* Of course, if Hollywood smells a hit somewhere else, perhaps it could make money by turning it into a movie (this is the logic behind turning books, plays, comics, and even video games into films: they all come with a built-in audience). And so, in 1968, Carol Reed's *Oliver!* won an impressive six Oscars, including Best Picture and Best Director. While I am a huge fan of the musical, for Reed to beat Kubrick to the Best Director statue when it was *Oliver!* versus *2001: A Space Odyssey* is just plain embarrassing for the academy.

It's strange but there's something about the social concerns of the early nineteenth century that keep being turned into hit musicals. Who would think poverty and crime in England (*Oliver!*) or social unrest in France (*Les Misérables*) or politics and corruption and scandal in America (*Hamilton*) could be the basis for some catchy tunes, but it turns out the genre just can't get enough of them. Of course, as soon as an entire crowd dances in precise choreography to "Food, Glorious Food," there is no pretense that this is real history. But what each one of these unlikely scenarios does is to highlight something that doesn't normally get into the conversation: the plight of the little man and the families on the breadline. And (spoiler alert for a 180-year-old novel/fifty-year-old musical) when Nancy is killed by Bill Sykes, we are stunned. Not everyone is going to make it out of this alive, and usually it's the nice people who are the most vulnerable. That is a tough lesson for a child to learn, but we all see it as kids when we watch the film.

A TALE OF TWO CITIES (1958)

A Tale of Two Cities (Paris and London) tells the story of the French Doctor Manette, who is imprisoned for eighteen years in the Bastille in Paris. He is eventually released and goes to live in London with his daughter Lucie, whom he has never met. These are the bare bones of a story that has at least a dozen central characters and one of the most famous opening lines of all times, "It was the best of times; it was the worst of times." As the tale is set around the French Revolution and the subsequent Reign of Terror, it has Dickens's most political of backdrops. It's one of the rare occasions when he goes back in history several generations to focus again on an ordinary person while pointing out that while France is in the grip of anarchy, England, by comparison, is doing nicely, thank you very much.

Indeed, Dickens's description of the bloody nature of revolutionary France has shaped the British narrative of those events ever since. In France the revolution was seen as necessary and the violence a minor price to pay to evolve into a republic after suffering for decades, if not centuries, under corrupt and inefficient Bourbon rulers. In Britain, by comparison, we focused on the deaths, the kangaroo courts, and the endless use of the guillotine. There was a total breakdown of law and order whose eventual calm coalesced in a career path for Napoleon, a man who would go on to fight wars against all the major powers of Europe for twenty years. Which is right? It's hard to say, but probably a bit of both. The summary executions should never be forgotten, nor should the state of the decaying French aristocracy in the late 1700s.

Starting with a short in 1907, *A Tale of Two Cities* received a lot of attention in the first half of the twentieth century, but interest waned as the century wore on (although there were multiple TV versions in the 1980s). There hasn't been a version in the twenty-first century, which probably means there's one in production as I write. Dirk Bogarde's 1958 movie is probably cinema's best take on the book, and like most films of the time, it's best not to list all the historical inaccuracies as they would take a chapter on their own.

A CHRISTMAS CAROL (1938)

The last story in this chapter has probably been remade more times than anything else in this entire book, and a review of the competition means that's saying something. I am, of course, talking about *A Christmas Carol*. This is a rare example of a piece of fiction not only reflecting history but making it too. Indeed, this whole story about Scrooge and his visitation by three ghosts is so famous I don't even need to tell you that because you know the plot like the back of your hand.

When Mount Tambora in Indonesia erupted in 1815, it knocked the entire world's weather system out of balance. This event did not make the British papers, and yet, its repercussions would have a significant impact on British culture, indeed, on world culture. Because of this eruption, Britain would have abnormally harsh winters for the next several years. This meant snow at Christmas, which was unusual in England. For the four-year-old Charles Dickens, this phenomenon would prove to be a seminal experience because, for the first few Christmases that he could remember, they were snowy and magical.

As such, *A Christmas Carol* is pivotal to the story of Christmas. As most of our contemporary Western European Christmas traditions come from the pages of Dickens's book, Christmases in the eighteenth century and earlier would have looked very different from anything we know today. The story takes place in an unusually snowy London, which recalls Dickens's childhood memories. Exchanging presents, roasting a large bird, eating Christmas pudding—putting all these together was a surprisingly novel idea. In 1843, the book's year of publication, Sir Henry Cole made and sent the very first Christmas cards. The German tradition of the Christmas tree had only recently been introduced to Britain by Prince Albert; but by 1842, there were adverts for them in the London papers.

A goose was then the most common bird served for the Christmas meal. While turkeys had been in Britain since the sixteenth century, they only became popular holiday eating much later in the nineteenth century. Christmas celebrations had, for centuries, been nothing like anything the first Christians would have recognized; but these earlier festivities would have been alien to us too. In just a few short years in the Victorian era, the Christmas celebrations we recognize today had been turned into something "traditional." So, it's probably fair to say that modern Christmas celebrations have more to do with Charles Dickens and Victorian England than first century AD Palestine.

The name Ebenezer Scrooge was apparently inspired by a tombstone in a Scottish cemetery Dickens visited: "Ebenezer Lennox Scroggie—a meal man."[4] But Dickens misread the last part as "mean" and apparently began to wonder who could be so terrible that "mean" was the summary of his life, preserved for eternity on his headstone. And so a legend was born.

Once again, the productions of this story are almost as old as narrative cinema itself, with the first silent short coming out in 1908. In 1938, there was a very solid version of the whole story, but you really can take your pick. A lot of people like 1992's *The Muppet Christmas Carol*, which has Michael Caine singing as Scrooge. Then there's the updated (for 1988) *Scrooged*, which has Bill Murray in top form as a completely amoral TV producer (is there any other type?). Or how about a computer-animated 3D version starring Jim Carrey as Scrooge in 2009's *A Christmas Carol*? In 2020, we get Jacqui Morris's delightful version which takes real actors and interplays them with several types of animation. But enough already! There are at least sixty-four movies, TV movies, and short series based on this one short story. That's more than one new version every other year since the original 1908 short. And that's not including one-off Christmas TV specials, such as 1988's *Blackadder's Christmas Carol*. No matter what you are looking for in the retelling of this story, I'm going to say it already exists. Please, can everyone stop remaking this?

NOTES

1. W. S. Baring-Gould and C. Baring Gould, *The Annotated Mother Goose* (Open source: Bramhall House, 1962), 35.

2. Alexander Kazhdan, ed. *De Ceremoniis*: *The Oxford Dictionary of Byzantium* (New York and Oxford: Oxford University Press, 1991), 595.

3. Nick Collins, "*How Wuthering Heights* Caused a Critical Stir When First Published in 1847," *The Telegraph*, March 22, 2011.

4. "Revealed: The Scot Who Inspired Dickens' Scrooge," *The Scotsman*, December 24, 2004.

Chapter 7

The Not So Civil War

The civil war that erupted in Russia during World War I lasted longer than America's civil war and killed at least seven million people. The political aftermath of the communist victory changed the course of the twentieth century. But that civil war is all about Russians and communists, so in American filmmaking, it barely gets a mention.

The Spanish Civil War was a testing ground for the weapons and tactics of World War II. It was an emphatic victory for fascism and a sign of the terrible things to come and yet, according to Hollywood, it is of no consequence.

The English Civil War (1642–1651) combined politics and religion and culminated in the execution of a king. That's a good story. However, it is well known in Britain that books, TV, and movies about the topic never do well. This civil war is box office poison.

And yet the conflict from 1861 to 1865 in America, which had less global impact than any of the above-mentioned conflicts, is not only box-office dynamite, but to this day, is still a hotly contested subject. It is also inextricably linked to the history of Hollywood, and definitely not in a good way. The correct name for this war is the US Civil War (most countries have had at least one), but as it has become known as the Civil War and you will know which country I am discussing, it will be called the Civil War in this chapter.

THE BIRTH OF A NATION (1915)

In 1915 one of the first feature-length films to come out had scenes of great technical skill and composition (at three hours fifteen minutes it's long even by modern standards). It is epic in scope, size, and length, with large-scale battles and a cast of dozens of characters. It was, in effect, the first step from the infancy of movies into more accomplished filmmaking. Had the Oscars existed in 1915, there can be no doubt it would have swept the board with golden statues.

Today the film is rated U in England, which means it is "suitable for all": There is no bloody violence, it's silent so there is no bad language, and the viewers of the age would have been appalled at any sexual content. The film is *The Birth of a Nation* and is one of the most overtly racist movies ever made.

Regrettably you read that right: The equivalent of American filmmaking's graduation photo is one of the most blatantly racist pictures you could ever see. This is not surprising as it's based on Thomas Dixon Jr's novel *The Clansman: An Historical Romance of the Ku Klux Klan*, clearly a biased source. President Woodrow Wilson is often quoted as saying, "It's like writing history with lightning. My only regret is that it is all so terribly true."[1] It appears not to be a real quote, although the man himself was racist even by the standards of the day.

The film is set during the aftermath of the Civil War when Dixon grew up in a Christian fundamentalist family in North Carolina. His grandfather had been a slave owner, and his father and uncle were some of the first to join the Ku Klux Klan, which formed in the immediate aftermath of the war. It is therefore unsurprising that Dixon combined his love of God with his hatred of African Americans to become a white supremacist.

What needs to be explored is how the book and the movie perpetrated the myth of the "lost cause." It started the day the Confederate South surrendered on April 10, 1865, when General Lee released this famous order to be distributed to all Confederate forces:

General Order No. 9

After four years of arduous service marked by unsurpassed courage and fortitude, the Army of Northern Virginia has been compelled to yield to overwhelming numbers and resources.

I need not tell the survivors of so many hard fought battles, who have remained steadfast to the last, that I have consented to the result from no distrust of them. . . .

. . . By the terms of the agreement, officers and men can return to their homes and remain until exchanged. You will take with you the satisfaction that proceeds from the consciousness of duty faithfully performed, and I earnestly pray that a merciful God will extend to you his blessing and protection.

With an unceasing admiration of your constancy and devotion to your Country, and a grateful remembrance of your kind and generous consideration for myself, I bid you an affectionate farewell.

General Grant of the Unionist North allowed Lee to leave with full honors. It was as if the South had paused its fight with the North rather than been emphatically beaten (which it had). American military historians generally agree it was not if the North would win, but when. It had more men, money, resources and the factories to produce armaments.[2] That the war lasted so long was due in part to General Lee's effective leadership, but also in part to the North's largely incompetent military leaders. It is almost shocking that the Union took so long to win.

Today, you can still visit plantations from the Civil War era, where the role of slavery is barely acknowledged, and the cause of the war is said to be "states' rights." While the South was indeed fighting for these rights, they weren't fighting over fishing quotas or sales tax but the right to own people. Their economy was based on slavery, and the rich landowners of the South faced certain financial ruin if they had to change their business model.

The destruction wrought on the South both during and after the war (with the release of all slaves from bondage) meant the North had to funnel huge amounts of money into Reconstruction. Within this maelstrom of hurt pride, economic collapse, and the ascendancy of the urban industrial North, bitterness in the South began to form and is still evident today. And it was in this toxic environment that Dixon grew up, obviously seething at the injustice of it all (from his perspective), and wrote a novel that became a smash hit across the country.

So how bad are the movie's politics? The simple answer is very. The Klan is seen as the bringers of peace and justice, a paramilitary group keeping decent, upstanding white people safe from evil African Americans—yes, it's that bad; there are no sympathetic Black characters. I will give no specifics because they are all the most racist of tropes. Also, the number of actual African Americans on screen is kept to a bare minimum, with many Black characters being portrayed by white people in blackface. This is the problem Hollywood has. If it wants to point to the film that started movies as spectacle, where an entire afternoon was spent being whisked off to another time and place, it starts here with *The Birth of a Nation*, but to the modern viewer it is unwatchable. It is also a sign of the engrained racism in America that when the film was released, it was financially successful, and not just in the South.

GONE WITH THE WIND (1939)

The uncomfortable facts keep coming for Hollywood, because show business is not just about the show but also about the business. Studios love to talk about grosses even more than reviews. So, if we are looking at hit movies, the biggest-grossing movie of all time (adjusted for inflation) is *Gone with the Wind*, another highly problematic film set in the South during the Civil War and its aftermath.

If you want to point to a film that gets more hand-wringing in Hollywood than any other, it's *Gone with the Wind*. Unlike *The Birth of a Nation*, it has been shown again and again in cinemas and on TV. The story around the making of the film is almost as famous as the movie itself. The strong, liberal women in my life all love it. Scarlett is, after all, one of the most complex and well-rounded female characters in movie history. It is well documented that it was the hottest role for any actress in the late 1930s and that it went to the relatively unknown British actress Vivien Leigh, shocking Hollywood. Some of the lines have seeped into the public conscience ("Frankly, my dear, I don't give a damn"), but when I last watched it, Amazon had posted an opening statement to say that its racial views were "of its time" and that viewers might find some content distasteful. It's a good way to get around the fact that the film is racist, but because of its unparalleled success can't be erased from the annals of Hollywood history. On HBO the film even has accompanying videos to put it in context and explain the reality versus the twisted version of events portrayed. That's a lot of effort to put into a film, underlying its importance, as well as its problematic nature.

Once again, we see a movie reinforcing myths set up by the South in the nineteenth century. Slaves are seen as stupid, obedient, and happy. The fact that they had, at best, a poor education would be true, but that doesn't make someone stupid, and everything else is flat-out wrong. Not once do we see physical coercion or abuse, and the scenes with slaves in the fields seem sometimes to be played as light relief. The movie is based on the bestselling book by Margaret Mitchell, and Mitchell, like Dixon, was from the South. Scarlett was based on her grandmother who had been a Southern belle living on a slave plantation at the time of the war.

At least this time the film's Black characters are played by African Americans, which brings us to Hattie McDaniel, who played Mammy. She was the first Black actor to be nominated for and win an Academy Award. However, it's the story of what happened to McDaniel which shows how, in some ways, the Civil War was and is still being fought generations later. Most people are aware that due to segregation, when the film premiered in Atlanta, she was unable to attend. To be fair to Clark Gable, when he found out, he wanted to boycott the premiere of what everyone knew would be one of the biggest films ever made.[3] It was McDaniel who talked him into going. What is less well known is that when you see footage of her receiving her Oscar, it was done in a ceremony separate from the main one.[4]

You would think the Oscar win would make McDaniel a role model in the African American community, but there was an understandable outcry by some for portraying a racial stereotype in a film which is problematic for its portrayal of slavery. McDaniel's response was awesome: "(I'd) rather make seven hundred dollars a week playing a maid than seven dollars being one."[5]

Gone with the Wind is another biased view of what happened in 1860s America. It's not completely historically inaccurate as it correctly shows that the burning of Atlanta was the result of Confederate orders rather than wanton destruction by the Union. As Confederate general John Bell Hood was withdrawing, he ordered the destruction of supplies including a train carriage full of ammunition, to stop it falling into Union hands, the resulting explosion destroying houses and starting fires. Sherman never wanted to burn Atlanta, but due to damage from the battle and the withdrawal, that's what happened. The scene where Clark Gable drives his horse-drawn wagon through the inferno (a stunt performed by the legendary Yakima Canutt, more on him in another chapter) is impressive even by today's standards. It is also a literal piece of film history, as this was well before CGI effects, so to portray a city on fire, MGM grabbed every unused set it could find and . . . well, burned it. It was a one-shot take thing, which, if it had gone wrong, would have been so expensive to reshoot it probably would have meant the end of the film. One of the pieces of scenery used was the great wall from *King Kong*, so linking two of the most famous movies of the 1930s together rather unexpectedly.

Ashley Wilkes needs a brief mention. Set up as part of the love triangle with Melanie and Scarlett, he is the man we should be rooting for as, unlike Rhett Butler, he fought in the war. Today we would describe him as having PTSD on his return, but he never seems to gain much sympathy, with all of the women I know saying actor Leslie Howard even looks like a drip in his role. To counter this, it should be remembered that Howard left Hollywood to help the British war effort and was shot down and killed on a civilian transport in 1943.

12 YEARS A SLAVE (2013)

Next, we come to a film that while technically not about the Civil War, is a two-hour reminder of why *Gone with the Wind* is so problematic and why a war needed to be fought over the injustices of slavery. I am talking about *12 Years a Slave*. Finally, we get a film about Black people directed by a person of color. Steve McQueen (not that one) started out as a British video artist, even winning the Turner Prize for his work; it was inevitable that he would turn to movies. But now, having a Black man's eyes on slavery brings us all the anger, brutality, and scathing judgement needed for the topic of slavery in America.

12 Years a Slave is a vital retort to *Gone with the Wind*; perhaps the two should be shown as a double bill. The film is based on the autobiography of Solomon Northup, whose story must be the nightmare of every African American. Born a free Black man in the state of New York, he had a comfortable life. He had land and he had the opportunity to become a professional violinist, but when he was offered the chance to perform in Washington, DC, he was drugged, taken south, and sold into slavery. Northup had done nothing wrong. His only crime was to be an educated Black man and some saw this as a threat, something to fear.

There has been criticism of the film's title because it is a summary of the film itself: We know he's going to be captured and we also know he's going to escape. But to those misanthropes I say, a story is about the journey, not the destination. And what a terrifying journey it was (he is played to perfection by Chiwetel Ejiofor, another British talent). Northup had a number of owners in his time in the South, but none was more despicable than Michael Fassbender's Edwin Epps. If you want to see the myth of the acceptable nature of slavery laid bare, then this is the performance to see. Epps is utterly loathsome and Fassbender had a tough time playing the character. Like most actors, he's a nice person, with liberal values and an inclusive view of the world, but McQueen had already worked with Fassbender on several other films and goaded him into being the most venal racist ever portrayed on the screen (probably). Epps was a real man, and when Northup was finally freed, he only mourned the loss of his property and not the feelings of a man who had been enslaved for over a decade.

The brutality, and the use of human beings as objects to be used, tortured, and discarded, is a hard watch for anyone. Lupita Nyong'o, who plays fellow slave Patsey, is just as tragic as Northup and sets the screen alight. She would go on to win a Best Supporting Oscar for her role, while the film won Best Picture and Best Adapted Screenplay Oscars.

While Northup finally escaped his nightmare situation in 1853 and made it back home, what happened next is not so edifying. His family were aware of his plight and had been petitioning for years to get him back; that had won him his freedom but not justice. The slave trader in Washington, DC (where slavery was still legal) who had taken him south was arrested and tried but acquitted because District of Columbia law at the time prohibited a Black man from testifying against a white person. The other men involved were identified, but their cases were dragged out over years and were all eventually dismissed. No one paid for the crimes inflicted on Northup.

A year after escaping his terrifying experiences, he wrote and published *12 Years a Slave*. It was a bestseller and he went on tour, becoming an outspoken abolitionist (which seems pretty mild considering everything). He later became a carpenter, but exactly what happened next isn't clear. It's most likely he died while the Civil War was being fought, so let's hope he died knowing the South's fate was sealed.

The Civil War didn't do well as a topic in Hollywood after World War II. Many westerns referenced it; quite often a character had been a soldier in the war and was now a cowboy, but there weren't any grand biopics for the likes of Grant or Lee or even Lincoln.

HOW THE WEST WAS WON (1962)

How the West Was Won was not just about the war, but it uses the interesting device of telling the story of a family over multiple generations and splitting up the 1800s over five different segments, directed by multiple directors. The third segment is about some of the family members embroiled in the war, including a re-creation of the very bloody Battle of Shiloh. One of my own ancestors, a captain on the Union side, fought in this battle, and we have his letters written from that time. Soldiers don't usually know the name of the battle they are engaged in; they are too busy fighting and tend to leave that to the generals and the historians. However, in this case, the captain correctly guessed that as the battle was near the town of Shiloh that would be its name.

How the West Was Won was one of the most epic westerns ever filmed, with a cast of virtually every well-known actor of the day: Henry Fonda, James Stewart, and John Wayne to name some of the biggest. It was hugely ambitious and expensive, but it was also a smash hit. Reviews at the time did reflect an interest in the segment on the Civil War, but the movie's success didn't trigger a renaissance in films on the subject. It is also worth noting that all the main characters were, of course, white. This was how the West was won from the perspective of white settlers.

GLORY (1989)

To have a positive view of African Americans in a film about the Civil War had to wait for the end of segregation and progress in the Civil Rights Movement. Which means we now jump to 1989's *Glory*. Directed by Edward Zwick, this is the true story of the Union's first all-Black volunteer company, the 54th Massachusetts Infantry Regiment, to fight in the war. The South feared the mobilization of the African Americans in this conflict as much as it feared the inevitable emancipation of the slaves. In other words, the South saw both as an existential threat, and as such, no Black soldier could expect mercy if captured by the Confederates.

The film finally makes Black men the heroes of the story; these are men with their own agency rather than being victims. Saying that, it's not perfect. The headline name on the poster of the movie? Matthew Broderick, who plays the real leader of the regiment, Colonel Robert Gould Shaw, the son of an abolitionist and the perfect man to lead the Black soldiers. Now Broderick is a fine actor and *Ferris Bueller's Day Off* is a 1980s classic, but his career never made a big impact beyond the 1980s, so to see Broderick get top billing over Denzel Washington and Morgan Freeman, well let's just say it hasn't aged well. Washington would go on to win the Best Supporting Actor Oscar as his cast-against-type troublemaking ex-slave Trip and unlike McDaniel, he could pick up his award in front of a packed theater of Hollywood elite.

In the modern world where the focus is often on social media reactions to the latest Marvel trailer, *Glory* has become a forgotten gem. Many critics at the time thought the opening battle scene was the direct inspiration for the following year's *Dances with Wolves* (more on this film in the next chapter). The battle scenes are visceral and accurately re-create the real events of the company. It is true that their initial engagement happened at a similar time as the Battle of Gettysburg, but as the events were separated by weeks, it's unlikely that Gettysburg (which happened in early July 1863) drowned out the events of the Battle of Grimball's Landing (yes, that's the real name of a real battle) on July 16. However, it's true that the regiment didn't get as much coverage as similar white regiments.

It is also true that initially Black soldiers were paid less than white ones, showing that the American government really didn't do itself any favors even when it was doing the right thing. The final battle scene at the Second Battle of Fort Wagner was as bloody as portrayed on screen. *Glory* is an earnest portrayal of a little-known but hugely significant moment in American history. If you haven't seen it, give it a watch; you owe it to yourself.

GETTYSBURG (1993)

If you want the most Civil War of US Civil War films, then that has to be *Gettysburg*. Coming in at an eye-watering four hours and nineteen minutes, this manages to make *Gone with the Wind*'s three hours and fifty-eight minutes look positively breezy. A distinct advantage of *Glory* is that at two hours and two minutes, it is both a good and comparatively short film about the Civil War.

Gettysburg's buttock-numbing run time is an indication of its intention. It is so careful in its reproduction of the most pivotal battle of the entire war that it is, at times, more the driest of dry documentaries than it is in any way . . . y'know . . . an entertaining film. Most of the actors are under an avalanche of facial fur, which while historically accurate, doesn't help the viewer in working out who is who.

And here comes an important aside about facial hair and why everyone was covered in it during the Civil War. The reason was due to another war fought about a decade earlier on another continent. The causes of the Crimean War (1853–1856) were highly political and complex (basically, and I'm not making this up, it was over a stolen Christmas decoration in Bethlehem; that was the trigger, but of course, it was what the ornament symbolized that counted), but the result was that Britain, France, and the Ottoman Empire went to war with Russia. Many innovations came out of the war, including the balaclava (named after a battle), the cardigan (named after a general), and the invention of the cigarette. It was also the first war to have a war reporter and the first major war to have photographs taken on the front line. William Howard Russel would send almost daily updates to *The Times* newspaper, his stories sometimes accompanied by images of British soldiers. The logistics of the British army into the Crimea were desperately inadequate, so sanitation was poor. Even though it was standard practice for soldiers to shave daily, so many men were falling ill to infected cuts that for the first time in the history of the British army, men were told not to shave, and so beards became normal. However as these were the first photos of British soldiers in action, everyone back home saw these soldiers covered in facial hair and assumed that the army always looked like that. Also, as soldiers were the epitome of bravery, it became fashionable for civilian men to start growing facial hair.[6] As Britain in the nineteenth century was the number one global power, the fashion soon spread to other countries, including America, where, a decade after those first photographs, we see bearded men in the US Civil War. One unremarkable Union general had particularly luxurious mutton chops (thick whiskers on the side of his face). He was General Burnside, whose name was flipped to give us the term *sideburns*. His grooming legacy is better than his military one.

But back to *Gettysburg*, a truly noble endeavor. Having four hours (plus) to show a three-day battle gives the director Ron Maxwell enough time to explain why the battle was being fought there as well as the ebb and flow of the epic clash. It is a surprisingly old-fashioned work for the 1990s. To put it in context, it came out the year after *Reservoir Dogs*, but *Gettysburg* is so safe and earnest it could have been made in the 1950s.

Real Civil War reenactors were used to shoot the battle scenes, filmed on location at the Gettysburg battlefield. Uniforms, weapons, tactics, and even some dialogue are 100 percent accurate even if most of the uniforms are a little too clean and crisp. While the director takes great care to be as realistic as possible, the film offers nothing new; the audience has seen it all before, done better in other movies. However, the same team returned ten years later with *Gods and Generals*, a similarly earnest retelling of the career of General Thomas "Stonewall" Jackson in the war at a comparatively breezy three hours, thirty-nine minutes.

UNCLE TOM'S CABIN (1927, 1965)

12 Years a Slave was the real deal, a true story about slavery. It was held up by abolitionists as a compelling reason to end that blight on the country, but another book from the time carried the same message and was turned into multiple movies: *Uncle Tom's Cabin*.

Written by Harriet Beecher Stowe, the book came out just over a year before *12 Years a Slave* was published. It was a smash hit (estimates of the book's sales probably made Stowe the bestselling author in America in the whole of the nineteenth century), but it has aged like fresh milk left out in the sun. To be clear, *Uncle Tom's Cabin* did more to forward the abolitionist cause than *12 Years a Slave* as it was all but a battle cry for the Union leading up to and during the war, but today it's problematic in its own way. Unlike any of the other books mentioned in this chapter, the title character is used today by African Americans in a negative way. "Uncle Tom" is slang for a Black person who is particularly servile to whites, because that's exactly what the character is like in the book . . . to the point of forgiving his tormentors. This is meant to be a Christ allegory but instead, today, just seems misplaced. Other racial stereotypes stem from this book and are best left unsaid. Putting it simply, Stowe meant well, but she was a product of the times.

Interestingly, the enormous success of the book led to Southerners writing books that were rebuttals, showing how radical Stowe's work was for the mid-nineteenth century. But if *Uncle Tom's Cabin* is now deemed racist, those other works are now unreadable and rightly forgotten.

With all that said, it was inevitable that such an important work would get the Hollywood treatment. The first major attempt was 1927's version, clocking in at nearly two and a half hours, with a reported budget of $1.8 million, making it the most expensive production up to that point—and it was an early talkie. It shows that even in the 1920s, Hollywood loved a book adaptation but was aware of the desire for movies with a conscience. Considerable care went into the making of the film, and here we have a smash hit where the Black title character is played by an African American (James B. Lowe), rather than a white actor in blackface. It was a huge success and received glowing reviews.

It's a fascinating piece of movie history. Despite it being an early talkie, there are numerous title cards with the dialogue. It's an example of the seismic shift happening as the industry moved to full audio. But the film, like the book, is full of racist stereotypes, and while it means well, it is basically unwatchable to a modern audience.

Then in 1965, there was the rather strange *Uncle Tom's Cabin*. This was a European version in English—and now in color—but it's a perfunctory version which is less authentic than the much earlier black and white one. Herbert Lom played the despicable slave owner Simon Legree, and his performance was good enough for him to play the same role in the next version.

There's a 1987 TV movie which has Samuel L Jackson in it as George, not Tom, but the most recent Hollywood version is a rather truncated ninety-minute effort from 1977. The reality is that these are likely to be the last versions of this book (without a *major* rewrite). With a growing confidence in representation and more and more African American filmmakers, *Uncle Tom's Cabin* isn't relevant. Nobody has any desire to remake it, and it certainly doesn't speak to modern cinemagoers, Black or white.

LINCOLN (2012)

When Americans are asked to rate the greatest president of all time, Abraham Lincoln consistently takes the top spot. He served as president during the time of the Civil War, his policies would change American society forever, and he was the first president to be assassinated. With all of that going on, it is remarkable that he doesn't have movies about him coming out all the time. They exist, but he's far less a cottage industry than the war itself.

With that in mind, it is surprising that two films about Lincoln came out in 2012: *Abraham Lincoln: Vampire Hunter* and the far more historically accurate *Lincoln*. I will not be discussing the former except to say that the title and the premise are better than the film.

Lincoln, directed by Steven Spielberg, is a salient reminder of why he is the greatest director ever. That's not to say this is his best film, but this quiet biopic is set largely in rooms where bewhiskered middle-aged men talk about governmental policy, and yet he makes it interesting. Compared to his *Saving Private Ryan*, *Jurassic Park*, *West Side Story*, or *Jaws*, *Lincoln* is about as different a movie as anyone could imagine. Kubrick was just as diverse, but it often took him five years or longer to make another one.

In terms of drama, the problem with *Lincoln* is that it's what the man stood for and what he said rather than what he did that makes him important; and therefore, while America owes this president a huge debt of gratitude, he's not that cinematic. Spielberg uses every trick in the book to make what could be a very dry analysis of the man at a pivotal moment in his career involving and watchable.

It helps that Spielberg got the most special effect of all, Daniel Day-Lewis, to play Lincoln (the role won him his third Best Actor Oscar). Day-Lewis is so mesmerizing in this film, it's not hard to believe that you really are watching Lincoln. Once again, a master director ensures natural light is used, and all clothing/props/settings are era appropriate. There was no way that Spielberg was going to make this look anything other than 100 percent authentic.

That's not to say they got everything right. There are some military terms that are anachronistic, and eagle-eyed viewers can spot a bust of Woodrow Wilson in the Virginia state capitol where filming took place. Wilson would not become president for about fifty years. But these are minor quibbles about one of the most impressive and adult views of Lincoln's presidency.

Like a number of films with the "middle-aged white man" problem (this will come up again in the discussion of *Darkest Hour* in a later chapter), there are scenes to put some much needed and literal color into the film. In *Darkest Hour* we know the scene is a complete fabrication; with Lincoln there's a touching scene between Lincoln and Black men in uniform. Could this have happened? Yes, but there's no evidence of it. They chat pleasantly about the end of the war, a scene that has weight beyond its words as we know Lincoln survived only until a few days after the war ended (the shot that killed him could be considered the Civil War's last shot), and the plight of African Americans would not be resolved by the war either. The scene also mentions the discrepancy of pay between white and African American soldiers.

Spielberg chose not to re-create the scene of the famous Gettysburg Address. This was probably for the best as Spielberg was going for realism, and the truth around the Gettysburg Address is almost farcical. First of all, as the film is set later than November 19, 1863, Spielberg would have had to either rejig the facts or show the speech in flashback. Instead, he alludes to it in a conversation with African American soldiers. The point of that day in November 1863 was the dedication of the Soldiers' National Cemetery in Gettysburg, Pennsylvania. There were hymns, sermons, and the main event was "The Battles of Gettysburg," a much-anticipated oration by the great speaker Edward Everett.

Everett was the main event, and the president of the United States, Abraham Lincoln, was to make "Dedicatory Remarks" (from the program). Everett roared his speech to an engrossed crowd for a full two hours. It was said to have gone well. Lincoln followed and with his rather thin voice proceeded to deliver one of the greatest (and shortest) speeches in the English language. Its poetry, profundity, and brevity are peerless. However, as nobody was expecting much, many of the crowd missed it. Indeed, there are only two pictures of Lincoln speaking and in one of them he's sitting down. The official photographers missed it.

It wasn't until a couple of days later, when the speech was reproduced in newspapers, that people realized its importance, but to the crowd at the time, it was something of a nonevent.

History has not come down on the side of slavery. It is just plain wrong. Even the British Empire had worked that out and abolished it in 1807, but it took America two more generations and a bloody civil war to come to the same conclusion. The resulting catastrophe was (at least) twofold: Although the war brought an end to slavery, it is a tragedy that so much blood had to be spilled to take the morally right course of action. And secondly, the war was only the starting point in the fight for equality and civil rights; these would take more than a century to come close to some kind of parity. That fight goes on.

NOTES

1. Mark E. Benbow, "Birth of a Quotation: Woodrow Wilson and 'Like Writing History with Lightning,'" *Journal of the Gilded Age and Progressive Era* Vol. 9, no. 4 (October 2010), 509–33.

2. Carl Zebrowski, "Why the South Lost the Civil War," Historynet, August 19, 1999.

3. Anna Robinson and Matt Reigle, "The Truth About Clark Gable's Relationship with Hattie McDaniel," grunge.com, July 13, 2022.

4. Seth Abramovitch, "Oscar's First Black Winner Accepted Her Honor in a Segregated 'No Blacks' Hotel in L.A.," *Hollywood Reporter*, February 19, 2015.

5. "First Black Oscar Winner Honored with Stamp," CBSnews.com, January 26, 2006.

6. Jem Duducu, *The Sultans: The Rise and Fall of the Ottoman Rulers and Their World: A 600-Year History* (Gloucestershire, UK: Amberley Publishing, 2018), 244–52.

Chapter 8

How the West Wasn't Won

The expansion of the American frontier largely occurred from the 1850s to the 1890s, a time when America was not seen as a world power. It had no empire to speak of, and it had to wait in line to become industrialized after Britain, France, and Germany. America's potential was there, but it would have to wait a few generations to be realized.

The Wild West was contemporary with the Franco-Prussian War and the reign of Queen Victoria. What appealed to industrialized Europe was the savagery of the American frontier; it was very exciting to read about gunslingers, cattle rustlers, and Indian attacks. But then newspapers or books would be put down, and as the readers stared out of their windows to see the smokestacks of industry, they were reassured that life was better in their sprawling metropolis.

THE GREAT TRAIN ROBBERY (1903)

As mentioned earlier, the very first motion picture considered to be a narrative movie is the twelve-minute-long *The Great Train Robbery*. In the film a group of bandits holds up a train and is subsequently chased by a brave posse. It's the first movie and it's a western, which tells us that the cowboy film is in the very DNA of Hollywood.

The strange thing about cowboy films is that they portray a very specific time and place. The idea of herding cattle on horseback did not originate in America. It was first recorded in Islamic Spain in the Middle Ages, but I am aware that it's difficult to imagine a Muslim peasant cowboy riding around in the 1300s, stopping periodically to get down from his horse to pray toward Mecca. Where's the hat? The gun? The Americanness of it?

The truth is that the cowboy era in America is like the time of chivalry in Europe or the age of the samurai in Japan—except it is a lot shorter. The periods are genuine, and we have genuine stories of contemporary heroism and bravery, but they are also times that have inspired and generated myths. And just as King Arthur and his Knights of the Round Table are exaggerations of days gone by, it is the same for the second half of the 1800s in America and the stories from the American frontier.

The big difference between the myths from other eras and those from the Wild West is that those from the latter were often knowingly created by the players of the time. There was money to be made by the writers who followed colorful characters and reported lurid and highly inaccurate accounts for publication back east, where the population enjoyed stories about lawless territories, frontier dangers, and bad-boy gunslingers.

Racial biases of these accounts infiltrated the movies. In reality, about 25 percent of cowboys were Black, and after the Civil War, many of them were freed slaves looking to start life anew away from the South. That story is rarely told, and a Black face is a rarity in a western film in the first half of the twentieth century. Also, because horses were small and nutrition wasn't the best in the nineteenth century, most of the cowboys were short, so the two giants of cowboy movies, John Wayne and Clint Eastwood, both comfortably over six feet in real life, do not accurately portray the physique of a typical cowboy. But they are who we think of when we hear *cowboy*, right?

Before we get to famous examples, the cowboys themselves were not above altering their image, and photos of the era show men in their best clothes. A photograph was expensive and quite often used in correspondence with a young lady (mail-order brides were also nothing new), so the occasion demanded a shave, a bath, and a flattering outfit, often with a pistol strapped to the hip, gunslinger style. Rare photos taken in the field show scruffier versions of these men, with their pistols on their belts like any other tool. The derby (the bowler hat in Britain) was the preferred headgear of the time as it was designed to be a riding hat and offered some protection if thrown from a horse. The classic ten-gallon hat existed, but it was never as ubiquitous as the movies portray.

Buffalo Bill Cody is a famous example of someone who was part of the story of the Western frontier. He mythologized the facts and put a show on the road, where it was an instant success. From the early 1870s, the production got bigger and bigger as Bill went out of his way to get people who were part of the Wild West involved. As most of them were drunkards, wastrels, or defeated Native Americans, the regular paycheck and a warm bed under a roof was a pretty sweet deal. Chief Sitting Bull, Annie Oakley, Wild Bill Hickok, and Calamity Jane all appeared at various times. When the show traveled to Europe it was a huge success. The Prince of Wales liked it so much he demanded a performance for Queen Victoria, who also thoroughly enjoyed it. The Pope and even Kaiser Wilhelm II saw it (Annie Oakley shot a cigar out of the Kaiser's mouth and said later, after World War I broke out, she should have done the world a favor and shot him instead).

We forget that silent cinema developed not long after some of these events. Wyatt Earp lived until 1929 and was able to advise on films about his life and the famous gunfight at the OK Corral. He even met and befriended a young John Wayne at a time when the actor was picking up work as an extra. So, we now have an ouroboros where real people are exaggerating their stories, setting up the public to consume movies of their exaggerated exploits and increasing the appetite for more of the same.

It's also worth mentioning that most "cowboys" as depicted in western movies are not realistically portrayed; the job of a cowboy was cattle herding and there is very little of that in most of these films. The roles most usually portrayed are those of a sheriff (or other law enforcement), bounty hunter, robber, gambler, bandit, prospector, tracker, soldier, ranch hand, and gun for hire. All these existed and sometimes people did more than one in a lifetime, but the Wild West era, which lasted perhaps twenty years from post–Civil War America to the late 1880s, was not just about moving cattle, with ranches, cows, shoot-outs, panning for gold, railway construction, and Native American attacks. If you believe Hollywood, those are the only things that happened in America from around 1865 to 1900.

For a tiny period in history the breadth of the genre is unprecedented. Think for a moment about *The Good, the Bad and the Ugly* (I know that as you read that, the music played in your head, that's how iconic the film is): It is set during the time of the American Civil War, a key part of the plot, but it is not a war film. Then there's the biggest-grossing movie of all time (adjusted for inflation), *Gone with the Wind*. This is also set during the Civil War and is a major part of the story, but again, it's not a war film. So, given the shared time settings, Clint Eastwood could, in theory, wander onto the Tara plantation, and no one would think him out of place. Except of course, he would be. It's hard to fit those very different films into a common image because that's how diverse films showing the Old West are.

STAGECOACH (1939)

The same year *Gone with the Wind* was released *Stagecoach*, another classic, also came out. John Wayne had been working for years on the periphery of the Hollywood film industry, but this was his big break. Already thirty-two, he played the Ringo Kid, and a legend was born when the camera zoomed in on him and he cocked his rifle. John Ford had directed other films, but this would be the first of his classic westerns, most of which starred Wayne. Technically, *Stagecoach* is a great film, starting with the claustrophobic atmosphere as the men are threatened from all sides by attack. The stunt work carried out by Yakima Canutt is breathtaking, particularly the famous scene where the Apache warrior falls between the galloping horses and lies dead on the ground as the stagecoach goes straight over his body. It is truly terrifying. When Canutt asked Ford if he got the shot he wanted, Ford replied yes, but later said he would have lied if he'd had to because now that he had seen the stunt he was certain that Canutt would be killed on a second take. It is a rip-roaring adventure even though the back projection isn't very convincing to the modern viewer.

But the specter of racism hangs over many of these movies. Their depiction of Native Americans as one-dimensional bad guys offends today's audiences even though the films are not a polemic about Native Americans. Here, it's the good guys versus the bad guys where the goal is to entertain. The problem is that the bad guys portrayed are a real people (most often played by white actors, so another layer of racism) and a race that was, at best, ethnically cleansed and, at worst, the victim of genocide. This complex topic is never broached in any of the films of this time. Even when I was kid in Britain we would sometimes play "cowboys and Indians" in the same way we played "cops and robbers," both of which meant playing the good guys versus the bad guys, and we didn't think anything about it. The films portrayed an era fifty years in the past but reflected the attitudes of the times when the films were made.

THE SEARCHERS (1956)

In one of the better representations of Native Americans in the 1950s, we get Wayne and Ford together again in the absolute classic *The Searchers*. Although the main members of the tribe are still not First Nations people but actors wearing toning makeup, this one does have a more nuanced view of Native Americans, and unusually for productions of the time, most of the extras were Navajo.

Many people are not aware that this film is based on real history. Throughout the nineteenth century, dozens of settler children were captured in raids carried out by Native Americans, a reminder that the Native peoples also carried out acts of violence against civilians. The story in the movie bears close similarities to the abduction of nine-year-old Cynthia Ann Parker by Comanche warriors in 1836. She was to spend twenty-four years with the Comanches and eventually married a chief with whom she had three children. During her captivity, Cynthia Ann's uncle devoted his time and fortune trying to find his niece. Then in 1860, the tribe was attacked by Texas Rangers who brought her back against her will. This is basically the plot of the film.

The obsessive hunt is conducted by John Wayne as Ethan, a man so hell-bent on finding Debbie and returning her to her home that he becomes a cold-blooded racist in the process, and by the end of the film he is just as savage and violent as the men who kidnapped Debbie. The movie is famous for its final scene where everyone gathers inside the house, everyone except for Ethan who, framed by the doorway, a bright light behind him, turns away from the homestead. He is a man of the Old West, and he no longer belongs inside with a civilized family.

The Searchers gives us an imperfect view of Native American life, but it was a step in the right direction, and Wayne's performance was his most nuanced to date. Levity is created with Ethan's sidekick Martin, played by Jeffrey Hunter, who at one point thinks he is trading for goods but discovers he's accidentally gotten married. The adult Debbie was played by Natalie Wood, who was still in high school at the time of filming. Occasionally John Wayne would pick her up from school to go to the set, which, of course, made her the envy of the entire school.

While modern audiences are racked with guilt about the simplistic racial stereotypes, it's worth noting that while making the film, one of the extras, a Navajo (not a Comanche) child became seriously ill and needed urgent medical attention. John Wayne had his private airplane on location and had his pilot take the girl to the hospital; she lived thanks to the rapid medical response to her pneumonia. Because of this the Navajos on the set named Wayne "The Man with the Big Eagle."

From *Stagecoach* to *The Searchers*, John Wayne created a persona before Schwarzenegger or Dwayne "the Rock" Johnson. They are hired to play a certain type, and all three of them are the very definition of "movie star" as opposed to "great actor." Their charisma oozes from the screen, but if they play a type too different from the familiar one, the movie quite often fails at the box office.

DANCES WITH WOLVES (1990)

To complete the transition from Native Americans being portrayed as pantomime villains to their rehabilitation as the genuine good guys, we have to look at *Dances with Wolves*. Kevin Costner directed the movie and starred as Lieutenant Dunbar. The film starts during the Civil War, when Dunbar was a Union officer who has been wounded and, as such, wants to die in battle (the terror of seeing a surgeon in the 1800s was very real). Quite by accident, he rallies the Union side to an unexpected victory.

And now comes an opportunity to talk briefly about the history of medicine: From the late 1700s to the mid-1800s there was a type of medicine known as "heroic medicine." The idea was to shock the body into wellness. Patients might deliberately be given a powerful emetic, forcing a violent purge through repeated episodes of vomiting, to "get the sickness out of them." Or worse, they might be burned with acids applied to the skin to force the sickness away through pain. George Washington had to endure this in his final hours as doctors tried desperately to keep him alive. We now know they were needlessly torturing a dying man in his late sixties. In such circumstances, a visiting doctor could be your last, worst hope.

Then there was surgery. Doctors at the time understood that shock and blood loss could be fatal, so the removal of a limb for medical reasons had to be fast. One Scottish doctor, Robert Liston, working in London in the first half of the nineteenth century, was known as "the fastest knife in the West End." He could amputate a leg in two and a half minutes. (Side note: He's the only doctor to have a 300 percent mortality rate. He was removing the leg of a man who died, when he accidentally cut off the fingers of one of his assistants who later died from infection, and as he was wielding his razor-sharp knives, he cut off the tails of a spectator's coat—in those days people would pay to watch operations—causing the man to have a heart attack. Some have cast doubt on this story, but it's there in the records of the time.) In the Victorian era of science and innovation, nobody knew about microbiology, and as such, cleanliness was regarded with suspicion. A surgeon did not clean his apron, thinking the dried blood proved he was experienced. Of course, now we know such practices were likely spreading infection.

With all that in mind, Lieutenant Dunbar would rather have died in battle than be butchered by a surgeon, but his heroics earned him a chance to go to the frontier "before it disappears." When he eventually arrives at Fort Sedgwick (a real frontier outpost in Colorado), he finds it deserted. But it's a long movie, so to cut to the important part of the film, he gets to know the local Lakota tribe and falls in love with a young woman, a captured white woman who was taken as a girl. Eventually Dunbar turns his back on settler life, seeing the Lakota as the more civilized people and their way of life one that appeals to him.

In 1990 the film was regarded as a huge risk because by then westerns no longer made money, and they were not seen as award contenders. But Kevin Costner proved everybody wrong: *Dances with Wolves* was the fourth-highest-grossing film in 1990 and won seven Oscars, including Best Picture and Best Director. If you have never seen *Dances with Wolves* or have not seen it for a long time, do so right now; it's a great film seemingly overlooked by younger generations.

THE LAST OF THE MOHICANS (1992)

After *Dances with Wolves*, Hollywood could not go back to the old-style westerns where Native Americans were the bad guys. So, next came 1992's *The Last of the Mohicans* (the ninth film version of this book by James Fenimore Cooper), where the English are definitely the bad guys (no rehabilitation for them, they are still the perennial villains), now with Hawkeye and his Mohawk allies the only voice of reason in a world gone mad. While Wes Studi as Magua (a Native American) is the final bad guy to beat, his motives have been well fleshed out. However, this is one of the rare films set during the Seven Years' War in the mid-1700s (known as the French and Indian War in America), which means it's set a century earlier than *The Searchers*, so the question becomes, is it a western or a historical drama? Or perhaps because it has several full-scale battles and the impressive siege at Fort William Henry (a real event from that conflict), it's a war film. You decide.

The Last of the Mohicans looks convincing, and certainly the depiction of the siege and the uniforms and locations are authentic, but it suffers from one mistake that is a regularly occurring flaw in westerns: the accuracy of guns used. In the movie, Hawkeye uses his musket like a sniper's rifle. That's not likely in the 1750s. Similarly, in the Sergio Leone spaghetti westerns, men are forever firing hats off people's heads or doing the classic rifle shot that cuts the rope to a noose around a man's neck. All of this is nonsense.

Reports from the gunfight at the OK Corral are quite telling in that these men, who knew their way around a pistol, had to be really close to each other to stand a chance of hitting anything. It's the same reason why soldiers formed long lines to fire away at the enemy in the US Civil War or the Napoleonic era, and it's all to do with physics. Firing a gun is a form of controlled explosion. A charge goes off behind a projectile, and that bullet then hurtles down the barrel of the gun. If the gun barrel is just a metal tube, that projectile will ricochet off the inside of the barrel, and while the shot will fire out of the gun, exactly which direction it will go after that is anybody's guess. This is why those long lines of musket men were so important. The bullets would be sent flying in so many different trajectories you needed fifty guys firing at the same time to hit any of the enemy soldiers right in front of you. The Brown Bess (the standard British infantry musket from the 1720s through to about 1850) was effective at a maximum range of just one hundred yards, and other armies' rifles were no better.

Revolvers like the Colt Navy pistol or the later Colt Single Action Army pistol were the classic Wild West guns. Both had those smooth barrels which meant they faced the same problem only more so as pistols generally aren't as accurate as muskets. The problem was remedied with the invention of rifling, an arrangement of spiral grooves on the inside of the barrel. Now, as the bullet travels down the barrel, it spins, which means it doesn't bounce along the barrel and therefore is far more accurate. Now it was possible to hit the intended target.

As for the classic shooting of the noose at a hanging . . . how many times has this been reported by eyewitnesses in all of the reliable tales of the Wild West? The answer is never and again it's for very good reasons: First, hitting a rope from three hundred yards would be an almost impossible shot with any gun. Second, a bullet (of any reasonable caliber) isn't as wide as a piece of rope, which means it simply cannot cut the rope cleanly. I once watched a documentary in which a Special Forces sniper tried to do it; he only managed to hit the rope once. His hit took a chunk of the rope out, but the hanging dummy was not released from its grim fate. He said that the only way to do it is to perfectly cut one side out with one bullet and then do the same to millimeter perfection on the other side, which he believed was simply impossible. But he didn't allow for Hollywood ingenuity which perfected the trick by tying the noose around a small explosive charge and running a wire up the rope. When the charge is triggered, it severs the rope cleanly every time.

POCAHONTAS (1995)

With *Dances with Wolves* and *The Last of the Mohicans*, Native American culture was hot in the 1990s, and in 1995 Disney released its animated classic *Pocahontas*, a project that had been started years earlier. That it is animated and has songs are warning signs that the movie will be light on history, but Pocahontas (voiced by First Nations woman Irene Bedard) and John Smith (voiced by an American who grew up in Australia, Mel Gibson) were both real, and theirs was a real story which Disney decided to largely ignore.

If *The Last of the Mohicans* isn't really a western because it is set in the 1700s, then as *Pocahontas* is set in the early 1600s, it's definitely not a western. The film emphasizes the idea that Native Americans are as one with nature, the idea personified by the beautifully animated and Oscar-winning song "Colors of the Wind." Pocahontas was the daughter of the chief of the Powhatan tribe, and she became, in essence, an ambassador to the English colonial settlement of Jamestown. It was here that she met the English explorer John Smith (forgettable name but really interesting guy). So far, so good with the film. But that's it for the history. The two most egregious issues are that we don't see her going to England, and at the end of the film, the settlers leave America!

Sadly, what actually happened was that Pocahontas was captured at roughly the age of sixteen and held for ransom in 1613. While in Jamestown she did act as a liaison between the settlers and her people and even converted to Christianity (she was baptized as Rebecca). She then married tobacco planter John Rolfe in 1614 at the age of about seventeen and had a son, Thomas Rolfe, in 1615.

In 1616, the family made the arduous journey across the Atlantic where Pocahontas was presented to English society as (and I do apologize to the readers for the next phrase) a "civilized savage." In England she became both a novelty and a celebrity, but she died suddenly in 1617, aged about twenty. Nobody knows what the cause was (if you heard syphilis, that's only one of many theories), and she was buried in a church in the very dull and very English town of Gravesend. So, all the actual history was left out of the movie.

PREY (2022)

In considering the role of Native American and First Nations people on film, we come to the counterintuitive franchise, *Predator*. This 1987 film is 1980s muscle action at its sweatiest, when a group of commandos are hunted by an alien with invisibility armor. One of the commandos is Billy, a Native American and expert tracker. Was this the inspiration for 2022's *Prey*? Who can say, but this *fifth* entry into the (main) *Predator* franchise gives us something completely unexpected: an historically accurate depiction of Comanche tribal culture from the early 1700s.

A little like *The Northman* (which also came out in 2022), the events unfolding cannot have happened, in this case because there are no such things as invisible aliens who hunt humans for their skulls to display them as trophies. But the effort in *Prey* to achieve historical accuracy is astonishing and uncalled for in such a pulp concept. This time around the human who must face a predator is Naru, played by Amber Midthunder. All the Comanche are played by actors of Native American or First Nations people ancestry. The film even has two different versions: one in English and one exclusively in Comanche. Comanche historians were on hand to ensure the war paint, tools, and clothing are accurate. It was also filmed on location, adding a further layer of authenticity to it. Naru wants to be a warrior and she is rejected, as would be natural in the Comanche culture, but through her fantastical ordeals, she proves her worth. So, like *The Northman*, if someone from that culture and that time were to watch the film, they wouldn't recognize the plot, but they would absolutely recognize the culture being portrayed.

Then we come to Clint Eastwood, who, while not in as many westerns as John Wayne, has been in enough good ones to get a reputation as the other icon of the genre. Eastwood has the notable distinction that while his list of westerns is lengthy, he never shot a Native American in any of them. I will be concentrating on the Dollars Trilogy and *Unforgiven*.

A FISTFUL OF DOLLARS (1964)

Clint Eastwood made his name in a cowboy TV show called *Rawhide*. The show was starting to wind down, so the ex-Marine who spent the Korean War as a swimming instructor decided it was time to branch out; the last thing he wanted was to be typecast as a cowboy. But then he was given the script of *A Fistful of Dollars*, and he loved how it was clearly a western remake of *Yojimbo*. He was excited by the project but was told to play down the similarities because the production company hadn't asked for permission or paid any royalties to Akira Kurosawa. He was also told that this western would be very different from the family-friendly TV show where he played a likeable cowhand called Rowdy Yates.

So, from 1964 to 1966, Eastwood played "the man with no name," who at times was called Joe or Blondie in Sergio Leone's groundbreaking, super bleak westerns. These cheap and violent cowboy movies were shot in Europe and became known as "spaghetti westerns" even though, while the director and crew were Italian, they were shot in Spain, with most of the extras speaking Spanish, not Italian.

Eastwood quickly realized that he was dealing with people who knew nothing about the history of the American frontier and whose point of reference was the movies made by John Wayne and Tom Mix, and other by-the-numbers cowboy films. There is no serious history to be found even though the final movie in the Dollars Trilogy makes some attempt to link the action to real events in the US Civil War. Some of the guns used were too modern, and the accuracy, as already discussed, is completely unrealistic. The sets and locations are all wrong, and from a different continent.

However, the first film did make cinematic history. Up until then, violence was very carefully regulated in Hollywood films, and critically, when it came to someone firing a gun, the audience would see the shooter firing before cutting to a second shot of someone crumpling over. There was a break between the action and the reaction. Leone didn't know this and there are many times when Eastwood fires his pistol and the target collapses in the same shot. This sent the American censors crazy, but audiences lapped it up. This was just one example of the shift away from the stifling moral codes that had ruled Hollywood for decades. And all of this was done to Ennio Morricone's masterful music, none of it contemporary. People don't scream in old songs from the 1860s, and the electric guitar was not invented for another century; none of it makes any sense, but it has become the quintessential music of the

Wild West. These films continued to replace the old myths while creating new ones and are about as historically accurate as *Ben-Hur*, but they are also great cinema and are my favorite westerns.

FOR A FEW DOLLARS MORE (1965)

The other two films are more important, as *A Fistful of Dollars* sets up the tone and *The Good, the Bad and the Ugly* becomes cinematic perfection. *For a Few Dollars More* represents a rise in ambition by Leone but not to the level of the last film in the trilogy. Again, the costumes, weapons, and geography are all over the place. There is no history here, only entertainment. Oddly Lee Van Cleef in this film survives, but is killed in *The Good, the Bad and the Ugly*, which as that is a prequel, makes no logical sense. But let's not let a little thing like logic get in the way of a great western.

THE GOOD, THE BAD AND THE UGLY (1966)

A final point needs to be made about safety: Both Eli Wallach and Clint Eastwood nearly died on set while filming *The Good, the Bad and the Ugly,* and it's forever preserved in the film. Wallach was told to lie near the train tracks and allow the train to break his chains. This was fine. But as the train approached, Leone realized that while there was plenty of clearance between Eli's head and the locomotive, that wasn't the case at the end of each carriage which had a metal step down. By now the train was too close to Wallach for him to hear the warning, but had he lifted his head just a little he would have been decapitated.

Eastwood was, as it turned out, a little too close to a bridge when it blew up (this was the second demolition as the first one happened by accident before the cameras were rolling, so they had to spend a fortune building a new bridge). When it blows, you can see real rubble raining down all over the area, and one rock falls just inches from Eastwood's head. Had it struck him it almost certainly would have killed him.

UNFORGIVEN (1992)

Finally, we come to Eastwood's meta commentary on his career as a cowboy and the legends of the Old West in *Unforgiven*. The title is ambiguous: Are the actions of Eastwood unforgiven, or are the actions of the assailants he is hunting unforgiven? Like the best movies, it allows the audience to make up its own mind. Eastwood not only starred in the film, but directed it too, and he had older actors play most of the key roles. Gene Hackman is the main antagonist, and he won a Best Supporting Actor Oscar (one of four for the film, including Best Director and Best Picture). This plus what had happened a few years earlier with *Dances with Wolves* meant that westerns had been elevated from cheap action films that Hollywood churned out with little fanfare to prestige projects with Oscar potential.

Unforgiven, like *Dances with Wolves*, was mainly interested in reassessing the legends of the Old West. There is no soaring music like that of *The Big Country* (perhaps the most rousing western score ever). Instead, it's dour, somber, and like so many more modern films, lit with natural sources of light. Nighttime is a time to fear because you can barely see your hand in front of your face—and that's in a saloon. The violence is brutal and sudden. No slow motion, no actions are reinforced with music. This feels like the real Wild West and it's full of mud, blood, and regret. Nobody wants to live in this place, which means it's a pretty accurate portrayal of the desperation of frontier life.

But before we leave the world of the spaghetti western, I must make mention of Leone's other classic, *Once Upon a Time in the West*. It may be better than *The Good, the Bad and the Ugly*, and the opening scene as the gunmen wait for the train to arrive is a master class in tension as they do . . . well . . . nothing, but it's riveting. And it has Henry Fonda in a rare role of the bad guy, positively reveling in his evil. We learn nothing about the nineteenth century from this movie. Like the Dollars Trilogy, fashion, technology, and even geography are all jumbled up. It is a historical soup of "stuff" that looks old and American. Saying that we certainly can learn a lot about how to shoot, plot, and pace a film. What's more, there's a quirk about this film that makes it important in cinema history, and that's the title. Leone used a version of the title for his last film in 1984's *Once Upon a Time in America.* By now his reputation was unassailable and versions of the title have been used in a myriad of films, from the 2011 Turkish film *Once Upon a Time in Anatolia*, to the 2003 *Desperado* sequel *Once Upon a Time in Mexico.* Quentin Tarantino used the intertitle "Once Upon a Time in Nazi-Occupied France" in the introduction to 2009's *Inglourious Basterds* and used it again in his 2019 movie *Once Upon a Time . . . in Hollywood* (and so the snake eats its tail again).

THE MAGNIFICENT SEVEN (1960)

Of course, while I've mentioned Kurosawa, I have to mention *The Magnificent Seven*, where Eli Wallach turns up in a potential sequel/prequel to his character of Tuco in *The Good, the Bad and the Ugly. The Magnificent Seven* was a huge hit, and as it's referencing a 1954 samurai movie which itself was based on no real history, this is not a historical movie, but it does have its own legacy: It was the film that brought Steve McQueen to the world's attention, and within a few years he had become a megastar. McQueen's way of getting noticed was genius. Yul Brynner was meant to be the star, and Brynner had the lion's share of the lines, but our attention strays to McQueen because even when Brynner is talking in the foreground, McQueen is cleaning his gun or checking his bearings or playing with his hat. The motion draws our eyes to him, and we think he's a more important character than he is. It reminds me of something Jack Nicholson once said in an interview, that to get more screen time he used to look in the direction he was about to move and only then walk off camera, giving us a second or more exposure each time. Genius.

The Magnificent Seven had multiple sequels, and in 2016, it had a reboot, with Denzel Washington putting the team together and Chris Pratt as the McQueen character. It was nice to see a Black cowboy in charge. There have been other attempts to put African Americans front and center in westerns. In 1993 there was *Posse*. After his 1991 directorial debut in *New Jack City*, I was a big fan of Mario Van Peebles. That was a gangster film with a very 1990s feel to it. So, when I heard his next film was going to be a Black western, I was first in the queue. Imagine my profound disappointment when I saw the most god-awful vanity project of my entire cinema-going life. I nearly walked out when Van Peebles caressed a naked woman with his gold-plated pistol (because women love the feel of cold metal on their bodies . . . sure).

DJANGO UNCHAINED (2012)

Quentin Tarantino added to the wealth of western films with *Django Unchained*, his first film based on an existing intellectual property. Leone opened the floodgates of the spaghetti western with his Dollars Trilogy, and in Spain and Italy directors cranked out gritty westerns of varying merit. One such movie was 1966's *Django* starring Franco Nero (who gets a cameo in this film). It was the kind of cult movie that appeals to Tarantino's sensibilities, so when it came to making his mark on the western genre, it was a great place to start. *Django Unchained* is not a sequel (of which the original had multiple) but more a reimagining. Franco Nero is white; Jamie Foxx is Black, and with that one change we get a very different film, one now based around slavery. The opening scenes of brutality against Django in the movie are unbearable and, sadly, all too accurate.

Leonardo DiCaprio plays the fictional Calvin Candie, a Southern slave owner who works his slaves on a brutally run plantation called Candie Land. DiCaprio is utterly convincing and utterly disgusting as the Southern

"gentleman" with a racist streak a mile wide. At one point during a confronta-
tion at the dinner table, DiCaprio smashes a glass, genuinely cutting his hand.
He stayed in character and completed the scene, creating a palpable tension
that was all too real.

The film is a power fantasy for an African American audience. Aided
by Christopher Waltz (his second film with Tarantino and his second Best
Supporting Actor Oscar), Django is out to get his wife back (the brilliantly
named Broomhilda von Shaft, the name a nod to the blaxploitation flicks
of the 1970s) without Candie realizing what's going on. Samuel L. Jackson
plays the utterly despicable house slave Stephen. He's an antagonist to
Django, so we want him to fail, but he's smarter than the Southern whites and
can tell that something isn't right. Like Cassandra of Greek myth, Stephen
keeps speaking the truth, but nobody listens to his warnings. The film also
portrays the Klan as a bunch of idiots, a decision guaranteed to put a smile on
almost every moviegoer's face.

So, *Django Unchained* has two types of history going on: the actual history of slavery in America but also film history, with all its references to past
movies. And on top of that, it's a great western, with several obligatory (and
bloody) shoot-outs.

HIGH NOON (1952)

Then there's *High Noon*. Gary Cooper plays Marshal Will Kane, who is the
lawman in Hadleyville, New Mexico. He knows that when the train arrives
at noon there will be killers onboard and they will be coming to get him. The
movie is revolutionary in many different ways, not least because it is filmed
almost in real time, and as bad as the gunmen are, they are not as unstoppable
or as inevitable as the march of time, the real enemy.

And then there's Grace Kelly. Women up to this point in westerns were
usually the damsel in distress or the hooker with a heart of gold, but Grace's
role has more agency and gives us a woman to admire in a genre usually
about six-shooters and men sleeping with their horses. The concept of the
mail-order bride actually evolves in the frontier era. Women who wanted to
escape the crushingly claustrophobic patriarchy in the East headed west hoping to find more agency to their lives and a little more freedom.[1] So, a strong
female character is likely to have been more of a norm than westerns set in
the 1940s and 1950s would make us think.

Finally, *High Noon* is an early example of a revisionist western, perhaps
not as obvious as the likes of *Unforgiven* but quietly revolutionary in its own
way. The narrative in many westerns is the settlers bringing "civilization" to
the Wild West. I don't have a chapter to debate this, so let's just say it's a

lot more complicated than that. However, just when the marshal needs them most, the townspeople all melt away, and Marshal Will Kane is left very much on his own. Going all the way back to Dalton Trumbo, the screenwriter on *Spartacus*, and the blacklisting of certain Hollywood left-wingers, this film offers a none-too-subtle allegorical reference to that era. (John Wayne was offered the main role in *High Noon* but turned it down as he supported the blacklisting of so-called communist sympathizers). So, once again, we have a movie set in a historical period which does nothing to accurately reflect that period but is a perfect encapsulation of the time in which it was made. It's tense viewing even today.

SHANE (1953)

Next we come to *Shane*, the most exciting movie ever made about agricultural land legislation. The plot centers on a gunslinger who wants to renounce his violent ways and arrives in town looking for a fresh start . . . but mainly it focuses on the Homestead Acts. There were two main ones: The first was passed in 1862 (nice to see the US government had enough time during the Civil War to pass land reform legislation), and the second and potentially more important one was passed in 1866 after the war. This second act applied specifically to freed slaves so that African Americans could be part of this release of land in an area that was huge, about 160 million acres or roughly 10 percent of what is today the continental United States.

The Homestead Acts were an expression of Northern politicians' desire to give individuals the opportunity to own their own land (160 acres), provided they undertook to improve it by farming, or homesteading as it was known. Successful applicants (in truth, anyone who applied) could acquire ownership of what had been federal land as a means of settling and developing millions of acres in the American West. But the act led to disputes between new and existing farmers who suddenly found themselves competing for land they hadn't bought because it had been government property. And there was also the little matter of the indigenous Native Americans who hadn't been told about any of this. The Homestead Acts are, in a way, the story of the American frontier and the settler experience in the latter half of the nineteenth century.

This is the background to and ultimately the cause of the conflict that draws Shane in. I have watched most westerns with my children who love a good John Wayne flick and have had enough patience to sit through *Seven Samurai*, but they hated *Shane*, finding the young boy Joey utterly irritating. We never got to the final showdown and the famous ride off into the sunset (is he dead or not?), which is a shame because that's definitely the best bit of the film.

BLAZING SADDLES (1974)

The far more successful attempt to put a Black man front and center in a cowboy film is a comedy that for nearly two decades was the biggest-grossing western of all time, *Blazing Saddles*. It's a typical western plot with a new sheriff riding into town to bring law to the lawless, except this time the sheriff is Black, and the townspeople are not happy about that. The hero of the film is Bart, played by Cleavon Little, and Gene Wilder plays a washed-up gunslinger who is now a drunk (another western cliché). But compared to the more serious Bart, Wilder gets to summarize racial tensions in the Old West in a poignant yet funny way:

> "What did you expect? Welcome, sonny? Make yourself at home? Marry my daughter? You've got to remember that these are just simple farmers. These are people of the land, the common clay of the new West. You know . . . morons."

Almost as a joke itself, in 2006, *Blazing Saddles* was deemed "culturally, historically, or aesthetically significant" by the Library of Congress and was chosen for preservation in the National Film Registry. I am not making this up.

CALAMITY JANE (1953)

But if you want real inclusiveness, how about a lesbian western from the early 1950s that's also a musical? *Calamity Jane* has the utterly clean cut and delightful Doris Day playing Martha Jane Cannary, better known as Calamity Jane. This is such a tour de force of musical brio that you may not be aware that she was a real person. Jane's life started as a reflection of the age. The family wanted to head west and establish themselves in the new lands recently opened up to settlers. It was a chance to make a better life for hundreds of thousands of people. However, by the age of fourteen, both parents were dead, so it was Jane's job to look after the rest of the family. She did this by taking every job she could get, from dishwasher to ox team driver to occasional sex worker. By the age of twenty she had become a scout for the US Army as it continued to clash with Native American tribes, and it was around this time she became known as Calamity Jane (there are multiple origin stories). For practical reasons, as she was riding, scouting, and sometimes fighting, she wore men's clothing. A trouser-wearing, gun-toting female scout got the attention of the press, and she became a celebrity. She was a part of the story of the Wild West and became one of the acts in Buffalo Bill's Wild West Show.

Jane ended up in Deadwood where she may have had a sexual relationship with Wild Bill Hickok. Even though she was an alcoholic, she was still involved in shoot-outs and worked, at times, both as security and sex worker in the local brothel. She died aged fifty-one in 1903 from a combination of inflammation of the bowels (a symptom of her drinking) and pneumonia. Jane's is the sad story of a woman trying to earn a living and survive, but she caught the public imagination and still turns up in movies and TV shows.

None of this bleak story makes it into the 1953 movie. Instead, we get a glossy musical very loosely based on the supposed love affair between Jane and Hickok. However, at one point in the film Jane sets up home with another woman, and the joke is that she's the one literally wearing the trousers as they create a pseudo husband and wife relationship. It was never meant to be interpreted as a lesbian relationship, but this part of the film is pushed further into the realms of a sapphic metaphor as Jane sings the song "A Woman's Touch." To a modern viewer these women are clearly a couple, but at the time of filming, the setup was seen as a joke.

TRUE GRIT (1969)

Back to John Wayne, who toward the end of his life, made *True Grit* (remade in 2010) and won an Oscar for playing US marshal Rooster Cogburn. The one-eyed, drunken Rooster seems incompetent but is hired by a persistent and stubborn teenage girl to find her father's killer and bring him to justice. Rooster turns out to be an excellent tracker and marksman, and the rest is cinema history. It even got a sequel in 1975, *Rooster Cogburn*, where John Wayne played opposite Katharine Hepburn, and the two of them bicker marvelously through the film.

True Grit introduced the concept of the US marshal, a branch of American law enforcement that still exists today and is unique in that there are no meaningful equivalents in other countries. In the nineteenth century they were the main source of day-to-day law enforcement in areas that had no local police of their own. It was the US marshals, as opposed to local sheriffs, who were key in keeping law and order in the Wild West. They spent most of their time hunting down troublemakers. Those "Wanted" posters were a real thing, but you only got the reward if you brought them in on your own. That money was called a "bounty," and the people who made it their main job to find these criminals were bounty hunters. However, if a US marshal got them first, well, that was their job so no reward for them. Although marshals today are required to have bachelor's degrees and police experience, things were a lot less formal in the 1800s, and some marshals were reformed criminals. They were tough men who brought tough justice to the frontiers.

One real marshal who needs a biopic made about him was Bass Reeves (he has appeared in a few films and TV shows, but always as a supporting character or as a highly fictionalized version of the man). Reeves started life as a slave but managed to become free at some point in the Civil War. He settled in Arkansas and until his late thirties Reeves was a farmer. In 1875 there was a drive to recruit two hundred more US marshals, and as Reeves could speak several Native American languages, he was perfect for working in "Indian" territory. Reeves worked as a US marshal until 1907, when at the age of sixty-eight, he became a police officer. He died in 1910 at the age of seventy-one. In his time as a marshal, he arrested over three thousand men and shot and killed fourteen (allegedly in self-defense). It's this Black US marshal who is thought to be the inspiration for the fictional Lone Ranger, who has always been played by a white man.

Another man who was an on-and-off-again US marshal (well, deputy marshal) was Morgan Earp, the brother of Wyatt Earp. Wyatt Earp, like Calamity Jane, did a little bit of everything. They were both trying to scratch out a living just to survive and raise a family, but that's not what Earp is remembered for. This leads us to one of the key moments in the Old West, the gunfight at the OK Corral. It was first immortalized in 1932's *Law and Order* but was done much better in John Ford's 1946 film *My Darling Clementine*. In 1957 the uninspiringly named *Gunfight at the OK Corral* was released, and more recently, there was *Tombstone* (1993) and Kevin Costner again in *Wyatt Earp* (1994). In 2017 we got an openly Kurosawa-inspired western *Tombstone Rashomon*, where the events are played out from different perspectives, just like the 1950 movie.

This famous gunfight lasted all of thirty seconds (remember that the next time you see a shoot-out sequence in a movie), not everyone involved was carrying a gun, and at the end, three men were dead. If you want to know more, I suggest starting with *Tombstone*. It's fairly historically accurate and does a good job of not putting the gunfight as the climax of the movie because there's more to the story than just thirty seconds of violence.

THE CONQUEROR (1956)

By the time John Wayne died in 1979, he had made dozens of westerns, but those were not the only films he made (he will get mentions in two more chapters); however, there was one piece of casting that was disastrous. In the 1950s, historical epics were big business, but as the Bible and the Romans had been done to death, Hollywood cast around for other great historical stories. The answer came in Genghis Khan. Great idea. He would be perfect for a number of epic movies: the battles, the conquests, the rise to power, all perfect for a matinee audience. Except he couldn't be too . . . y'know . . . Mongolian; white American audiences would not have accepted it. So they cast John Wayne as Genghis Khan. After all, they were both good with a horse. And who even knew what a Mongolian looked like, so they cast Native Americans as Mongol warriors because, well, they're basically the same thing, aren't they? Finally, Mongolia is quite a long way away from Hollywood, and in the 1950s, it was part of the Soviet Union, so they filmed it where they filmed all the westerns, in Monument Valley in Utah, USA.

As insane as the whole thing was, the project went ahead, and *The Conqueror* was unleashed on the world. Despite the limited tastes of American consumers in the 1950s and the box-office draw that was John Wayne, the cinema-going public didn't like it and it bombed . . . almost literally.

The locations chosen were the same locations where atomic bombs had been tested, and everyone on the set was unknowingly exposed to dangerous levels of radiation for weeks. Worse still, sixty tons of sand and soil from the area were shipped to the studios for the creation of sets to help with continuity. Everyone involved in the studio shoot was walking around in lethal levels of radioactive material. By 1980, ninety-one of the 220 cast and crew (including John Wayne) had developed cancer. Dozens died from it.[2]

The Conqueror was producer Howard Hughes's last film, ending a thirty-year career. He spent millions buying up every available copy because he didn't want anyone to remember it. John Wayne was honest about the mess, saying that the moral of the film was "not to make an ass of yourself trying to play parts you're not suited for." Racist, literally toxic, and historically incoherent, this is one film best left forgotten.

BUTCH CASSIDY AND THE SUNDANCE KID (1969)

Let's round off this chapter with the story of Robert LeRoy Parker and Harry Alonzo Longabaugh, perhaps better known as Butch Cassidy and the Sundance Kid. This movie shows Butch Cassidy and his gang called the Wild Bunch (and not the Hole in the Wall Gang, changed at the last minute because another classic western, *The Wild Bunch*, had been released just a few months earlier, and nobody wanted to confuse the two films) robbing trains and banks. To be fair, that's what he and the Sundance Kid did. However, it's safe to say they didn't do it with the panache, wit, and movie-star good looks of Paul Newman and Robert Redford.

The gang was formed in 1896, and these crimes came at the very end of what could be considered the Wild West. Cassidy and his gang were cold-blooded murderers, not cheeky scamps on fun adventures. One of the gang members shot and killed a sheriff; they were dangerous men. The film isn't far off the truth, but the tone is distinctly biased. We are meant to love these guys, even though you wouldn't ever want to meet them in real life. Butch Cassidy's younger sister Lula Parker Betenson was on the set during filming and would tell the cast and crew stories about her brother. Yet another reason to show these outlaws as relatable characters.

Tonally and utterly different, *The Wild Bunch* and *Butch Cassidy and the Sundance Kid* are about the same thing: the end of an era. By the start of the twentieth century, society and technology had caught up with the old ways. There was nowhere left to hide, and these men, who only knew one thing, were doomed by the unstoppable march of progress. The films also have similar endings, just shot in very different ways.

In the first half of *Butch Cassidy and the Sundance Kid*, the men are trying to escape a group of Pinkerton agents. Pinkerton was a genuine organization (which still exists today), and in the nineteenth century was the largest private law enforcement organization in the world. Their agents would do dubious things like infiltrate trade unions to disrupt them from within, but they also undertook regular law enforcement work (as shown in the film), where they acted like a cross between US marshals and bounty hunters. It was the gang's own fault that they were being pursued. In 1899 they had agreed to an amnesty with the governor of Utah: All they had to do was stop robbing trains. But they couldn't help themselves, and by the summer of 1900 they were at it again. In December of that year, the gang posed for a photo which gave law enforcement an up-to-date picture of its five members; these guys were much dumber than the film portrays.

It's true that Cassidy and Sundance managed to escape and wound up in South America. Etta Place, Butch's partner, was a real woman, portrayed in the film as a teacher, but she was, in fact, a sex worker. They set up in Argentina and by 1905, there were reports of two English-speaking robbers operating in the country.

By 1908 the two men plus Etta had moved hundreds of miles north into Bolivia, where they robbed the payroll intended for a silver mine. This got the attention of the local authorities. What happens next is the stuff of legend, and the final scene in the film is a freeze frame with the sound of volley fire over it. If you've seen the film, you know it takes dozens of Bolivian soldiers to bring down our two brave antiheroes. In reality, there were just three armed soldiers at the shoot-out. You read that right, three men, not thirty. It seems that once the gunfire stopped, soldiers entered the hut to find that Sundance had been mortally wounded and Butch had shot him to put him out of his misery, then shot himself.[3]

NOTES

The end of this film reflects the end of the Wild West. The stark contrast between the reality and the legends perpetuated by Hollywood come together in this one poignant moment from history. It's the perfect place to end the chapter.

1. Jem Duducu, *Slinkys and Snake Bombs: Weird but True Historical Facts* (Gloucestershire, UK: Amberley Publishing, 2021), 210.

2. Jem Duducu, *Forgotten History: Unbelievable Moments from the Past* (Gloucestershire, UK: Amberley Publishing, 2016), 263.

3. Bob Mims, "Did Butch Cassidy and Sundance Kid Die in Bolivia? Yes, But," *Los Angeles Times*, January 14, 1996.

Chapter 9

Oh! What a Lovely War

While the trigger for World War I was the assassination of Archduke Franz Ferdinand in Sarajevo in 1914, it only makes sense if you see the political concerns of the major powers. Germany feared encirclement, from the east by Russia, from the west by France, and in the North Sea by the Royal Navy. When Germany cast around for its own allies, a natural power base was the neighboring Austro-Hungarian Empire, and as Germany had been training the officer corps of the Ottoman Empire, one of the few European powers not to have gone to war with it while it was the weakest power in Europe, alliance with the Ottomans would ensure another front against Russia. The rest of Europe feared a rapidly industrializing and unified Germany with a militaristic Prussian core and armed forces.

After Ferdinand and his wife were killed, the alliances clicked into place over the summer of 1914, and the stage was set for inevitable conflict. At the time, most people in Europe thought it would be a good thing and sort out the primacy of the European powers once and for all (the term "the war to end all wars" was a reference to this and not to the massive cost in human life). Everyone thought it would be a short, sharp conflict, lasting a few months. Nobody in July 1914 knew what horrors lay ahead. By comparison when World War II began, the world had learned its lesson and there were no wild celebrations in the street. Everyone knew that this would be a bloody conflict; sadly nobody knew just how bloody.

U-571 (2000)

In the year 2000, the release of a World War II movie caused such an outcry the filmmakers were forced to add additional information later. The movie is *U-571*, starring respected actors Matthew McConaughey, Bill Paxton, and Harvey Keitel as well as soft rock legend Jon Bon Jovi. It's an action-adventure story set on a US submarine during the Battle of the

Atlantic. So far so harmless, but it was a strange movie that made lots of strange choices.

The crew were on a mission to recover an Enigma machine from an enemy U-boat, so they could crack the Enigma code. So far, so real history, but we now come to some *very* big differences. The U-boat in question was the U-110 not the U-571 (a minor detail); the Allied naval vessel was not a submarine but a destroyer; and the ship was not American, it was British (HMS *Bulldog*). But, most critically, the events happened in the first half of 1941. Why is the date important? Because this was the period in the war when Britain was fighting on its own. Germany would not be attacking the Soviet Union until the summer of 1941, and America would not be joining the war until December 1941 after Pearl Harbor (because it took America more than two years and a sneak attack from Japan to work out that the Nazis . . . were bad). In other words, we have an American film with such little regard for history that it erased the contributions of an Allied nation. So, before the end credits, a message was inserted about the role of HMS *Bulldog* to say, in essence, you know that film you just watched? Ignore it, it's all made up. Not a helpful marketing campaign. The film doubled its budget at the box office, but a key market (Britain) flat out refused to go see it. It was neither a critical nor a commercial success.

U-571 is to World War II what *Braveheart* is to the Middle Ages, except now we are getting to history that is just about within living memory or at least so engrained in cultures and societies that a push too far away from the perception means trouble. This chapter will be looking at the films about the world wars (and a little about Korea and the Russian Civil War, too) and how they shape our images of these major events.

LAWRENCE OF ARABIA (1962)

In the Shakespeare chapter, I discussed how the bard's play about Henry V plucked him from a dozen obscure medieval rulers to make him a well-known figure from history. The same can be said about David Lean's film *Lawrence of Arabia*. Colonel Thomas Edward Lawrence was not a key figure in World War I, but he is better known than most of the British general staff thanks to this one movie. David Lean shows every other director what can be done with a camera. The cinematography is so sharp that sixty years later, the sand dunes still glitter as if made from gold. Steven Spielberg calls it his favorite film, and many other directors have rightly paid homage to this utterly ambitious piece of filmmaking. Noel Coward was wittier, saying that if Peter O'Toole (who plays the titular character) was any prettier, "he would be known as Florence of Arabia."

It's a strikingly modern film, bringing Islamic politics to the forefront, something that had little coverage in the twentieth century but has become a major talking point after 9/11. It also shows that the problems inherent in the Middle East today started with the carving up of lands barely understood by Western powers drawing the borders on a map at the end of that war.

It is also one of the best movies about World War I because it breaks the conventions. Mention that war and people instantly imagine mud, barbed wire, and the pointless slaughter of millions. That was one reality, but it was by no means the whole story. The conflict between 1914 and 1918 may be the most misremembered event in history. There are many forgotten events (the Thirty Years' War? The War of Spanish Succession? Anyone?), but then there are the events people think they know but have either misremembered or have been told oversimplified or biased versions of them. Let's have a look at some of these:

One of the main accusations leveled at this conflict is the lack of problem solving by the high command. The common view is that British and French generals blithely sent troops to their death, hoping the same old strategies might still work. This is wrong. The First World War was a veritable laboratory of new ideas and technology. Flight was used for reconnaissance and later, there were air-to-ground attacks and even air-to-air fights, which earned the name "dogfights." This was all very new (the Wright Brothers's first flight was in December 1903), and while its application can be criticized (in hindsight) for not making enough impact, to have gone from brand-new invention to military application in the space of ten years meant there were always going to be teething problems. Had the generals really been set in their ways, they would have dismissed the novelty of aircraft and not used them at all. Instead, thousands of planes were used, anything to lead to a break in the stalemate.

Then there was J. F. C. Fuller and his invention of the tank. Critics point out that the early tanks could only grind along at four to six miles an hour, hardly the beasts of the blitzkrieg of World War II. This is not a realistic assessment. The tanks were slow, but they weren't slower than soldiers moving over rough terrain, so they allowed infantry to use them as cover as they moved along together. The initial German reaction was to run a mile when they saw these terrifying metal castles bearing down on them, their rifle fire harmlessly bouncing off. True, many broke down, but that's what happens with new technology.

Another innovation was poison gas, which turned out to be a waste of time. In order for it to work effectively, it needed perfect weather conditions and a guaranteed wind that moved it away from your own soldiers. War is rarely fought in perfect conditions. Rapidly improving gas masks meant that the memory of gas being used and its actual impact as a weapon are entirely out of proportion. Just 0.5 percent of Western Front casualties were caused by poison gas. That's not to diminish the horror of hearing the bell to warn of an incoming gas attack, but as an effective weapon, the simple rifle was better by far. However, it's another example of generals trying something new, something that has been exaggerated in poetry and films.

The fact that the Western Front solidified at all is another sign of new technology. Why hadn't this situation ever happened before? The answer is because of food. During Napoleon's time, keeping his soldiers fed was a huge logistical problem. He had either to depend on a massive baggage train of supplies or to keep moving and live off the land. Tens of thousands of troops will strip an agricultural area bare in no time, but the invention of canned food and railways meant that thousands of tons of preserved food were available to a mass of troops without them needing to go anywhere.

Because the trenches are just about the only things discussed in history lessons, I made the assumption (as many people do) that the troops lived most of their lives in the trenches. They didn't. The trenches were the front line, and as with any front line, the troops were regularly rotated to reequip them and allow them to rest. So, a unit would be up front for about seven to ten days before moving behind the lines for rest and recuperation.[1]

None of this is shown in *Lawrence of Arabia*, but what it does show is a completely different theater of war. In the Middle East, fighting the Ottoman Empire was largely about maneuvering, and the Ottomans were pretty good at it, which led to an obscure but important British defeat at Kut in 1916. The famous Allied defeat at Gallipoli (1915–January 1916) was down to Allied soldiers not maintaining the momentum of their attack and defaulting to the usual trench warfare.[2]

The film does a great job of portraying three-dimensional Arab characters, but it does a terrible job of showing the Ottomans as anything other than bloodthirsty or incompetent "Turks." The Ottoman Empire was a polyglot society encompassing multiple ethnicities. There was no such thing as "Turk" until the founding of the Republic of Turkey in the 1920s (there are ethnic Turks in the world, but they are in eastern Central Asia, a long way from this region). As a piece of cinema, it's perfection (even if it is more than three and a half hours long), and as a piece of World War I history, it's important.

DOCTOR ZHIVAGO (1965)

Lean followed up one epic masterpiece with another, *Doctor Zhivago*. Here we have a rare example of a Hollywood film (rather than a Soviet film) about the Russian Front during the First World War and the subsequent Russian

Civil War. What Lean did with sand in *Lawrence of Arabia*, he does with snow in *Doctor Zhivago*. The film accurately portrays the privations of Russian soldiers in World War I and how it evolved into the bloody mess of revolution, where at the time, it was not obvious who was going to win. It also highlights the importance of armored trains, used by a number of sides in the civil war. These were vital as the distances were vast.

The Russian Civil War was complex. Everyone knows about the Reds (the Communists) and the Whites (the Tsarists), but there were also huge battles with the Greens (massive peasant armies that grew tired of other armies rampaging through their farms) and the Blacks (urban-based bands of anarchists who specialized in mounting machine guns on horse carts for mobility) plus various nationalist groups attempting to break away from the Russian Empire. There were at least half a dozen separate powers vying for the future of Russia.[3]

If there's a problem with the film, it's only that it's all a bit too clean and sunny. We are once again rubbing up against the "it cost a lot of money, so we need to show it off" syndrome. Some of the events take place in northern Russia, so while it is light for half the year, it's very dark during the other half. But the interiors are always brightly lit from unknown light sources.

JOURNEY'S END (2017)

If there's one British play that defines the view of World War I, it must be R. C. Sherriff's *Journey's End*. The film has been made and remade multiple times, most recently in 2017. This version shows the psychological horrors of war more than the death and destruction. Set in the British trenches and dugouts near Aisne in 1918, Sherriff was writing from his own experiences. He had been seriously wounded, and the 2017 version is suitably gritty and an honest portrayal of the cost of war. However, my issue with it is that it is essentially a costume drama in that people sit around and talk for an hour and a half. It's all perfectly realistic and legitimate, but it's one of the stories that has led to the myth that soldiers spent all four years in the trenches, moaning about conditions, simply awaiting their doom.

Peter Jackson's 2018 documentary masterpiece *They Shall Not Grow Old* corrects this image with his lovingly restored footage and interviews that show there was laughter, camaraderie, and fun too. *Journey's End* is all one note for me, and the constant message that "war is bad" is not one I disagree with but on repeat for 100 minutes . . . well . . . it gets a bit dull and boring.

OH! WHAT A LOVELY WAR (1969)

Then there's Richard Attenborough's antiwar musical *Oh! What a Lovely War*. This film uses some of the popular tunes sung by troops in the trenches to fashion the story of three brothers who sign up to join the fight and slowly slide into despair as they live the reality of war.

The final shot takes place as they walk along a field with hundreds of white crosses (all before CGI so they had to be added by the props department). It's a strange film but was perfect for the counterculture. The only thing that 1960s' American counterculture and the Nazis have in common is that both "knew" World War I was a pointless stalemate where the men in the trenches were betrayed by their generals. That assumption was wrong, and this film in a way proves it. By 1969, the Tommies of the First World War were of retirement age, but they went to the film in droves and happily sang along not as a form of catharsis, but as a form of nostalgia. It may not have been "the good old days" exactly, but veterans were not looking back with bitterness at their time in the services.

THE AFRICAN QUEEN (1951)

Fun adventure films are rarely set in the World War I era; such fare more commonly uses World War II as a backdrop. But in 1951, *The African Queen* was released. The film starred Humphrey Bogart (who won the Oscar for Best Actor) and Katharine Hepburn, who spend a long river journey fighting each other as they try to escape German troops in Africa. The film is thousands of miles, both geographically and in tone, from a film like *Journey's End*. And it shows that the war was genuinely a world war and that the fighting in Africa (and the eventual loss of Germany's colonies in Africa to France and Britain) was an important part of the story. General Paul von Lettow-Vorbeck, who led German and colonial forces against vastly larger British forces, fought throughout the German East Africa campaign, and at the signing of the armistice in November 1918, was still undefeated and active on the field of battle. He returned to Germany a hero.

ZEPPELIN (1971)

There's also *Zeppelin*, starring Michael York. An adventure story can't be set in the trenches (not very cinematic), so in this film we get a rare view of the world of aerial combat and, in particular, the bizarre, almost steampunk notion of Germany sending gigantic hydrogen-filled airships over Paris and London to carry out mass bombings. Nearly seven hundred people in London were killed and nearly two thousand were wounded in these raids, in retrospect tiny numbers compared to what happened later in World War II. But at the time it was terrifying and a sign that with modern technology not even civilian populations in another country were safe from attack.

THE KING'S MAN (2021)

In 2021 (delayed from 2019 due to COVID-19) *The King's Man*, a prequel to the modern *Kingsmen* spy movies, came out. Starring Ralph Fiennes, it starts during the Boer War and shows one of Britain's concentration camps—an outrage where Boer families were kept incarcerated during this bitter war. It pulls no punches, showing the privations and deaths, and for these scenes alone it may be unique in Western cinema. It has a fairly accurate re-creation of the assassination of Franz Ferdinand by Gavrilo Princip, General Kitchener is killed at sea, and the Zimmerman telegram is shown as the key to getting America into the war. This is all surprisingly accurate. And while the film is a serious condemnation of war, the tone shifts to entertaining adventure. Tom Hollander has great fun in his roles as George V, Kaiser Wilhelm, and Tsar Nicholas, playing on the fact that the tsar and King George did look remarkably similar to each other, and it's true that they were all grandsons of Queen Victoria. But having Rasputin, Princip, and Mata Hari as part of a master plan for me was fun, while some found the retooling of real events and people tasteless. I would put it in the same category as *300*; the tone says this is not history, and yet, somebody had actually done the research in the background.

WONDER WOMAN (2017)

Not even the First World War is safe from superheroes, and there was the odd decision to have Wonder Woman fighting in the trenches. I suspect she was used because the area between the German frontlines and the Allied trenches was called "no-man's-land," the implication being that crossing it was impossible, but as she's not a man, she could do it, along with her magic shield and superpowers. Why didn't General Haig think of that? The film is great fun, but its logic, geography, and knowledge of the trenches is all over the place. First, the chemical plant in the Ottoman Empire has German planes; Germans had advisers and weapons in the empire, but there were no chemical factories or German-marked airplanes. Second, Themyscira is clearly set among the Greek islands, and yet the tugboat to London takes only a day to get there (that's faster than any naval vessel ever made could do). But the biggest issue is the trenches. To ratchet up the tensions there are civilians in danger. What? One of the strange things about the Western Front is that unlike almost any previous war, there weren't marauding armies roaming through towns in the area, so the number of civilians caught up in the war was tiny compared to almost any other conflict. The fact that Americans are now involved in the story means we are very near the end of the war, so the local populations would have left years earlier. No civilians would ever have been in the trenches, and yet, there they are.

1917 (2019)

The only kinetic movie set in the trenches is 2019's *1917*. Shot in what appears to be two continuous takes (there's a break in the middle), this is the story of two Tommies who must get to another unit before they go over the top. High command has discovered that it's a trap and the Germans are waiting for them; hundreds will die if the two messengers don't get there in time. It's a brilliant idea to create a race against time rather than men just sitting in a trench talking about how awful the war is. The story is loosely based on real history but is perhaps the most accurate depiction of the First World War ever put on screen.

Using clever editing and blending CGI models of real people to piece together separate scenes, we see the horrors of no-man's-land, with corpses of both men and horses and the gigantic shell craters and the superior trenches of the Germans. All of this is accurate. The Allies were desperate to retake the areas of Belgium and France under German control. As such, Allied trenches tended to be hastily built as the expectation was to move off from them and attack the enemy. The Germans, by contrast, had captured hundreds of square miles of enemy territory and built reinforced concrete bunkers and other similar defense works to ensure they could hold it.

As the story is, in theory, all done in one take and in real time, the distances between locations had to be compressed, but the equipment is accurate (right down to the planes in the sky), and there is mud everywhere. In my opinion, it's the best movie depicting the war and won three Oscars, including (quite rightly) Roger Deakins's for Best Cinematography.

ALL QUIET ON THE WESTERN FRONT (1930, 2022)

Perhaps the greatest example of a story from the First World War is Erich Maria Remarque's *All Quiet on the Western Front,* based on his own wartime experiences. I've already said *1917* is my favorite World War I movie, but this is my favorite book on the war and was made into a seminal film in 1930. It's an antiwar novel/film, and it shouldn't be forgotten that it was written by a German who is bound to have a pessimistic view of the war since the Germans lost (so proving that it wasn't a stalemate). It was regarded as so negative that the Nazi regime banned it, and I think we can all agree any book or film banned by the Nazis must have merit.

The film is an early talkie, and as the book was only published in late 1928, it shows the electrifying effect it had to be made into an English-language film less than two years after publication. The book is an unflinching portrayal of life as a front-line German soldier. It has all the profound sentiment of *Journey's End*, but this time the troops move location and even do some fighting, so it mixes antiwar sentiment with some actual drama. The film was a sensational hit and won Best Director and Best Picture Oscars. That said, as it was one of the first movies with sound, a lot of the acting is from the silent era, so it has not aged well. There was a TV movie update in the late 1970s that garnered respect at the time.

Then in 2022, Netflix released a German-language remake, the first version of this German story to be filmed in German (nearly a century after publication). The violence is gritty and bloody; the accurate depiction of French Saint-Chamond tanks is 100 percent accurate and rare in cinema. It is a masterpiece and everything that Remarque was trying to show the reader in his book, although structurally quite different. It is a horrifying and visceral depiction of the depraved nature of war.

A vivid scene in the book describes the soldiers sharpening their shovels in case of close-quarters combat (graphically depicted in the 2022 version). This utterly horrifying prospect, reducing these modern men to the savagery that would have been seen on a battlefield at the time of Ancient Rome, stuck with me. So, when I was writing my novel *Silent Crossroads*, a story about a man's moral journey through both world wars and his experiences in the Weimar Republic, I kept that imagery in during the section on World War I. Like this novel, we will now move from World War I to World War II.

THE GUNS OF NAVARONE (1961)

The strange thing about war movies of the 1950s and 1960s is they frequently starred men who were actual veterans of World War II, and yet to the modern eye the films seem tame. *The Guns of Navarone* is a completely fictitious account of a commando raid on a gun emplacement in the Mediterranean. One of its stars is David Niven, who by then was in his fifties, but during the war he had been a Royal Marine Commando carrying out these sorts of raids for real. *The Guns of Navarone* is a rip-roaring Alistair MacLean boy's-own adventure. It could have been set during World War II or during the Cold War, it didn't matter; it was there to entertain, nothing more.

WHERE EAGLES DARE (1968)

Perhaps the ultimate in this fantasy action version of World War II is another story by Alistair MacLean, *Where Eagles Dare* starring Clint Eastwood and Richard Burton. The plot is barely intelligible. There's one scene in a castle's great hall that leads to a double-cross, then triple-cross before our very eyes. Clint Eastwood, like the audience, is now thoroughly confused and just wants Burton to get on with it.

Where Eagles Dare was the perfect Sunday afternoon family film when I was growing up. It is a classic 1960s' action movie, more James Bond than serious attempt at explaining the events of the war. I shared it with my boys and realized that the first half of the movie only sets the stage. The Allied spies sneak around the German castle stronghold before it all goes wrong, and the second half is shooting, explosions, and fights on top of cable cars. My older son turned to me during the climax and asked, "Dad, is everything going to explode?" I smiled at him and assured him that yes, everything will blow up.

Although Eastwood had been in numerous, more violent movies, it's in this film that he has the most on-screen kills. It is reported that during the epic hallway shoot-out, he turned to the director between takes and sarcastically asked, "You do know guns have to be reloaded, right?"

The real hero of the film is Ingrid Pitt, born Ingoushka Petrov, a Polish Jew, who as a little girl survived a concentration camp and was clearly tougher than either of the two stars. She began her acting career in East Germany and eventually escaped over the Berlin Wall. She wanted to be in a big film with two of the hottest movie stars of the era, but when she signed on to play British spy Heidi Schmidt in *Where Eagles Dare*, she didn't realize just how many extras would be walking around in German uniforms. This made filming difficult for her as it brought back so many terrible memories. Later, Ingrid moved to Britain, where she carved out a successful career in British horror movies, appearing most notably in *The Wicker Man*.[4]

In *Where Eagles Dare*, the German uniforms are wrong, there's a helicopter from the Korean War, the explosive devices are pure Hollywood, and for the record, a Sten gun was a remarkably cheap and simple weapon to produce, so it has no separate firing pin (you'll understand why that's an important point if you've seen it). But it's got some great one-liners, rousing music, Eastwood and Burton with charisma by the bucketload—and it's never boring.

THE GREAT ESCAPE (1963)

There are loads of action films set during World War II, including *Operation Crossbow*, *The Eagle Has Landed*, *Von Ryan's Express*, and *The Dirty Dozen*. Take your pick and enjoy the action, but none of those films will teach you anything about the war. The movie that intersects real history with the war-time romp is *The Great Escape*, which arguably has the most uplifting music from any war movie and is still sung by England fans at football matches. Quick fact: The only actor to be in the three great "group" movies of the 1960s, *The Magnificent Seven*, *The Dirty Dozen*, and *The Great Escape*, is Charles Bronson, and he makes it out alive in every one. And another quick fact: Donald Pleasance is another example of an actor reliving his past as he had been in the RAF during the war, and was shot down over France where he was imprisoned and beaten in a POW camp. And there he is again as an RAF POW in *The Great Escape*.

The film is the true story of the mass breakout at the prisoner of war camp Stalag Luft III in March 1944, where the prisoners did, indeed, dig three tunnels called Tom, Dick, and Harry. Tom was discovered by the Germans and destroyed. Dick was never found, and when the Germans opened up a new area for more prison huts and fenced it off, it became redundant. But Harry was completed and used in the breakout.

Most of the techniques shown in the film were real. Clothes were dyed with ink and boot polish. Dirt was genuinely carried around inside trousers, bed slats were used to reinforce the tunnel walls. The list of ingenious ideas goes on and on. Steve McQueen's character is made up and is so heroic and dashing he doesn't really fit in the movie . . . and where did he get the baseball and mitt from? So, the motorbike chase, while an iconic piece of cinema, did not happen in the real escape. But the film pays homage to the horrific executions of the POWs who were recaptured. Fifty were shot in total.[5]

At nearly three hours long, *The Great Escape* is a strange film that probably wouldn't be made today. Almost everything McQueen's fictional character wears is not era appropriate, and yet the camp and the techniques to build the tunnels were painstakingly re-created. Today's production would be either the fun version or the gritty, historically correct version, but this film somehow gets away with dramatically different tonal shifts to create an absolute classic.

THE GREAT DICTATOR (1940)

A notable film about the war was made by Hollywood before America had even joined the conflict, and 1940's *The Great Dictator* is one of the most important movies ever made. Charlie Chaplin was the world's first movie star, and by 1920, he was the most famous person on the planet. He is best known as a silent movie star, but here, more than a decade after his prime, he returns in a "talkie" to deliver an antiwar speech that is one of the most important in cinema history. It had been observed that Chaplin and Hitler had the same moustache (it was a common working man's fashion at the time— look at Oliver Hardy). Chaplin leaned into this and played a Jewish barber impersonating Adenoid Hynkel, a thinly veiled Adolf Hitler.

The film was so incendiary that a neutral Hollywood in 1940 didn't dare give it a big release, and those who saw it considered it dangerous. A year later, once America had joined the Allies, it was widely released to thunderous applause. The scene where he plays with a globe-like balloon is interesting as Hitler had been photographed with a very similar globe, and it was one of the objects found in his bunker in 1945. The film was, of course banned in Germany, but we know Hitler saw it . . . twice.

THE SANDS OF IWO JIMA (1949)

One of the earliest films to depict the war and attempt to make it as realistic as possible was *The Sands of Iwo Jima*. How realistic is it? Actual footage of the battle is in the movie. And the iconic raising of the flag on the top of Mount Suribachi was re-created with the three remaining Marines who did this in March 1945.

Thinking he was too old at age forty-two (technically he was), John Wayne was reluctant to play the role of a Marine sergeant, but he got over it for this and other war films. In this one, his unit fights at Guadalcanal, Tarawa, and then Iwo Jima. These were three important battles in the Pacific conflict, but while any one Marine may have been transferred between units to fight in the three campaigns, no entire units were ever transferred, so it's historically inaccurate that his company could have been engaged in all three battles.

The Sands of Iwo Jima, while gritty for its time, is easy viewing by modern standards, and it has the first recorded use of the military term "lock and load." As most World War II films are set in the European theater, this film is important for its setting in the Pacific conflict.

LETTERS FROM IWO JIMA (2006)

Fast-forwarding nearly sixty years, Hollywood returned to the Pacific with Clint Eastwood and his two movies filmed back-to-back, both released in 2006: *Flags of Our Fathers* and *Letters from Iwo Jima*. *Flags of Our Fathers* is a competent retelling of the complexities around the famous planting of that flag on Mount Suribachi. The beach scenes were shot in Iceland, one of the few other locations with black sand beaches, and while this makes the landings look authentic, we can't help feeling that everyone looks rather cold to be fighting on a tropical island in the Pacific.

By far the more interesting and satisfactory movie is *Letters from Iwo Jima*, which tells the story of the battle from the Japanese perspective. This film is unusual in the Hollywood canon in that it is a sensitive and rounded portrayal of Japanese officers and soldiers fighting against the Americans. The sympathetic German officer had been a trope since the 1960s, but it needed sixty years to go by before Hollywood could do the same thing for the Japanese.

WINDTALKERS (2002)

Letters from Iwo Jima is certainly better than John Woo's *Windtalkers*, the fascinating true story of how American messages in the Pacific were not only in code but also in Navajo, with a Navajo speaker attached to each unit. This meant that even if the Japanese could crack the code, they still wouldn't be able to understand the message. It also meant that no Navajo translator could be taken alive; if it came to it, he had to die either by his own hand or by that of a fellow platoon member to stop him from falling into enemy hands.

Windtalkers was a chance to show the contributions of ethnic minorities to the US war effort, and John Woo is a master of action. The Navajo characters are dealt with sensitively. It is also clear that considerable effort was put into using the correct equipment and uniforms. Except his gun play is highly stylized and his type of gun-fu jarred with the way Marines would have been fighting in a real war setting. This is the silliest of action films dressed in the solemnity of *Saving Private Ryan* and those two types of films do not fit together. The film was a good idea, with all the right ingredients, but one that turned into a total mess.

MEMOIRS OF A GEISHA (2005)

Arthur Golden's *Memoirs of a Geisha* was published in 1997. It received rave reviews and hit the number one spot on the *New York Times* Best Seller list. Of course it came to Hollywood's attention, and in 2005, the movie version came out. The story follows Chiyo Sakamoto, a poor Japanese girl who becomes a geisha during a turbulent time in Japanese history, from the 1920s to the 1940s. It was an effective way to show the dynamic, highly patriarchal Japanese society of the age from a female perspective. Money and effort were thrown into the movie version, but it arrived heaped in controversy. None of the three central female characters were played by Japanese women. Zhang Ziyi and Gong Li were both Chinese citizens at the time of filming, and Michelle Yeoh is Malaysian. Japan's invasion of mainland Asia after the Meiji restoration resulted in a long list of horrific war crimes, both in China and Korea. The fact that Japan has been reluctant to acknowledge any of this has soured relationships with these nations to this very day. Then, to use Chinese women to portray Japanese women at the time when these crimes were being committed added insult to injury and meant that this appallingly insensitive decision overshadowed what is otherwise a respectful and beautiful movie.

The war itself is a backdrop; none of the characters are combatants. It shows the unfolding events from a unique perspective. This causes its own problems as the Japanese population were not told about the atrocities carried out by its imperial forces. Instead, the film is a little passive about the harsh realities. The irony is this would have been historically accurate, but it also looks like it's dodging the hard topics to a modern viewer.

Once the genie was out of the bottle, the Japanese critics piled on as well. Apparently, there are many errors in the etiquette and ceremonies depicted, and even though you really have to know your Japanese geisha history to spot them, it was enough for the Japanese to dismiss the film.

HACKSAW RIDGE (2016) AND *THE BATTLE AT LAKE CHANGJIN* (2021)

Finally, in the Pacific there was *Hacksaw Ridge*. Directed by Mel Gibson, this has all his favorite interests on display: bloody violence, religious faith, and Christ allegories. But Gibson also knows how to entertain. The opening scene is one of utter carnage, as if to say, don't worry, I'll give you the battles, but first you must know the man. Then, for a little over half the movie's run time, we get to know Desmond Doss. This is the true story of the only conscientious objector ever to win the Medal of Honor, America's highest citation for bravery.

We see Doss grow up (played with immense charm by Andrew Garfield) and meet the girl of his dreams, an utterly luminous Teresa Palmer. He wants to join up for the war effort, but because of his religious beliefs, he will not take up arms so decides to be a combat medic. His drill sergeant (played with relish by Vince Vaughn) does the second-best chewing out of the new recruits in Hollywood history (number one is in the last chapter). The sergeant puts Doss through hell, and the other recruits turn on him, seeing him either as weird or dangerously unreliable. This is where I want to pause. There will be more on this in a later chapter, but one of the things Hollywood does not get enough credit for is its criticism of its own country. Yes, this is ultimately a story of heroism, and any hero's journey must be filled with adversity, but it isn't usually from your own soldiers. The film is being honest that the US Army is not a nice place; it's there to turn you into a weapon to kill the enemy. By showing the flaws in the US military it's saying America, too, has flaws.

Compare this to 2021's Chinese monster hit (the second-biggest-grossing film worldwide of that year) *The Battle at Lake Changjin* (and its 2022 sequel which was filmed at the same time and proved to be another monster hit—the target was different but tonally everything else remains the same). In this film the Chinese soldiers go through hell, but it's worth it because they are there to save China; they are united in their love for China, and China loves their bravery. Meanwhile, the Americans they are attacking are bad, and they have no right to be in Korea, so the good Chinese soldiers will go and kill the bad Americans. Add some explosions and that's the plot. No criticism about China's incredibly unimaginative tactics that led to the needless loss of life among their own troops, a proven fact from the Korean War. No nuances about the war itself or why China was fighting in Korea (if the Americans have no right to be there, why does China?). Hollywood gets accused of oversimplifying conflicts, but to be fair, when we look at how most other countries portray the battles in their history, Hollywood comes across as surprisingly nuanced.

But back to *Hacksaw Ridge*, where Doss eventually goes to court to earn his right to be a medic, and he is allowed to go to war his way. The second half of the film is a full-blooded (and I mean that both literally and meta-phorically) war film. Blood and viscera fly through the air like the goriest horror films. The effects of a flamethrower on a human body are graphically shown, and when demolition charges detonate in a bunker, it erupts in a roiling orange explosion (this is completely unrealistic as demo charges will emit smoke and debris, but a reinforced concrete bunker will not simply blow apart). The film jumps to a time when Doss has already been awarded two Bronze Star medals with a "V" added for "exceptional valor." It was for his later heroism at Hacksaw Ridge in Okinawa that he won the Medal of Honor for working behind enemy lines to transport more than fifty wounded soldiers back to safety. It's the perfect story for the modern cinema viewer. We want the heroics, but we don't necessarily want to see the soldier who won the medal mowing down the enemy like blades of grass. Doss puts himself in harm's way with no way to defend himself, not to kill but to save lives.

THE ENGLISH PATIENT (1996)

Then there's *The English Patient*. This Oscar winner (it won nine) is my favorite romantic movie. It's *Lawrence of Arabia* meets *Romeo and Juliet*, only better than that comparison. It shows the North African and Italian campaigns as well as other less well remembered aspects of the war, such as bomb disposal. It is based on real history and archaeology. In 1933, László de Almásy, a Hungarian count, discovered the cave of swimmers in the Sahara Desert. This was an incredibly important series of cave paintings thought to be over ten thousand years old and proof that the Sahara region was a lush area with water at the end of the last Ice Age. The depiction of these multinational archaeological expeditions is entirely accurate. These men were concerned with the science and not the politics of the day, and their work was all the rage in the interwar era.

During the war, Almásy was involved in mapping North Africa for the Germans and helped several German spies get to Cairo. Unfortunately, that's it for accuracy as there was no love affair, no plane crash with debilitating burns to his body, and slightly disappointingly, László de Almásy died of dysentery in 1951. It's another case of "inspired by" rather than "based on." But for the record, what an inspired piece of filmmaking it is (I cry every time).

THE DAM BUSTERS (1955)

Richard Todd is another example of a man who fought in the war and ended up fighting it all over again on the big screen. First, there's *The Dam Busters*. This is the true account of the development of a new type of bomb and the mission to drop a payload of them on German dams in the Ruhr Valley to disrupt the German war machine. Michael Redgrave gets to play the charming and ingenious Doctor Barnes Wallis who created the "bouncing" bomb.

The Dam Busters has been edited twice since release due to racist language. The problem is Wallis's dog. It's a black Labrador and when I first saw the film as a boy, I loved Wallis right up until he called to his dog, and I thought, wow, he's a racist, so now I don't like him. So, the dog's name was changed, but by the 1990s the new name was also thought to be racially insensitive. Now, when you watch the movie, the dog's name is Trigger.

Once the bomb was created (and in 1955 the bouncing bomb was still covered by the Official Secrets Act, so it's shown to be spherical, whereas they were actually similar to oil drums), the movie changes to the mission to drop them. The leader of the 617 Squadron of Lancaster heavy bombers was Wing Commander Guy Gibson, played by Richard Todd. The final third of the film portrays the nail-biting attempts to blow up the dams. Multiple planes were shot down as they made their bombing runs under heavy antiaircraft fire. George Lucas was a big fan of this film, and he pays homage to these final scenes in the trench run in 1977's *Star Wars*, a sci-fi version of this mission.

At the end of the film, Wallis congratulates Commander Gibson on a successful mission. Todd thanks him but tells him that now he will have to write letters to the families who have lost men. Todd said in a later interview that it was a tough scene to do as he had had to write those very letters during the war.

THE LONGEST DAY (1962)

Staying with Richard Todd, we come to one of the most ambitious war films of all time, *The Longest Day*. This is the story of Operation Overlord, known more commonly as D-Day. Entire sections are filmed in German and French, and we see the Normandy landings from the British beaches as well as the American ones. It's one of those films that has everyone famous at the time in a brief cameo. Sean Connery, hot from his success as James Bond, gets to play a Scotsman, so the accent finally fits. John Wayne plays Lieutenant Colonel Benjamin Vandervoort of the 505th Parachute Infantry Regiment. The lieutenant colonel was at the premiere, and while he was pleased to be played by Wayne, he was frustrated that in 1962, he was only a little older than Wayne was in the film depicting him eighteen years earlier.

Todd had an odd experience on the set because he had been a paratrooper who was dropped (by glider) onto Pegasus Bridge on D-Day, and in the film he played his own commanding officer, fighting the very same battle. He didn't need the costume department to provide him with the beret; he brought his own from the original battle, which I'm going to say is one of the coolest moments in movie history.

Meanwhile, with reference to the first chapter, while Richard Burton twiddled his thumbs waiting for *Cleopatra* to start up again, he played an RAF pilot back at base but later shot down and wounded. For a film he wasn't meant to be in, he was his usual charismatic self.

Despite being filmed in the 1960s when color was standard, *The Longest Day* is in black and white, which echoed the norm of wartime footage and was meant to give an authentic feel to the film. The entire project reflected the full force of Hollywood's intention to make something worthy and use its stars—Robert Mitchum, Henry Fonda, a young Robert Wagner, to name a few more—to bolster its credentials. As a result, *The Longest Day* is the best cinematic depiction of the overall strategy and movements of D-Day, recognized in its Oscar for Best Cinematography. It also won Best Picture along with three other Oscars.

SAVING PRIVATE RYAN (1998)

The next film may be more realistic about World War II combat, but it assumes we already know why the men are there and why they are fighting. *Saving Private Ryan* is the greatest war film of all time. If you disagree, I would love to know what's better. The opening shows the cost of war: a huge cemetery with its simple white crosses in neat rows and a silver-haired man in tears (this was actually filmed on location in the modern cemetery in Normandy so is about as historically accurate and poignant as you can get). He is surrounded by the graves of his fallen comrades; he has lived his life and grown old; they never got that chance. It's making a powerful statement before we even get to the opening scenes of combat as the landing craft come onto shore: it's June 6, 1944.

But already there is a technical error: The sailor calling out to them is American. In reality, all landing craft were run by the Royal Navy. The only time the British are mentioned is when someone comments that "Monty is overrated." The reason for the error is unknown, and the comment may prick British pride, but it was an accurate reflection of what the Americans thought of the British at the time.

The sheer genius of the next sequence on Omaha Beach is not just that it is a tour de force in guerrilla filmmaking, showing the callous and brutal deaths of so many young men, some drowning in the Channel before they even had a chance to set foot on dry land. No, its genius is in the unexpected. I remember sitting in the cinema with a friend, both of us certain of what was coming. We had seen *The Longest Day* a bunch of times, so we knew what to expect. Instead, we saw something more visceral and savage than *Platoon*. By the 1990s, World War II had the reputation of being the "good war" versus Vietnam being the "bad war." Now we were watching as men were torn to pieces. This was an antiwar film, which at the same time was saying this needed to happen so we could defeat the Nazis. My friend and I came away shaken. We had seen similar things before, but we had never seen World War II portrayed like that.

American actor and military adviser Dale Dye was on set to ensure realistic military action, but most unusually, we saw American soldiers behaving brutally as prisoners were gathered up and some shot on the Normandy beach. Later in the film, there's a debate about executing a prisoner, and at the climax, one soldier sits down and cries rather than helping a desperate comrade. This film is authentic down to the sound a bullet makes when it hits a body (several cows sort of made the ultimate sacrifice as cow carcasses were fired upon with live ammunition and recorded to ensure authentic sound effects).

Steven Spielberg redefined the cinematic depiction of war, and from then on, *Saving Private Ryan* cast a shadow over all other war films, regardless of the era. The film won five Oscars, including Spielberg's for Best Director. For some inexplicable reason however, *Shakespeare in Love* won Best Picture, the Academy making yet another insane decision.

DUNKIRK (2017)

If *Saving Private Ryan* is about the Allies arriving on the beaches, then Christopher Nolan's *Dunkirk* is about leaving them. This film tells the story of the mass evacuation of British and French troops at Dunkirk in 1940. Nolan likes stories around time, and the idea of showing three different time lines in one film is clever. The beach perspective covers one week, the ships in the Channel cover one day, and Spitfires in the sky cover one hour. This plus Hans Zimmer's score (including an audio illusion called a Shepard tone) leads to a nerve-shreddingly tense film. However, it's not without its problems, the main one being Nolan's resistance to using CGI (I agree), but this leads to the beaches looking . . . well, empty. About 330,000 men were evacuated, so where is everyone? The chaos depicted in *Atonement* is a better re-creation of the beaches at that time.

DARKEST HOUR (2017)

Strangely, in the same year, there is another depiction of the same events, but this time from Churchill's point of view. Gary Oldman plays the prime minister in *Darkest Hour* (which won two Oscars, one for Oldman for Best Actor and one for the makeup that transformed him), a film that explains the strategy while *Dunkirk* shows what happened. A clever film editor should fuse the two to create the definitive version of the Dunkirk evacuations.

Oldman brings Churchill to life. His clothing, mannerisms, and even receding hairline are all quite accurate. You could argue that he is a bit of a caricature, but the reality is Churchill had deliberately refined himself into one. Churchill was sixty-five when he had become prime minister in 1940. As a young man he had been involved in Imperial actions on the Afghan border, a cavalry charge in Sudan, and had been a prisoner during the Second Boer War, and all of that was before his time in the admiralty and trenches in World War I. He made himself the living embodiment of the British Empire with all the positives and negatives that brings. Oldman is able to instill this in his performance of a man who was the very definition of a legend in their own lifetime.

When it comes to World War II, there's a reason why there's no debate that the Nazis had to be stopped: the Holocaust. What's widely considered to be the greatest movie on the subject is the ten-hour-long documentary *Shoah* (the Hebrew word for disaster, it's now sometimes the preferred term as *holocaust* is the Greek word for a burnt offering to the gods, and that is *not* what the Nazis were about). But this is a documentary, so it's not relevant here.

SCHINDLER'S LIST (1993)

The first place Hollywood takes a look inside the camps is in *Schindler's List*. By day Spielberg was shooting this film, and in the evenings, he was going over the edit of *Jurassic Park*. This shows Spielberg's genius, as there can be no two more different films to hold in your head simultaneously and get them both right.

Spielberg said of the Holocaust, "Nobody can take it all in, so I put it behind a wall, and I drill a small hole in that wall and let you look through that hole. That's what *Schindler's List* is." Spielberg had tried serious topics before in *The Color Purple* and *Empire of the Sun*, but he hadn't quite got that sort of filmmaking perfected yet. They are earnest, but there's something about them that stops them being classics. With *Schindler's List*, Spielberg, a secular Jew, reached out to his Jewish roots and made an honest connection that sears across the screen. Ralph Fiennes is mesmerizing as the concentration camp commandant Amon Goeth. He isn't a cackling madman; he's far more normal than that, which makes him even more chilling. Once again, the Academy dropped the ball and gave the Best Supporting Actor Oscar not to Fiennes, but to Tommy Lee Jones for *The Fugitive*.

Schindler's List is perfect and heartbreaking and entirely accurate. As Spielberg said, "This is just a tiny part, but the liquidation of the ghetto and the arbitrary brutality of the camps will now be preserved for everyone to see, to witness how low we can stoop without human empathy."

LIFE IS BEAUTIFUL (1997)

There are three other Holocaust movies worth a brief look. First, *Life Is Beautiful*. This is not a Hollywood film, but an Italian movie directed by and starring the Italian comedian Roberto Benigni. He won the first Best Actor Oscar awarded for a role in a foreign-language film. The film also won another two Oscars. It's a gently comic situation where a Jewish father and son are put in a concentration camp, but to protect his son from the horrors around him, the father pretends that the whole thing is a game, and if they can get to one hundred points, they win a tank. Just like Spielberg, Benigni knows that to get the horror across, the story must focus on the small, so we, like the son, aren't allowed to see too much, and it's all the more affecting for that. At the end, when they are liberated by the Americans arriving in tanks, the boy knows the game is over. It's a wonderful touch that allows the overwhelming emotions to include a moment of levity.

THE DIARY OF ANNE FRANK (1959)

Of course, if you are to explain one of the greatest crimes in human history to children, the introduction must not be so overwhelming as to be off-putting. The perfect way to do this is with a German girl called Anne Frank.

Anne was not a key player in the war. She fought in no battles, cracked no codes, and had no political power. In her lifetime she was a complete unknown. And yet this young teenage girl has become world famous and a key figure in understanding World War II.

Anne was a German Jew, and after Hitler came to power, her family fled to the Netherlands. But in 1940, the Germans invaded and forced their racial laws on the occupied country. Anne and her family now had a death sentence hanging over their heads. As the Nazi authorities started closing in on them in 1942, they went into hiding with other Jews and ended up in a cramped attic in Amsterdam where Anne started keeping a diary. Much of it contains the everyday thoughts of a teenage girl as she writes about her first love, clashes with her mother, and the irritations of communal living. It's the honesty and relatability of the text that makes it one of the great literary works of the war even though it was never meant to be seen by anyone.

The family's luck ran out in August 1944, when they were captured and sent to a concentration camp. Anne hung on, but just months before the end of the war, she perished in Bergen-Belsen, aged just fifteen.

Hollywood's first attempt to adapt the book for the screen was a huge success, with Millie Perkins playing Anne. The film won three Oscars. including

Shelley Winters's award for Best Actress in a Supporting Role as Mrs. Petronella Van Daan.

The movie was deliberately filmed in black and white, and the long shadows the monochrome film throws adds to the tension and claustrophobia in the movie. At three hours, it was given a run time to let the characters come to life on the big screen. It was everything you could expect from a 1950s' production, including some very mawkish music that wouldn't have been out of place in *Gone with the Wind*. But that was a stylistic choice of the time. In terms of accuracy, seriousness, and respect for the heroine and the context, it has stood the test of time.

THE PIANIST (2002)

Finally, there's *The Pianist*, directed by Roman Polanski. Polanski was a Jewish Pole who, in the 1940s, lived in the ghetto that Spielberg re-created in the 1990s. Polanski was separated from his family, and considering that 90 percent of Poland's Jews were killed in the Holocaust, it was a minor miracle that he not only survived, but was reunited with his father after the war. Therefore, putting on screen the true story of Polish-Jewish pianist and composer Władysław Szpilman and the traumas he suffered were very personal for Polanski. We witness Szpilman's hell trying to avoid the ghetto and struggling to survive the Treblinka death camp and the Warsaw uprising (an ultimately unsuccessful but incredibly intense conflict between the Polish resistance and German forces). Szpilman was a concert pianist, someone who had no skills to survive such brutality, but he was lucky and made the right choices and managed to live through it, much like Polanski. Toward the end of the film he's asked why he is wearing a German army coat; his response is pure pragmatism: "I'm cold."

Unlike other Holocaust movies, this one doesn't end with grim statistics but, instead, gives us hope. We see Szpilman at a grand piano in a dinner jacket, playing for an audience. He's survived the catastrophe that interrupted his life; now he can get on with what he loves and was born to do. *The Pianist* won the Palme d'Or at Cannes and three Oscars, including Best Director for Polanski and Best Actor for Adrien Brody in the title role. And that message of hope is the perfect place to end this chapter.

NOTES

1. Jem Duducu, *The Busy Person's Guide to British History* (Seattle: KDP, 2013), 318–19.

2. Jem Duducu, *The Sultans: The Rise and Fall of the Ottoman Rulers and Their World: A 600-Year History* (Gloucestershire, UK: Amberley Publishing, 2018), 276.

3. Anthony Beevor, *Russia: Revolution and Civil War 1917–21* (London: W&N, 2022).

4. Ingrid Pitt, *Darkness Before Dawn: The Revised and Expanded Autobiography of Life's a Scream* (Baltimore: Midnight Marquee Press, 2008).

5. Paul Brickhill, *The Great Escape* (London: W&N Military, 2000).

Chapter 10

Badfellas

This is another chapter where so much ground is covered it's virtually impossible to summarize. But let's start with what is meant by the "Cold War." A "hot war" means actual combat is taking place between the two sides. After World War II the world generally fell into two camps. One side was communist, largely under the power of the Soviet Union, or after 1949, Mao and the Chinese Communist Party. These were ideologically aligned, left-wing dictatorships (Cuba was the same only much smaller, with better weather). In the second camp were the democracies of "the West," meaning mainly Western Europe and the United States, but which also included other places that had a democratic outlook such as Australia and Turkey.

At the conclusion of World War II, the so-called Cold War broke out between the two camps. This consisted of political hostilities, including threats, propaganda, and other tactics, everything short of open warfare. And all this led to the industrialization of spying. All sides needed to know what the other side was thinking because in a world of nuclear weapons, the stakes had never been higher. As the Cold War rumbled on, technology reached new heights. The space race not only supported the arms race but was also a way to show which camp had the technological upper hand. Superfast spy planes like the SR-71 Blackbird were first flown in the 1960s, but these were eventually replaced not by another aircraft, but by spy satellites.

Looking at the chapter heading, it may seem strange to put these three groups together, but there is logic behind it: Both gangsters and pirates do essentially the same job. Pirates can also be smugglers, and some smuggle for gangsters. Sometimes pirates are paid by governments to carry out raids against an enemy nation's shipping or their ports (these pirates are called privateers). Similarly, many spies work in some morally dubious areas. It is alleged and confirmed by eyewitness accounts that the CIA was involved in the drug trade in Southeast Asia in the 1960s and 1970s.[1] Employees of a US government agency acted as spies and smugglers and worked with gangsters. At other times spies needed smugglers to get to restricted locations. So, there is a strange but undeniable interconnectivity among these groups, and no matter what distinctions we might make, Hollywood doesn't see much difference. The plotting and the emphasis on action is the same in a film about gangsters, pirates, or spies.

In the 1930s and 1940s, pirates and gangsters were big business in Hollywood (spies less so). However, both labels are just other names for bandits and robbers: one does it on the sea and the other does it on land. They could be from any era.

Let's start with pirates and that classic book by Robert Louis Stevenson, *The Sea Cook: A Story for Boys*. Hang on, that title isn't very inspiring, so let's change it to *Treasure Island*. The story was originally syndicated in newspapers but came out as a complete book in 1883. It has a tropical island with buried treasure, the black spot, galleons and muskets, and a pirate with a wooden leg and a parrot on his shoulder. The entire genre was created in this one story.

The strange thing is there have been pirates in every era and in every sea in the world. The period from the late 1600s to the early 1700s has been called "the golden age of piracy," but try telling that to the Romans. In the first century BC, pirates were everywhere, and at one point, they were so bold they plundered a port town near Rome. As a young man, Julius Caesar was kidnapped by pirates and held for ransom. He performed his Stoic poetry for them and got angry when they didn't appreciate it (pirates aren't famous for their love of Stoic poetry). Then he argued with them that his ransom was too low, and it was rumored that he "entertained" the pirates too. On his eventual release he told his captors that he would hunt them down and crucify all of them. When he went to the local governor and found no help, he assembled his own fleet, hunted them down, and crucified them all.[2] This is a great story which has never been put on screen. Roman pirates only get a mention in the Asterix animated films.

Or how about Zheng Yi Sao, a female pirate leader at the start of the 1800s, who terrorized the South China Sea. She led the Red Flag fleet, comprised of some five hundred Chinese junks. Her enterprise encompassed at least seventy thousand people, and she made it a rule that if a man forced himself on a woman, he would have to marry her. The Chinese emperor eventually negotiated with her and allowed her to retire because no one could beat her. There have been several Chinese movies about her, but she is virtually unknown in the West.[3]

Instead, thanks to Stevenson, a pirate wears a tricorn hat and operates exclusively in the age of sail, mainly in the Caribbean. The real pirates of this age were violent men who robbed, murdered, and raped. And yet bizarrely, this image has been deemed child friendly. Preschool children, who would never be allowed to dress up as Mafia hitmen or as members of dangerous paramilitary organizations, are happily given tricorns, eye patches, and plastic cutlasses, and that's okay. When one of my boys was little, I asked him why he wanted to dress up like a pirate, why he wanted to be a bad guy. His reply was, "I'm not a bad pirate, I'm a good pirate" . . . of course. So that was the golden age of piracy, a period when the Royal Navy (the most powerful maritime force in the world at the time) didn't have enough ships to protect its growing global trade interests.

TREASURE ISLAND (1950)

Treasure Island itself has been made and remade countless times. Generally speaking, there are two types of pirates: the cunning, colorful character (less action-oriented) pirate like Long John Silver and Captain Jack Sparrow, or the second type who is the braver, more dashing pirate fighter like Captain Blood or the Dread Pirate Roberts (from *The Princess Bride*). The first serious effort to tell the story was in 1934, and in 1935, Errol Flynn was swashbuckling as *Captain Blood*. But perhaps the film most likely to be regarded as a classic pirate film is the 1950 version of *Treasure Island* with Robert Newton doing an era-defining performance as Long John Silver. Disney has two versions: 1996's *Muppet Treasure Island* and the 2002 sci-fi version *Treasure Planet*. *Treasure Planet* was hugely ambitious and is beautifully hand animated, but it came out during the rise of computer-animated films and was one of Disney's biggest animation flops (pirate movies that flop will be a theme).

CUTTHROAT ISLAND (1995)

In 1983 Graham Chapman of Monty Python fame starred in *Yellow Beard*. It was written by the very best comedy writers and featured the best comedians of the time. The problem was that it wasn't very funny and it flopped—hard. Then in the mid-1990s, Carolco, the production company behind *Terminator 2*, the *Rambo* films, and *Basic Instinct* as well as other flashy popcorn movies, decided to greenlight a $100 million pirate movie that starred a female pirate played by Geena Davis called *Cutthroat Island*.

While it's true that there were examples of a number of female pirates being very efficient at pirating, this was based on no history. Davis's character Morgan Adams isn't even the name of a recognized female pirate. This was all meant to be swashbuckling fun. It was satisfyingly progressive. Davis was meant to be the hero, bailing out Matthew Modine in what was basically a gender reversal of the damsel in distress character. It came out in 1995, the same year as *Showgirls* for Carolco. Both were huge flops, but as *Showgirls* cost substantially less, it was *Cutthroat Island*'s massive costs that ultimately bankrupted this previously successful production company. The joke in the industry was the only thing *Cutthroat Island* managed to sink was Carolco. After that, pirate movies were toxic for years.

PIRATES OF THE CARIBBEAN: THE CURSE OF THE BLACK PEARL (2003)

Then Disney decided to take a major risk with *Pirates of the Caribbean: The Curse of the Black Pearl*. It was still hurting from *Treasure Planet*, and *Cutthroat Island* was less than ten years earlier, but the execs decided to throw $140 million at a pirate movie based on one of their theme park rides. The stars would be Orlando Bloom, hot off the *Lord of the Rings* movies, Keira Knightley, who was gaining some heat after *Bend It Like Beckham* and a TV adaptation of *Doctor Zhivago*, along with the well-respected indie actor, but not exactly box-office dynamite, Johnny Depp.

Depp didn't want to be a standard pirate and came up with a dreadlocked, makeup-wearing dandy based on Keith Richards of the Rolling Stones. Meanwhile, during the filming, boats sank on reefs, and Keira Knightley was so sure she would be fired she only brought a few clothes along. Depp kept ad-libbing about eunuchs, and the whole production had the feel of another *Cutthroat Island*. However, when it was released, this fun fantasy-action romp was a huge hit and was so successful they are still making variations of it.

While no discernible history can be taken from a movie with zombies and magic, the uniforms and weaponry are, somewhat surprisingly, authentic for the period. Similarly with the film's slightly fictionalized East India Trading Company (the real name was The East India Company EIC). The EIC did brand men found guilty of piracy with a "P" on the forehead, while in *Pirates of the Caribbean* it's on the arm. So even in a film as silly as this one, there is real history lurking, rather like a kraken.

CAPTAIN PHILLIPS (2013)

Perhaps the most historically accurate and refreshingly different pirate movie is *Captain Phillips*. How can I call this a pirate film? Where are all the pointy hats and doubloons? Well, as previously stated high seas piracy is a global crime that has happened throughout history, right up to today. This is the true story of the 2009 hijacking by Somali pirates of the MV *Maersk Alabama* cargo ship. While this is very much a modern movie, showing a contemporary event, as time goes on it becomes almost a documentary, a time capsule of real issues facing that area in the early twenty-first century. Captain Phillips was an adviser on the film, so all the clothing and technology are accurate because it was what was in use at the time. Somalia was a failed state and many of its people were desperate, capable of doing whatever it took to survive. If that meant capturing passing ships for financial gain, then we might as well use the term *piracy* to describe what it was. But it's telling that when people dress their children as pirates, they don't put them in faded shorts, T-shirts, and flip-flops and give them replica AK-47s, while saying, "Now you're a Somali pirate."

The movie is very careful not to cast the pirates as two-dimensional bad guys. We understand they are acting out of sheer desperation. The film portrays real security measures such as having a marksman onboard if the ship is likely to travel anywhere near the Somali coast. However, the first line of defense was the fire hoses pouring out pressurized seawater to push the pirates away. The fact is that these super cargo carriers are so big they cannot be easily maneuvered, and once fast boats get alongside, they are likely to be able to hijack the ship. The military response portrayed is realistic because the situation unfolded as shown and was expertly re-created by the director Paul Greengrass.

With the exception of *Captain Phillips*, a pirate movie basically means action and adventure, one where the audience revels in the vicarious delights of seeing a bad boy on screen. The same could be said about the gangster movies of the first half of the twentieth century, but then, with the advent of *The Godfather*, they suddenly became prestige pictures, where the best actors of the day vied for roles in ambitious productions. But we are still in the world of the criminal, whether they are wearing tricorns or trilbies.

The Eighteenth Amendment to the United States Constitution was ratified by the requisite number of states on January 16, 1919 and became law a year later. The amendment prohibited the sale and consumption of alcohol in the United States; it was now illegal to have a whiskey with friends or a beer at a bar. The Eighteenth Amendment was repealed by the Twenty-First Amendment in 1933. It is the only amendment ever to be repealed.

The period in between these two amendments was called Prohibition, and just as there was a golden age for piracy, this was a similar period for gangsters who fulfilled the demand for alcohol. The Roaring Twenties was big business for the gangs who smuggled alcohol across the border from Canada and through the docks along the East Coast. The legendary Al Capone, and a little later, Bonnie and Clyde, are names that emerged with as much mystique around them as King Arthur or Robin Hood—only these were real people.

ANGELS WITH DIRTY FACES (1938)

Angels with Dirty Faces examines the poverty in America at the time as well as the inherent glamour a criminal would have to the kids in the neighborhood. It's a complex moral tale, particularly for the 1930s. James Cagney is the star but rising up the order of players is Humphrey Bogart. One of the most famous movies showing this era was *The Roaring Twenties* (confusingly, made in 1939). James Cagney manages to outshine Humphrey Bogart in this exciting drama where a group of men try to monopolize the liquor business during Prohibition.

It is worth pointing out that in the early days of Hollywood, there was no such thing as blanks in guns. Cagney nearly died in the filming of *Angels with Dirty Faces* because the director wanted a marksman to fire real rounds near him. At one point a ricochet almost hit him in the head. Movie guns sadly are still dangerous as shown by the tragic death of Halyna Hutchins, killed by a movie pistol on the set of the western *Rust* in 2021.

Perhaps the most iconic version of James Cagney's gangster persona is 1949's *White Heat*. Cagney plays a sociopath with an unhealthy mother complex called Cody Jarrett. This film isn't so much about Prohibition as it is about causing chaos and destruction. It has the famous scene at the end of the movie where he is standing on top of a burning chemical plant, screaming either in defiance or delirium, "Made it, Ma! Top of the world!" It's interesting that these films show elements of reality among the dated scenes of violence, and some are more morally complex than movies made fifty years later.

BONNIE AND CLYDE (1967)

Then there's *Bonnie and Clyde*, where we see the repurposing of real people to make a point about current attitudes. The film is another example of "when the truth becomes legend, print the legend" (from *The Man Who Shot Liberty Valance,* a great western I didn't have the space to include). Warren Beatty and Faye Dunaway are impossibly cool and good looking as the titular characters, but the real couple were substantially less attractive than their Hollywood counterparts. The events in the film are loosely realistic, but it's the tone that's important here.

At the time of their crime spree across America (1931–1934), there was a general feeling of sympathy for the couple. America was in the grip of the Great Depression, so the idea that these two glamorous robbers were taking money from the banks (which had ruined the country) and staying one step ahead of the law gave them a modern-day Robin Hood quality. When they were gunned down, some saw them as martyrs. It was said that the largest bouquet of flowers at Bonnie's funeral was paid for by newsboys in recognition of all the extra papers that were sold because of their story.

While the pair were part of the Barrow Gang, this is very much Bonnie and Clyde's movie. The crimes are cheeky, almost comical, and the couple are always having fun as they "stick it to the man." Tonally, the film has more in common with other counterculture classics such as *Easy Rider* and *The Graduate* than *Angels with Dirty Faces*.

When I saw this film on TV as a child (I have no idea how I got to see such an adult film at an early age), I loved how brave and cool the duo were, always one step ahead of the cops . . . until the ending. As they are ambushed and mercilessly gunned down by law enforcement, I (like everyone else watching it for the first time) was appalled at the callous brutality unleashed on this beautiful young couple. It left me with a sour taste in the mouth not for the gangsters, but for the law. Which is exactly the feeling Arthur Penn, the director, was going for. *Bonnie and Clyde* may have been set in the 1930s, but it was about the 1960s and the seismic social changes taking place in America, specifically, the antiwar protests and the Civil Rights Movement. Young people felt disenfranchised from an older generation that was sending them off to Vietnam to fight . . . for what, exactly?

THE HIGHWAYMEN (2019)

If you're going to watch *Bonnie and Clyde*, I recommend a double bill with 2019's *The Highwaymen*, starring Kevin Costner as Frank Hamer and Woody Harrelson as Maney Gault, two washed-up Texas Rangers who helped in the manhunt for Bonnie and Clyde. The film is a strangely impassioned rebuttal to the 1967 movie some fifty years later. It strips away the metaphors, the glamour, and the myths. Bonnie and Clyde are hardly in it, and Clyde has a limp (which he did after cutting off some of his toes with an axe to avoid hard labor in prison). It's a gritty retelling of the story, with two highly watchable Hollywood stars now past their prime.

This time the film dwells on the violence committed by the duo; they didn't just kill cops, they killed "ordinary people," too. Bonnie and Clyde were dangerous and damaged people. Clyde was repeatedly raped in prison, which everyone agreed changed him, and Bonnie was married six days before her sixteenth birthday, which was unusual even for the 1920s. At the time of the final ambush, the two are not portrayed as a couple of lovebirds on their way to some bit of innocent fun, but two dangerous criminals armed to the teeth with military-grade hardware (Clyde particularly liked using a BAR, a Browning Automatic Rifle). When the bullet-riddled car is removed to a nearby town, the locals go wild trying to grab any memento they can, tearing at the dead couple's hair and clothing (it isn't shown in the movie, but some of their fingers were removed in the frenzy for keepsakes).[4] This is the real story of Bonnie and Clyde and is a thoroughly underrated film.

SCARFACE (1932, 1983)

Which brings us to *Scarface* . . . the 1932 original. The plot concerns a bootlegger who hires a guy called Tony to be his bodyguard. Tony eventually becomes the crime boss, and he violently suppresses all opposition. It was an incredibly dark and violent film for its day. It was proudly promoted as being based on real events and features a re-creation of the 1929 Saint Valentine's Day Massacre. The film was made while Bonnie and Clyde were still on the streets breaking the law, and as such, the bad guys are bad, really bad; there's no nuance here. The famous 1983 remake, directed by Brian De Palma and starring Al Pacino, follows a similar storyline, but instead of drink, it's now drugs. In the 1932 version there are no chainsaws and no "say hello to my little friend," but there is the svelte platinum blonde Tony meets in a nightclub. I will put myself out there and say that the ending of the 1983 movie is, for me, the most satisfying movie ending of all time.

AL CAPONE (1959)

The man whose real nickname was Scarface was Al Capone, and the original movie *Scarface* was made barely a year after his arrest. The reason why the main character isn't named Al Capone is probably because the studio wanted to use his notoriety but not unnecessarily annoy his associates, who were still very much active as gangsters. There followed multiple films where characters were based on Capone, but he didn't get his own name in a movie until 1959's *Al Capone*. Besides gangsters, another thing to fear in Hollywood is getting sued. Capone's sister sued the studio for "invasion of privacy" for an eye-watering $10 million. The case was eventually thrown out in 1962, but a lawsuit is not something any studio wants to attract. As such, movies about Capone tended to come out later in the century when everyone involved was either very old or very dead.

THE UNTOUCHABLES (1987)

Perhaps the most famous version of the story of Al Capone is *The Untouchables*. Here Brian De Palma plays fast and loose with real events. Eventually Capone does (famously) get taken down for tax evasion, and Eliot Ness and his team, who were nicknamed "the untouchables," did try to take down Capone's criminal organization. Frank Nitti really was the name of one of Capone's men (he wasn't killed by Ness but committed suicide just before going before a grand jury in 1943). Perhaps the key issues are that Ness and Capone never met, so their tense standoffs in the movie are pure mythmaking. Then there's the rather uncomfortable piece of reality that the tax evasion case wasn't actually run by the Untouchables. So there wasn't much historical accuracy, apart from the fact that Ness was running the Untouchables and Capone was running his criminal empire.[5] The music is by Ennio Morricone in top form; the suits are by Armani and look fabulous; De Palma uses every cinematic trick in the book and the movie is always gorgeous. De Niro was clearly enjoying his role as a Chicago mob boss with a Brooklyn accent (to be fair, Capone was from New York but didn't speak with that accent), and Sean Connery finally won an Oscar (it was an interesting decision by Connery to play an Irish American cop with a Scottish accent).

The film will not help you with the history of Prohibition or the rise and fall of Al Capone. But it is an amazing movie. Whether it's been ages since you've seen it or if you have never seen it, sit down and watch it tonight. Go on. You can find me on twitter as @jemduducu and you can thank me afterward.

So, while *The Untouchables* can't help you with events in the 1920s, it can help you with film history and does pay homage to one of the great sequences of silent cinema. In the jaw-droppingly tense shoot-out at the train station, the pram clattering in slow motion down the stairs is a direct reference to Sergei Eisenstein's 1925 movie *Battleship Potemkin*, and the Odessa Steps montage where a baby's pram rattles down the steps as revolution and chaos break out.

THE GODFATHER (1972)

The filming of *The Godfather* series has been the subject of entire books, so rather than talking about all the behind-the-scenes issues, I want to put the movies into the context of Hollywood crime movies and the eras they are portraying in the films.

A little like pirate films, the gangster flick was not in good shape in 1970. Cheap crime thrillers arrived from Europe, but in America, little effort was put into the genre. That changed when Francis Ford Coppola was brought in to adapt Mario Puzo's book, not because of Coppola's lengthy career and string of hits leading up to this point because that didn't exist, but because he was of Italian heritage and he knew where to point a camera. Puzo's book was a *New York Times* Best Seller and while Hollywood would always take a chance on one of these, the book wasn't exactly Shakespeare. *The Godfather* came out in 1969, and as always with book adaptations, a quick turnaround was essential before everyone forgot about it. The movie came out in 1972, an amazing undertaking given the scope and ambition of the film.

Most people forget that the opening line of the first movie is "I believe in America." The scene is set during Don Corleone's daughter's wedding, and we have a local man explaining that his daughter has been attacked and raped by two white men and asking the Godfather for justice. The scene is fictional, but it's the immigrant experience, so vividly shown here and even more so in the second film, that makes it timeless. For the first time Hollywood is showing what it's like in America when you weren't born there. Speaking as the son of immigrants, I find it fascinating to understand the almost arbitrary bits of culture that get fused from the old world and the new one. For example, my father is Turkish and knows no English language nursery rhymes, but I remember him singing to me as a child, "Come on baby light my fire," "Hello, I love you, won't you tell me your name," and "We all live in a yellow submarine." I was a teenager before I knew those weren't actual nursery rhymes.

This opening scene shows us how vulnerable immigrant communities are and why they tend to stick together. We see how organized crime grows as it provides a very practical service of protection from the outside world—but that protection comes at a cost. Another story from my father: By the late 1980s, he and my mother had a delicatessen in Portobello Market in London; they also had a wholesale business with a regular supply of and a good price for duck eggs. So, knowing that duck eggs are important in Chinese cuisine, Dad went to London's Chinatown to see if he could get some new customers. Every place he went, the restaurant manager agreed that he had quality eggs at a good price, but he was also told he would have to deal with a Triad (Chinese Mafia) middleman. My father never went back to Chinatown.

The film then, while a piece of fiction, accurately shows how organized crime works: the hierarchy of a Mob family, the gatherings of the family; a structure known as "the commission" created by a rival to Capone, Charles "Lucky" Luciano, in the 1930s as a way to settle disputes between the families without a gang war. The research was meticulous, very rare for something technically fictional. It was alleged that the producers reached out to the Mafia to get their blessing and, again allegedly, their only condition was to remove the word *Mafia* from the script. Whether this is a legend swirling around a legendary film or true, the fact is that in a film about the Mafia, the word is never used once and it in no way diminishes its impact.

THE GODFATHER: PART II (1974)

The immigrant story is even stronger in the second film, and now we have a film running over multiple time lines. When Vito Corleone comes over to America as a child, there's confusion over his name, and as a result, his home-town becomes the family name (this was not uncommon). The scene was shot on Ellis Island, and the clothes worn by the immigrants and even the uniforms worn by police officers are accurate for the time. The apparently mute Vito even gets an authentic chalk cross on his coat, a sign the inspector believed the person had a mental defect.

Immigrants tend to speak in their own language, and this caused problems for De Niro, who couldn't speak Italian. So he went to live in Sicily not only to learn the language, but to pick up the island's specific dialect as Coppola wanted everything to be authentically Italian. As a result, De Niro barely speaks any English in the film, and now there are whole chunks of the movie needing subtitles.

The other unusual piece of history in the film and one that is key to the second movie is the Cuban revolution. This is another moment in history that is rarely shown (unless it's after the revolution and focuses on the Cuban Missile Crisis), but in *The Godfather: Part II*, we see the Batista government fail to quell the popular and disciplined rebel fighters led by Fidel Castro. There's a key scene where a man kills himself with a hand grenade but takes a military police officer with him. This convinces Michael (Al Pacino) that the government cannot stop the highly motivated rebels, no matter how much money or tacit support either he or the US government give Fulgencio Batista. If you ever want to see a minute-long metaphor on why America's foreign policy from Cuba to Afghanistan has failed, it's in this one scene. This is a moment of cinematic perfection that ages like fine wine.

THE GODFATHER: PART III (1990)

The third film is not even close to the quality of the other two, but it does take us to some interesting history, depicted on screen for the first time. The Institute for the Works of Religion is not an organization you are likely to have heard of, but you may know it as the Vatican Bank. In the movie we get a fictitious link between the bank and the Corleone family. That senior figures

of the church died because of corruption is also portrayed. It is worth pointing out that in 1978, Pope John Paul I lasted all of thirty-three days before
dying. Much has been made of his death, with the Vatican saying, of course,
it was due to natural causes, but it seems odd that the most important man
in the Roman Catholic Church would have died so suddenly . . . which has
led to lots of conspiracy theories, many of them linked to organized crime's
involvement in the Vatican Bank. Any rejection of these theories is not helped
by the fact that the bank did have two real scandals around this time, one in
1974 and another in 1982. So, the suggestion of foul play linking money,
power, and religion (which could be the tagline for the Vatican for most of its
existence) was not unrealistic. There is no hard evidence to link the death to
any financial irregularities, but the movie makes some valid points, and the
bank continued to be hit by scandal until a restructure in 2010. Fortunately,
since then, the Catholic Church has not faced any other scandals or serious
allegations of any kind. . . .

GOODFELLAS (1990)

Then there's Martin Scorsese, who has created multiple gangster movies,
usually based on real events and real people. The standout film of the genre
has to be *Goodfellas*, the true story of Mafia mobster Henry Hill (played by
Ray Liotta), who was arrested and turned FBI informant. The film spends
little time on events after his arrest and wallows in his criminal life instead.
This movie is one of the greatest ever made, with tour-de-force performances
wrapped up in a killer soundtrack and astonishing direction from the master himself.

Goodfellas takes us through the 1950s and into the 1970s. It would be
impossible to cover everything, and Hill's three-year stint in the Army was
an interesting time where even as a soldier he continued to hustle, but it is
not mentioned in the movie. In 1967 he was pivotal to the Air France robbery,
and Hill believes that was the job that got him the respect he wanted from
the Mafia. In the movie version, Hill was peripheral to the event, and that's
what stops mobster James Conway (played by Robert De Niro) from killing
him. Apart from Henry Hill all the names have been changed to protect the
not so innocent. The film shows spectacularly well the everyday life of a
Mafia mobster. It's social history in the same way that *Jane Eyre* or *Pride and
Prejudice* are, except these aren't little women, these are wise guys.

Goodfellas is a masterwork of classic scenes and perfect direction. From
the opening scene when Hill slams shut a car trunk containing a freshly
killed man, to the narrated line, "As far back as I can remember I always
wanted to be a gangster," to the one-shot entrance to the club through the

bustling kitchen, to Joe Pesci's "funny how" scene, this is one of Hollywood's crown jewels.

In the very last scene, Joe Pesci looks straight at us as he fires a gun into the camera. This moment always confused me until I saw the same last scene in the 1903 film *The Great Train Robbery*. Scorsese was linking the criminals he had just depicted to the very first narrative movie ever made, showing our strange fascination with very bad men.

Bizarrely this wasn't the only film about Henry Hill in the witness protection scheme to come out in 1990. There was also the Steve Martin / Rick Moranis comedy *My Blue Heaven*. Far more family friendly, and definitely funnier, it's a weird quirk that these two films would come out within months of each other. The comedy makes no attempt to depict anything approaching a real story (and indeed they change Hill's name to Vinnie Antonelli). One of these films has been remembered as a cinematic masterpiece, the other has been largely forgotten, I'll leave it to you to work which is which.

Scorsese is often referred to as a crime moviemaker, and it's true that some of his greatest successes are in that genre, but he has spent most of his career documenting the past. *The Irishman*, *Hugo*, *The Last Temptation of Christ*, *The Wolf of Wall Street*, *Gangs of New York*, *Raging Bull*, *Kundun*, *The Aviator*, and *Casino* are all about past events and people. 2016's *Silence* is a look at Christian faith in seventeenth-century Japan and is the only Western film to have ever looked at the persecution of Christians under the Tokugawa Shogunate; it could happily fit into Kurosawa's later work. *The Age of Innocence* is a beautifully made if rather flat film in the style of female writers of the nineteenth century, so about as far away as it gets from *Goodfellas*. The problem with *The Age of Innocence* is it has neither the wit of *Pride and Prejudice* nor the elemental power and emotion of *Wuthering Heights*. In the end it's just an achingly beautiful movie about people sitting around in period rooms in period-appropriate clothing. So, not all of his films were successful (I'm looking at you too, *Kundun*), but I find it interesting that almost no one thinks of Scorsese as a historical filmmaker, and yet his passion for the past is clearly there on screen, again and again.

AMERICAN GANGSTER (2007)

While the immigrant experience has been discussed, the story of Black gangsters doesn't get anything like the same level of attention as that of other ethnic minorities, unless it's based around hip-hop. This was rectified with the high-budget and very ambitious movie *American Gangster*. This Ridley Scott–directed, $100 million film may be too little too late, but it is one hell of a movie. Here we have a highly respected director and not one, but two leading men: Denzel Washington is Frank Lucas, the titular gangster, and Russell Crowe is Richie Roberts, the lawman coming after him. The film is packed with lots of familiar faces and all are on form.

Frank Lucas is portrayed as an utterly pragmatic man. He is not a vicious sociopath, nor is he high on his own supply. If he had been given the opportunity, he could have been the CEO of IBM, but he was never going to get that chance growing up in 1940s North Carolina, where life was bad if you were Black: As a child he witnessed his twelve-year-old cousin being murdered by the Ku Klux Klan. Later Lucas moved to New York and started doing petty crime, which grew in ambition as he grew in age. Of course, as we know from these other films, organized crime in New York in the 1960s was under the control of Mafia families. So Lucas decided to cut out all the middlemen involved in the smuggling of heroin and flew out to Southeast Asia, while the Vietnam War was going on, and negotiate directly with the drug producers to get the drugs back to America.

Exactly how he did that has been contested. The most popular story (and to be honest, the most pragmatically effective option) is that he put the drugs into the coffins of dead soldiers being flown home. This is a disgusting desecration of young men who gave their lives in a somewhat pointless war. It was, however, a clever plan as the US Army was good at logistics, and nobody was going to open the coffins of dead GIs. The other possibility is the drugs were hidden in furniture that was legitimately shipped to the United States. Either way, Lucas now had direct control of the majority supply of heroin coming into the East Coast. Because he could control the quality and the price, he went from small-time hustler to major crime boss. He used family contacts and close friends from North Carolina to help in his criminal endeavors, but he was arrested in 1975 with over half-a-million dollars in cash in his home.

This was thanks to the man on the other side of the law, Richie Roberts, head of the Federal Bureau of Narcotics task force. Law enforcement had noticed a new, high-quality heroin on the streets called "Blue Magic," and a criminal investigation was launched to find out which criminal organization was smuggling it into the country. Roberts was real, but the *American Gangster* version of him is almost entirely fiction.

Lucas was on set during the filming of *American Gangster* and helped Washington portray him in a realistic way. He was thrilled that Washington was playing his younger self (well, who wouldn't be?), but he said that a lot of liberties had been taken with his life story. This seems to be the general point raised again and again by these movies, where the formula seems to be to take a remarkable and compelling true story, simplify it (because life is messy, and nobody can follow multiple characters/plot lines in a two-hour movie) and then make up a bunch of stuff that's cool and add that in.

Now for the world of espionage. It may seem odd to put spies in the same category as pirates and gangsters, but this is the perfect example of "one man's hero is another man's traitor." Spying is as old as history. In Ancient Greece important people would pass secret messages to each other (and beat the spies) by shaving the head of a slave and tattooing the message on the scalp, then wait for their hair to regrow before sending the slave to the intended destination. It was an ingenious method, but unsuitable for anything urgent.

Of course, if we are going to discuss spies in movies, we have to talk about the elephant in the room and the vodka martini at the bar, one James Bond. Again, entire books have been written about the origin of the character, the name, and Ian Fleming's wartime record.

James Bond teaches us nothing about spycraft from any era, nor is he ever put in a historical setting; he is always "now." Of course, this means that as the decades roll on, he is very much a reflection of the time in which a particular movie is made. Individual Bond films are not something we can necessarily go back to and enjoy as we might have done first time around. These are time capsules of the culture and fashions of an era, and they are not always positive reflections.

DR. NO (1962)

Take one throwaway scene in the first film, *Dr. No*. Once Bond is at Dr. No's lair he walks past and looks at a rather prominent Goya portrait of the Duke of Wellington. Why it's there is never explained, nor is it ever referenced again. This was an in joke for a 1962 audience as the painting had recently been stolen. So it was a throwaway visual sign that Dr. No was committing all sorts of crimes including art theft. As the painting was eventually recovered it makes no sense to a modern viewer (unless you're me doing a deep dive on this inconsequential stuff).

GOLDFINGER (1964) AND YOU ONLY LIVE TWICE (1967)

Next some examples from the "timeless classic" *Goldfinger*. Before I ruin it for you, I would agree that the theme tune is amazing, the laser scene is great fun, and the final fight in Fort Knox provides a suitably tense climax. But now onto the bad stuff: Bond is talking to Felix Leiter when his girlfriend turns up and tries to join in the conversation. Bond rebuffs her, saying it's "man talk," then slaps her on the bottom and sends her on her way. That hasn't aged well.

Then there's the line, "There are some things that just aren't done, such as drinking Dom Perignon '53 above the temperature of 38 degrees Fahrenheit. That's just as bad as listening to the Beatles without earmuffs." In 1964 this would have got a chuckle from parents taking their kids to see the movie, but to a modern audience Bond sounds like an old fuddy-duddy. And still with *Goldfinger*, we have a woman called Pussy Galore. Classy. Some prime objectifying of women there. Today only a porn star would have such a name, and their names don't tend to be as unsubtle as that.

In *You Only Live Twice* Bond has plastic surgery to look Japanese— oh boy! Then in the same film we get this exchange between a Chinese woman and Bond:

Bond: Why do Chinese girls taste different from all other girls?

Ling: You think we better, huh?

Bond: No, just different. Like Peking duck is different from Russian caviar. But I love them both.

Ling: Darling, I give you very best duck.

More recently, in 1987's *The Living Daylights*, Bond fights side by side with the Mujahideen in Afghanistan, which is jarring for today's viewers, but the makers of James Bond movies are never trying to offend. The films are hugely popular around the world, but societal norms change, and attitudes from the past, uncomfortable for today's audiences, are preserved in these family-friendly movies. Alas, we must conclude that Bond is not like a bottle of Dom Perignon that gets better with age; rather, he's more like a bottle of milk left out in the sun.

The Bond films also reflect the tastes of moviegoing audiences at the time. From the 1960s to the 1980s, nobody could do action like Bond. But then, in the late 1980s, Hollywood started producing a slew of classic action movies, a trend that continued into the 1990s. Especially noteworthy is 1994's *True Lies*, where Arnold Schwarzenegger and James Cameron create the best Bond film ever made. It took the humor and kinetic action and outdid any gag or set piece Bond had done yet. It made the producers realize that the moviegoing public's expectation of action and excitement had changed over the decades. This resulted in the Bond producers ramping up the action in Pierce Brosnan's first Bond film, 1995's *GoldenEye*, which achieved both critical and commercial success.

Ian Fleming was a strange man who had some strange ideas. In one James Bond book, it is claimed that homosexuals can't whistle. What? While Fleming was an intelligence officer in World War II, he wasn't interested in creating a realistic spy; he wanted to create something fun and thrilling for people. That idea worked! According to Fleming, Bond has a Scottish father and Swiss mother (so Sean Connery could use his accent to his heart's content and it fit perfectly), but he was orphaned after they died in a skiing accident (the story of so many orphans). He was educated in the British private boarding school system and is, therefore, very much part of the British establishment. With that background, Bond is a poster boy for enough British clichés to satisfy the entire world. In 1977's *The Spy Who Loved Me*, Bond outsmarts and outfights his enemies while skiing, only to ski off a cliff and escape certain death when a parachute emblazoned with a Union Jack opens up. This amazing stunt was done for real, and while it's absurd, it's also thrilling and jingoistic in a harmless kind of way. Bond's popularity seems to grow as Britain's importance in the world shrinks.

THE BOURNE IDENTITY (2002)

It took America a long time to come up with a rebuttal to Bond that wasn't just a ripoff, but in 2002, Hollywood released *The Bourne Identity*, with Jason Bourne as the anti-Bond. This gritty, in theory, more realistic spy (which compared to Bond's heavy-drinking, promiscuous, luxury-car-driving, gadget-using escapades wasn't hard) caught the public imagination, and the film was so successful it launched a franchise with five films (four with Jason Bourne) and a TV show. Bourne has no high-tech gadgets, and while he globetrots around the world, he always ends up in a cheap hotel rather than a chateau. And he is far more dangerous than Bond, beating people to death with books or stabbing assassins with pens. Bourne doesn't have the inclination to seduce women, there are no racial stereotypes (unless you count a Russian assassin), and the bad guys are his old employers at the CIA. It's everything that action-hungry fans, turned off by the misogyny and casual racism from Bond, could want.

Just as *GoldenEye* was a response to Hollywood action films of the 1990s, Bond's producers once again took note, this time of Bourne's grit, and in 2006 Daniel Craig starred in his first Bond film, *Casino Royale.* Now the action is more muted, and the gadgets are at a bare minimum. We see Bond fall in love and cuddle his girlfriend. He is captured and tortured, but the villain has no lair in a volcano. Craig's Bond was the first one to have an overarching story to his five films. So, while in the first film there is clear DNA being shared with Bourne, by the fifth film, 2021's *No Time to Die*, we have been on this long journey with Craig so will accept that this Bond can meet a villain in a lair on a remote island, just like Roger Moore would have done in the 1970s in a safari suit. Right now, Craig's Bond feels peerless, but make no mistake, just as we now cringe at the casual sexism of Connery or roll our eyes at the ludicrous set piece of *Moonraker*, in twenty years' time, there will be something in these films that future audiences will scoff at.

ZERO DARK THIRTY (2012)

A real ex-CIA operative reviewing a Bourne film would point out that Bourne, despite the apparent harsh realism, is just as fantastical as Bond. While the spycraft is believable, the CIA doesn't have ninjas. And what is meant by that is best shown in the next film, *Zero Dark Thirty*. The film is the true story of the ten-year manhunt to find Osama Bin Laden after the 9/11 terrorist attacks. The film opens with a completely black screen with a genuine recording of a woman trapped in one of the Twin Towers talking to the operator, understanding that she is going to die. It is perhaps the most sober opening to a film ever. This isn't Hollywood; this is real. Filming was delayed because just as they were about to start, US Special Forces launched a raid in Pakistan and killed Bin Laden. So, the film now had to have a completely different third act.

The first act is a hard watch as we see the CIA using "enhanced interrogation" techniques (a euphemism for torture) on a member of Al Qaeda. These scenes caused huge controversy: Some saw their inclusion as making the case for torture because intel was eventually retrieved from the subject; others thought they were anti-torture as almost nothing came from brutalizing the victim. I would say, if both sides saw the scenes as supporting their point of view, the conclusions reached reflected the attitudes of the viewer rather than the filmmaker. Depictions of waterboarding and keeping prisoners awake with loud, heavy metal music are all accurate. So, too, are the bombings depicted, whether in Pakistan or London. Authenticity is enhanced when real news footage is intercut with movie scenes.

This film shows the genuine work that spies do. Much of their time is spent searching for clues and sifting through raw data until they find a pattern that indicates something of interest. If it's a person, they could be a link in the chain, a link field agents follow. If they are a prime target, special forces like the SAS or, in the case of Bin Laden, Seal Team Six will be sent to take them out. The ones doing the spying aren't the ones doing the shooting; they are two completely different skill sets and training people to do both would be a waste of time and money.

The final act of *Zero Dark Thirty* is the raid on Bin Laden's compound. At the time of filming, it was a secret mission so some of it is conjecture. In the real raid, one of the mission's helicopters did crash, which meant the team had to set demolition charges to destroy it, but the remains clearly showed a previously unknown stealth helicopter which had to be best guessed for the movie. It appears that in the real raid, Bin Laden was one of the first to die, but this is Hollywood, so he goes down last in the film. However, there's no slow-mo of the body being riddled with bullets, no soaring music, no triumphant high-fives over the corpse. These scenes were supervised by members of the Special Forces so are as accurate as possible in a Hollywood film.

At its core, *Zero Dark Thirty* has the same plot as a Bond film: a villain carries out an unspeakable act of violence which gets the world's attention. Spies hunt him down and there is a final shoot-out at the villain's secret hideout. But everything else couldn't be more different, and *Zero Dark Thirty* shows just how unrealistic both Bond and Bourne are.

BRIDGE OF SPIES (2015)

Another example of a realistic spy movie comes from Steven Spielberg with *Bridge of Spies*. Here we have Mark Rylance playing Rudolph Abel (a role that won him a Best Supporting Actor Oscar), a Soviet spy (who was English born) in America. He passes his secrets on not with any high-tech spy gadgetry, but with a hollow nickel that conceals his tiny pieces of paper. This is a true story, and this is what real spying looks like—no martinis or Aston Martins. Abel wouldn't last thirty seconds in a fistfight with Sean Connery, let alone James Bond. He is a quiet, insular person, everything he needs to be in his work. He's also an example of the "bad spy." Like a pirate or a gangster, he is doing harm not with physical violence, but by helping a foreign power with a diametrically opposing ideology. He wants to bring down the government, democracy, and the free market.

The film shows his capture and incarceration before we are introduced to the real hero of the movie, James Donovan, played by the ever-charismatic Tom Hanks. Donovan had the unenviable task of acting as the defense counsel for a foreign spy caught red-handed at the height of the Cold War. This is all true and, unsurprisingly, Abel is found guilty and imprisoned.

Fast-forwarding a few years to 1962, a downed U-2 pilot is in a Soviet prison and another American is caught in East Germany. Donovan is tasked with negotiating a prisoner exchange, Abel for the other two. The film all but spells out that spying during the Cold War was scaled up to an almost industrial level, an idea that was reinforced in the Bond films. Prisoner swaps at places like Checkpoint Charlie in Berlin were regular affairs. On this occasion the prisoner exchange happened at Glienicke Bridge, another regular site used for these swaps. The scenes in the film were shot at the actual bridge (it doesn't get more historically accurate than that), but simply saying that belies the Herculean effort required to get the paperwork in order. It took one person five months to obtain the necessary permits from twenty-three different agencies in order to film there.

Bridge of Spies is meticulous in its authenticity, with everything from the clothing to the story of the construction of the Berlin Wall carefully researched. Spielberg even kept the historically accurate terrible cold Donovan suffered while he was in Berlin. Generally, when people are sick in a Hollywood movie, it's an epic disease which will kill them; the illness is invariably part of the plot, but here we have an extra layer of suffering for a man who is already finding it hard, and haven't we all had to deal with that cold while we got on with the day job?

Because *Bridge of Spies* is a modest film, with a modest budget, and never had ambitions to be the biggest film of the year, it is rarely discussed and has now been largely forgotten. That's a shame as not only is it a very good historical reconstruction of events from the middle of the twentieth century, but it is, quite simply, a good spy thriller. And Spielberg did it without ever feeling the need to include an attractive blonde double-agent or an Aston Martin DB3.

RED SPARROW (2018)

Finishing off this section we come to a film that while fictional is an adaptation of a novel of the same name by a retired CIA operative. The film stars Jennifer Lawrence who in 2018 was one of the hottest properties in Hollywood.

The film revolves around Lawrence as Dominika Egorova, a Russian spy who has been to "Sparrow school." The concept of the "honey pot" goes back a long way. An attractive young woman sleeps with an important man who lets slip things during the pillow talk. Nobody walks away in this situation with much dignity.

So this is a very different film to the others in this chapter. Seduction as spycraft is a real tactic, and has proven to be quite effective and not just with men. In Berlin during the Cold War, the STASI (East German secret police) trained men to hook up with the women who were stationed in the Western parts of Berlin who acted as administrators and secretaries and therefore had access to all kinds of classified documents. These men would sometimes even "marry" these women with the STASI supplying fake priests to marry them. Some of these women even started families with these men only to find out years later the whole thing was a sham. This level of deception feels to me even worse than the affairs some female spies had with important men. If you feel like this is all a thing of the past, there was quite a scandal in the 2010s involving a woman called Anna Chapman who was trying to basically sleep her way into the Obama Administration.[6]

So, the element of seduction in the modern world in the movie is completely realistic, and as for historical accuracy that's it. While exactly what training these women receive is still a closely guarded secret, we know that none of them are seductresses/secret ninjas. We are back to the James Bond impossible archetype of hitman, spy, and seducer all in one. That just doesn't exist. Also, Lawrence gamely tries a Russian accent, but it's not great. In essence this film is *Black Widow* with bloodier violence, some nudity, and an R rating.

NOTES

1. Alfred W. McCoy, with Cathleen B. Read and Leonard P. Adams II, The Politics of Heroin: CIA Complicity in the Global Drug Trade (New York: Harper & Row, 2003), 385.

2. Jem Duducu, *The Romans in 100 Facts* (Gloucestershire, UK: Amberley Publishing, 2015), 48.

3. C. R. Pennell, *Bandits at Sea: A Pirates Reader* (New York: New York University Press, 2001), 253–82.

4. Jeff Guin, *Go Down Together: The True, Untold Story of Bonnie and Clyde* (London: Simon & Schuster UK, 2012).

5. Luciano Iorizzo, *Al Capone: A Biography* (Westport, CT: Greenwood Publishing Group, 2009).

6. Maria Berry, *Spycraft* documentary series, 2021.

Chapter 11

I Have a Dream?

The story of civil rights is a specifically American one. While there was, of course, racism in Europe, there were no laws prohibiting an affluent Black family from living where they chose or sending their children to whatever school they wanted. There were no whites-only restaurants in Paris or whites-only hotels in London. But like the next chapter on Vietnam, America's regular examination of this period of internal social change has made other countries of the world feel like it happened to them. The reality is that every country has a sad story of racial tensions and complex race relations with either indigenous or immigrant communities, but each story is different. The civil rights story is America's story, not the world's.

As we have so recently seen, racial tensions still exist in America today, highlighted by the new Black Lives Matter (BLM) movement. The difference between the films of this genre and those of the other chapters is stark. This subject is as serious and significant as it gets in America. As such, there are no comedies about the Civil Rights Movement or Black Lives Matter. And because much of this is within living memory, the attention to historical detail—the clothes, cars, and technology—are all 100 percent accurate. Some of these films are the most accurate to ever have been created by Hollywood, but that's not to say they are flawless or not without their own distortions as they attempt to tell complex stories in two hours.

First, let's examine a group of movies about these events as seen from the perspective of white people. There is a trope in Hollywood known as the "white savior," and it is not meant to be a compliment. The message of these films is that the solution to the problem was down to that white man over there. This may play well to a white audience, but it takes away from Black people the impetus, power, determination, and recognition of the solution from those who had considerably more on the line than anyone white.

MISSISSIPPI BURNING (1988)

This is the perfect example of a white-savior movie. This is an Oscar-winning film, directed by the respected British director Alan Parker. Gene Hackman, Willem Dafoe, and Frances McDormand are the three main cast members, and all were nominated for Academy Awards. All are phenomenal talents and, of course, all four are white.

The film is based around the true story of the FBI investigation into the disappearance and eventual murder of three civil rights activists in 1964. The three young men, two white, one Black, were attempting to increase Black voter registration in response to local Ku Klux Klan intimidation.[1] On this occasion, the white activists suffered the same fate as the Black one, and the movie itself is everything you could want from this story. It is well acted, serious, and a chilling look at institutional racism in the American South. But in its roughly two-hour run time it's hard to find any people of color. It meant well, but today it feels like the movie is looking in the wrong direction. *Mississippi Burning* was a big hit, with excellent reviews, but the times have moved on, and today it is largely forgotten.

GREEN BOOK (2018)

The Green Book of the title refers to a publication that listed hotels that did not bar Black people. Of the three white-savior movies under appraisal here, this is easily the weakest. It's the true-ish story of a small-time heavy called Tony Lip who was the driver/bodyguard for Dr. Donald Shirley, a well-known Black pianist, who was touring the South in the 1960s.

The film is shockingly trite for something to come out two decades into the twenty-first century. At several points in the movie, Lip bullies odious white racists into submission. Is this gratifying for the audience eyes? Maybe, but we all know that the racists won't be changing their ways just because one guy is bigger than the other guy. It's almost like it was made as a segregation movie for beginners: enough tension to qualify it as a drama, but nothing too shocking. It could be used in schools for a class on the Civil Rights Movement for twelve-year-olds.

This subject always gets the Academy's attention, but there are times when it is obvious the Oscar is awarded not because of the quality of the movie, but to show the world that Hollywood knows racism is, well . . . bad. Unbelievably, this film won three. Mahershala Ali (Dr. Shirley) won Best Supporting Actor, but Viggo Mortensen (the white guy) had been nominated for Best Actor in a leading role. So, in a movie about segregation, the Black man plays second fiddle to the white man.

TO KILL A MOCKINGBIRD (1962)

This is probably the most significant of the white-savior films. Based on the 1960 novel (of the same name) by Harper Lee, both the book and the film sent shockwaves through white America. To this day they are considered classics.

The story is told through Scout's child eyes as she watches her father Atticus defend a Black man accused of rape. Set in the Deep South in the 1930s, the result of the case is never in any doubt. A Black man accused of raping a white woman is so incendiary that even though we all know Tom couldn't have committed the crime, he is convicted.

The problem again is that the story is seen through the eyes of white people, and the noble grace exuded by Atticus (played by Gregory Peck to perfection in the movie and winning him an Oscar for his efforts) is pretty much the personification of the "white savior." The scene where the Black community stands up for Atticus as he leaves the courtroom tends to put a tear in the eye of the white viewer, but to the Black viewer, it is all too reverential for a man who failed. Saying that, if you want a white audience to engage, they need to anchor onto something, and far better than a hundred *Green Books*, *To Kill a Mockingbird* is still the best way to show a white audience that justice is not color-blind.

A TIME TO KILL (1996)

Sometimes there can be a strange rebuttal to movies made years earlier. In *To Kill a Mockingbird*, the shocking premise is the gross miscarriage of justice. We all know Tom Robinson is innocent, but the racist jury can't see beyond their prejudices. In *A Time to Kill* two crimes are committed: First, we see a Black child being raped and beaten, followed by the subsequent court case with the focus on the furious father, Carl Lee Hailey, played with all the fire you would expect from peak 1990s Samuel L. Jackson. When justice is not served, Hailey guns down the perpetrators in the courthouse in front of dozens of witnesses. Now we have a Black man we know is guilty, but guilty of murdering men who beat and raped his little girl. We are meant to feel that his vigilante justice is acceptable. He is badgered while being cross-examined and even says under oath, "Yes, they deserved to die, and I hope they burn in hell!"

Things are not looking good for Carl. Meanwhile, outside the court, there are two rival crowds, one composed of white supremacists and members of the Ku Klux Klan, and the other side, well, normal, decent people who are a mix of races. Molotov cocktails explode as punches are thrown. The tension is nail-biting.

This film is loud when *To Kill a Mockingbird* is quiet; this is violent when *To Kill a Mockingbird* is calm. But in the end, Carl Lee Hailey is found not guilty. There's a palpable feeling that he gets the justice Tom Robinson never got.

MALCOLM X (1992)

So, moving away from films that have problematic issues, let's turn to a Black filmmaker who doesn't always make a five-star movie but always has something to say, Spike Lee. Here, all the problems of authenticity evaporate. Spike Lee's desire to share Black history and culture to as wide an audience as possible is there to see in most of his films. He is never better than when picking at the façade of white privilege and bias, and he is capable of being both funny and shocking in the same scene. He often takes a topic we think we know something about, and then shows it to us from a different angle so we can think again.

Saying that, *Malcolm X* is a surprising film even for Lee. When it was first announced, everyone assumed he would bring his signature individualism to his first biopic, but what came out was a more than three-hour epic, which structurally and cinematically had more in common with *Lawrence of Arabia* or a sword-and-sandals epic of the 1960s than his 1989 film *Do the Right Thing*.

In the film we are taken from Malcolm X's early days as a small-time criminal who, when he eventually goes to prison, meets members of the Nation of Islam, a religious and political organization founded in America for African Americans. Malcolm X, then Malcolm Little, converts to Islam and describes his family name as one from a white slave master; because he can never discover his true family name, he replaces Little with X. Cassius Clay, who also became a member of the Nation of Islam, did the same thing and changed his name to Muhammad Ali.

There are sometimes accusations that the central characters of biopics are lionized, but Lee vociferously defended himself against any such charges. He correctly pointed out that had he wanted to portray Malcolm X as a saintly figure, he wouldn't have spent the first thirty minutes of the movie showing him to be petty, vain, and a troublemaker. Of course, the story of faith lifting a sinner from such an amoral background is an age-old theme, but to those who say this is a sanitized version of events, I think the evidence is there on screen to refute this.

From that start, we follow Malcolm's journey from ex-convict to political activist, to civil rights advocate. The whole story is told in chronological order, and while Lee's direction shines, and Denzel Washington is mesmerizing as Malcolm X, the whole thing could have been made at the same time as *Spartacus*, cinematically speaking. *Malcolm X* came out in the same year as Richard Attenborough's *Chaplin*, the biopic of Charlie Chaplin. Here was an old-school British filmmaker, in the business since the 1950s, producing work that tonally was the same as that of this exciting young New York director who first came on the scene less than ten years earlier. What Lee has alluded to in interviews, and what I would guess, is that by telling the story in a "standard" way, Lee was saying that Malcolm X is as important to history as Cleopatra or Lawrence of Arabia. The film was an act of reverence, sealed by the fact that at the end, he cuts to a school in South Africa where Nelson Mandela recites one of Malcolm X's speeches (although he does not include the controversial ending that raised so many headlines in the 1960s, "by any means necessary"). Mandela at this time had only just come out of prison and had yet to become president of South Africa. So, we come from a biographical account of one Black rights activist to the then living embodiment of Black rights. This was the ultimate stamp of approval.

I am a big fan of Spike Lee (although I admit some of his films are harder to love than others), but when my mother (who is American and remembers all of this from the time) and I went to see it on the big screen, we were the only two white people in an otherwise full theater.

BLACKKKLANSMAN (2018)

Continuing with Spike Lee, we jump forward more than twenty-five years to *BlacKkKlansman*, the true story of officer Ron Stallworth (played with incredible confidence by Denzel Washington's son John David Washington), the first Black police officer in Colorado Springs. And he decides to communicate with the local Ku Klux Klan, who convince him to join. As insane as this sounds, it's all true. Obviously, his cover would be blown if he attended the meetings in person, so a white officer was sent in his place. In the movie the white officer is played by Adam Driver, a Jewish man called Flip Zimmerman. In reality, the man was not Jewish and was known as Chuck.

This is one of several factual inaccuracies in the film. One practical change to the facts is that some of the correspondence was via letter, but that doesn't work on film, so phone calls are the main medium of communication. Making the Chuck character Jewish is an important creative choice as it shows that while the Ku Klux Klan is known to be racist against people of color, they are also rabidly anti-Semitic, so placing both men in potential peril. Before these events, Stallworth was sent undercover to see a speech made by a former leader of the Black Panthers (more on them coming up), but the relationship with a woman portrayed in the film is fictional, which also means the whole subplot around her and her safety are also a work of fiction.

It is, however, some of the most unbelievable moments that turn out to be true. When David Duke (a leading figure in the white supremacy world) went to Colorado Springs, Stallworth was assigned to him for personal protection and even cheekily got a photo with him. Proof that fact can be stranger than fiction. I find this one of the most impressive films on the topic of civil rights because there are times when it's genuinely funny, but the seriousness of the situation is never far away. It's easy to pile misery on top of injustice, but if there's too much, it can be too emotionally draining. With this movie, you get the point, empathize with the right people, but still have the emotional strength to get through the rest of the day.

There are other artistic choices that fly in the face of the facts. The events themselves occurred in the late 1970s, not in 1972 as portrayed in the film, but this allows Lee to put in a scene to wax lyrical about blaxploitation films and include the funkiest of songs for the soundtrack. Stallworth did have an afro, but it was not as large and luxurious as Washington's. Also, for the sake of the film, the Ku Klux Klan begin to suspect they are being watched by law enforcement. While many of the group are portrayed in the film as dumb, in reality, they were so stupid and incompetent nobody suspected a thing.[2]

Just as he did in *Malcolm X*, Lee throws in a shocking ending when he skips forward in time, in this instance to footage from the Charlottesville rally in 2017. We see here that white supremacy is still a blight in America, and people are still dying over this issue.

JUDAS AND THE BLACK MESSIAH (2021) AND DETROIT (2017)

The Black Panther movement comes front and center in *Judas and the Black Messiah*, which won two Oscars, including one for Daniel Kaluuya, playing the very young and charismatic deputy chair of the Panthers, Fred Hampton, who at the time of the events in the film was only twenty-one (although Kaluuya was thirty when filming). This Shaka King film is one of the newer films where an African American story is told largely by a Black cast and crew, with Black producers and writers. Putting it simply, the people who made this cared and wanted to tell the story. This was not just Hollywood cynically pushing out potential Oscar bait, like 2000's *The Legend of Bagger*

Vance, which may have starred Will Smith, but he was surrounded by a white cast, a white crew, and the white director, Robert Redford. If you haven't seen or heard of the film, there's a reason for that.

The film itself does not have Hampton as the protagonist, but Bill O'Neal, a small-time criminal who has struck a deal with the FBI to get his charges dropped in return for informing on Hampton. As Hampton was shot by the police in his own home in December 1969, this makes him a martyr to the cause, which would make O'Neal his Judas. The clever title reinforces that the central character is morally conflicted. O'Neal doesn't really want to be there and certainly does not want to see this firebrand speaker murdered, but at the same time, he is not a convert to the cause. It's one of the most morally complex stories about the various civil rights groups that made it to film. Comparing this to *Malcolm X*, where we know who we are rooting for, here, do we really want O'Neal to succeed? When we see the bloody results, there is no admiration for him. This is a genre that will make you sick to the stomach over the injustices portrayed.

Similarly, there's 2017's *Detroit*. This Kathryn Bigelow–directed movie depicts true events around a police raid on a hotel during the 1967 race riots in that city. The police brutality is shown in real time, with the middle hour reconstructing the hour-long ordeal the police inflicted on the hotel occupants. By the end of the movie, several people have been executed by the police. The film is incredibly powerful and more stomach churning and terrifying than the goriest of horror films. Both *Detroit* and *Judas and the Black Messiah* are almost too authentic, too honest. Both also have important roles for Black British actors (John Boyega and Daniel Kaluuya). In their retelling of these terrible moments in American history, the films are so brutally stark as to be almost unwatchable, but they are essential and important viewing, a testimony to the institutional racism in American law enforcement. They are films to endure and respect rather than rewatch.

ONE NIGHT IN MIAMI (2020)

After the sheer intensity of the previous films, let's lighten things a little. *One Night in Miami* is based on a 2013 play of the same name written by Kemp Powers. The film version is directed by Regina King (female directors are all too rare although they are slowly coming to the fore, but a Black female director is a real rarity), but unlike the other movies about real events, this one poses a what-if. It is February 25, 1964, and Cassius Clay has just won a title fight with Sonny Liston. Clay meets up with Malcolm X, Sam Cooke (the singer/ songwriter), and Jim Brown (an NFL player).

All we know is they met and that all played their roles in the Civil Rights Movement. Did they chat? Sure, but what was said has remained among the four of them. This is another example of a film "inspired by real events," so by now we know to treat such stories with caution from a historical perspective. But playwright Powers uses the circumstances to let his imagination run riot. He can foreshadow events that were to happen later, he can put words of encouragement or sometimes doubt into the mouths of icons. The entire play happens in one room where events are described, but King knows there's only so much you can do in a room and film is a different medium, so we get flashbacks and some slick camera work to keep the audience engaged in what is essentially a ninety-minute conversation.

One Night in Miami is a thought-provoking rather than a shattering viewing experience, but it's nice to have a civil rights movie where nobody at the end is dead or brutalized by an uncaring police force. It's a story about young men in their prime, with plans for the future . . . but we know that some of these young men will be gone too soon.

There is no footage proving that one night in Miami ever existed, or what the four famous men said to each other, but without such documentary evidence it allows Powers to use his creativity. And what he does with his play is an example of what happens with the so-called historical films in this book: The moment there's a conversation behind closed doors, the historical records do not record it. We know almost nothing of the conversations between Julius Caesar and Cleopatra, but as they had a child together, we know they must have meant something to each other, and it couldn't have been a relationship conducted in total silence. But as soon as they start chatting in the movies, it's speculation and as fictitious as Kemp Powers's play.

HIDDEN FIGURES (2016)

Again, keeping things a little less life-or-death, we come to the true story of three African American women working for NASA during the space race. The story was first highlighted in the book *Hidden Figures* by Margot Lee Shetterly.

I have worked with a number of engineering companies during my years as a business consultant in Britain, and the reality is they are all full of white men. That's not to say they are racist, but the biases of education and aspirations and role models have created an industry that does not attract women or people of color. It has also led to the shocking complaint I keep hearing from managers of engineering departments that, at the time of writing, 50 percent of Britain's engineers will be of retirement age in the next ten years. And Britain isn't the only Western nation to have this dangerous imbalance.

Therefore, millions have been spent to encourage both women and people of color to consider what is intellectually challenging, rewarding, highly skilled, and well-paid work.

Of course, representation is all important in the recruitment drive. If I never see anyone like me in a role, I assume it's not meant for me. Therefore, the importance of *Hidden Figures* showing not just women, but women of color actively engaged in the single greatest engineering endeavor in the history of humanity is uniquely powerful for these underrepresented groups.

The three women at the center of this story are Katherine G. Johnson (played by Taraji P. Henson), Dorothy Vaughan (played by Octavia Spencer), and Mary Jackson (played by Janelle Monáe). Katherine G. Johnson was ninety-eight when the film came out and was delighted with the movie. Henson said that portraying a person who was still alive added extra weight and pressure to the role for her.[3]

While the real-life story is inspirational, the movie is by the numbers (couldn't resist the pun). What these women did was incredible, and the way they have been written out of the narrative is a crime. The film itself is extremely reverential to our three heroines, although their supervisor Al Harrison (played by Kevin Costner) once again is an example of a white savior character. This is a little trickier because the women did work in a predominantly white environment, but Hollywood couldn't help framing the relationship with the old trope. Its heart is in the right place, but the direction is workmanlike, and the score swells when we need to feel something. The complexities of life are distilled into easily digestible Hollywood clichés. It's not bad, it just lacks the bite of *Judas and the Black Messiah* or the wit of *BlacKkKlansman* or the playfulness of *One Night in Miami*.

Hidden Figures is a solid, worthy biopic of three forgotten but important women. But, in truth, the historical facts are more surprising and inspiring than the film.

42 (2013)

A similar story to *Hidden Figures* can be found in *42*, the story of Jackie Robinson who, in 1947, became the first African American to play major-league baseball. Robinson was signed by the Brooklyn Dodgers, and unsurprisingly, caused a sensation. Indeed, in his first season he won Rookie of the Year, and in 1949, he was the first African American to win the National League's coveted Most Valuable Player award. In case you're wondering why the movie is called *42*, it was his jersey number. In 1997, Major League Baseball retired that number across all teams in honor of his memory.

Chadwick Boseman plays Robinson in this movie and is sensational in the role, but American sports films do not travel well. The film was well received in the United States and became Boseman's calling card, but the rest of the world had yet to discover his talent as Jackie Robinson is of little interest to a world where the most popular team sports are football (what Americans call soccer), cricket, and rugby.

The film, like *Hidden Figures*, shows the institutionalized racism blocking Robinson at every turn. Only his talent, moral fiber, and willpower see him through. While this is something of a Hollywood cliché, in Robinson's case it's all true. And also like *Hidden Figures*, both films were directed by white men. Again, it's a solid film with a great central performance. The film sticks close to established facts but again suffers from a cookie-cutter biopic format and lacks the urgency and earnestness we see in the best of this genre. Jackie Robinson is one of the greats of baseball; *42* is not one of the greats of cinema.

And speaking of standard format films, let's not forget musical biopics, which also follow a shockingly repetitive structure. What do Elvis Presley, Ray Charles, Johnny Cash, and the British rock band Queen have in common musically, culturally, ethnically? Not a lot, and yet if you watch *Elvis* (2022), *Ray* (2004), *Walk the Line* (2005), and *Bohemian Rhapsody* (2018), they are the same story: a troubled childhood, a stuttering start into music, initial rejection of their musical genius, then the rise and adoration before the cracks appear in relationships due to drink or drugs and a final redemption, all to a jukebox soundtrack of their greatest hits. Cut, print, send out to theaters and watch the money and Oscars come rolling in. Of course, there are colossal differences between a blind Black boy in America and a Parsi-Indian boy attending a British boarding school, but musical biopics have essentially the same predictable formula as sports biopics, and their three-act structure would make a lecturer in screenwriting proud.

SELMA (2014)

Moving away from the solid but not groundbreaking movies of that genre, we come to one that is important in so many ways. *Selma* is the true story of Martin Luther King Jr.'s 1965 march from Selma to Montgomery (in the state of Alabama) to secure equal voting rights, a plague that still blighted the American South a century after the Civil War.

While many of the stories told in the films listed in this chapter are, at times, ancillary to the Civil Rights Movement, here we see an event at the heart of it, led by the defining figure of that movement. But before we get into the history portrayed in the film, let's look at the history made by the film. There was a general feeling that the 2015 Academy Awards showed a consistent bias against people of color. This film would win an Oscar, but that was for the song "Glory." Its live performance on the night seemed less about that moment in 1965 and more a condemnation of the academy. *Selma* received a nomination for Best Picture as well as the song, but none of the acting talent or the director Ava DuVernay (again, that rarest of sights, a Black woman) were even nominated.[4] The other shocking fact is that for such an important person in twentieth-century American history, this was the first ever Hollywood-produced biopic about King. (I know. This is so counterintuitive I had to go away and double-check that fact.)

Hollywood is very proud of its liberal stance on most topics, but in this instance, it looked quite old-fashioned and, well, racist. Action was needed and the Academy admitted an influx of new members, mostly women and people from ethnic minorities. The result was a noticeable increase in the number of films produced by African Americans post 2015. *Selma* changed Hollywood.

The movie itself is a fastidious reproduction of those events. David Oyelowo does an incredible job of bringing to life one of the greatest orators of the twentieth century. When we hear King's speeches, they sound like a sermon; they have the same vocal pyrotechnics of a fiery Baptist minister because that was King's day job. To have a Brit, born in Oxford, sounding utterly convincing as this American icon shows how much care and attention went into not just re-creating the events of that march, but even the vocal coaching. Therefore, to look again at the controversy around the 2015 Academy Awards, for Oyelowo not even to get an Oscar nomination was a clear sign of how myopic the Academy had become (he was unlikely to have won as Eddie Redmayne picked up the golden statue that year for playing Stephen Hawking, and the Academy loves it when an actor plays a person with a disability).

Selma doesn't just focus on King's march; we also see things from President Lyndon Johnson's perspective too. The president is even mentioned in the famous "We March" speech, again lovingly re-created in the film. It also is that rarest of biopics because it shows the subject's flaws by laying out the facts and letting them speak for themselves. King was not perfect, so to recognize the flaws makes him more human and more relatable. The movie has its limitations, mainly to do with a modest budget, so there are times when the sweeping shots of crowds and the famous bridge scene aren't as crisp as they would be in a mega-budget blockbuster, but it's not for lack of trying or general attention to period detail. This is important and serious history, and the film treats it as such.

THE WOMAN KING (2022)

The Woman King is a terrible name for a great movie. The "woman" of the title is a member of the Agojie, a group of female warriors married to the king. They were an elite unit who fought in battles, just like any other military unit, but the fact that they were women caused much interest among Europeans who started describing them as Dahomey Amazons, a reference to the legendary Greek female warriors.[5]

I have been aware of their story for years and always thought what an interesting movie it would make, but I also knew that if better well-known European history had yet to get the Hollywood treatment, then a story about an extinct kingdom nobody but a few academics knew anything about was never going to make it to the big screen. That was until 2022, when it was announced that the story of these female warriors would indeed be made, with the cream of Hollywood's Black talent both in front of and behind the camera.

Of course, the story of a West African kingdom in the early nineteenth century has, technically, nothing to do with the twentieth-century Civil Rights Movement in America. But the making of the film absolutely does. After the *Selma* debacle at the Oscars, Black filmmaking was finally hot. Hollywood wanted to make amends, and the checkbook was open for stories about Black history. After years in development *Black Panther* made it to screens in 2018 and was a monster hit. Wakanda may be a fictional country, but it galvanized the African American moviegoing masses to flock to the cinema. It was the first non-Avengers movie for Marvel to gross more than $700 million domestically and would go on to make more than a billion dollars globally.

In *The Woman King*, Viola Davis plays the titular character with the name of Nanisca. How often do Black women in their fifties get to play an historical action hero? Never. It was the role of a lifetime for her, and she grabbed it with both fists and body-slammed the movie into submission. The whole film is a war cry of African American confidence.

The battles are kinetic and the acting is strong. The camera pans and zooms, letting us soak up a different time and place. We see an African civilization in its prime. No need for an imaginary Wakanda, this movie shows the world the truth, that Africa has had multiple powerful and complex civilizations to be proud of. Not every Black history story needs to be about slavery or civil rights or social injustice.

So how historically accurate is it? Well, for the first time in this genre, the answer is not very. And that is why this film makes it into this chapter— because only now, after decades of deferential Black-history storytelling have Black writers allowed themselves to cut loose. To hell with the facts, let's make a thrill ride where Black comes out on top. Two words hang together every movie in this chapter so far: the first is *earnest*; all these films have a deep sincerity to them. The other word is *serious*; none of the previous films are fun and carefree. In fact, some are so intense you might need a lie-down afterward. So why not make a film that eases down the throttle on the earnestness level and dials up the fun factor?

The fact is Dahomey was a traditional kingdom. The Agojie were part of a battle formation designed to conquer and control. Their king was an autocratic dictator who enslaved subject people. The Dahomey system was like that of the Roman Empire or Imperial China, and its politics are deeply unsavory to a modern liberal democracy like America. So how to deal with these uncomfortable facts? Ignore them.

While the film gets the look of the era mostly right, their firearms are missing; perhaps they had yet to acquire them although that is unlikely. And it is true that they trained with fire and thorn bushes (some African types are like natural barbed wire). All these things have a ring of authenticity about them. The real King Ghezo (played magnificently by John Boyega) was, however, a warmongering slave trader. Why they picked him rather than another, perhaps more easily adaptable, Dahomey ruler is unknown. So, he's completely repurposed to be the king who needs the guidance of Nanisca. He's likeable and just relatable enough to make him one of the "good guys."

The film created a cottage industry of new historical works on Dahomey. Check Amazon and you will see at least half a dozen books all coming out in 2022. As this book shows, it's important not to take any movie's historical interpretation of events as the gospel truth, but at the same time, it's great to see so many people picking up on this opportunity to add real historical veracity on the back of a crowd-pleasing film.

It's taken decades, but finally Hollywood has made a Black *Spartacus* or an African *Gladiator*. The topic is wholly new and refreshing, but the big, sweeping storytelling, using traditional storytelling tropes, are satisfyingly old-fashioned. Never before has there been an historical drama about Black warrior women (two of whom have a gay subplot), told with all the historical abandon and dedication to fun as *The Adventures of Robin Hood*.

NOTES

1. www.fbi.gov/history/famous-cases/mississippi-burning.

2. Julie Miller, "*BlacKkKlansman*: The True Story of How Ron Stallworth Infiltrated the K.K.K.," *Vanity Fair*, August 10, 2018.

3. Kara Harr, "'Hidden Figures': 10 of the Film's Stars and Their Real-Life Inspirations," *Hollywood Reporter*, January 30, 2017.

    4. Kevin Fallon, "The Whitest Oscars Since 1998: Why the 'Selma' Snubs Matter," *Daily Beast*, January 15, 2015.

    5. Maeve E. Adams, "The Amazon Warrior Woman and the De/construction of Gendered Imperial Authority in Nineteenth-Century Colonial Literature," *Nineteenth-Century Gender Studies* Issue 6.1, Spring 2010.

Chapter 12

'Nam

In the second half of the twentieth century, superpowers on both sides had nuclear weapons, so world wars such as were fought in the century's first half were no longer an option. The term MAD, Mutually Assured Destruction, applied and the implications were chilling. Instead, there were lots of proxy wars, mainly civil wars where the great powers picked a side believed to be amenable to their ideology and gave them money, weapons, and sometimes soldiers to fight their cause. This is the backdrop to the Vietnam War. The AK-47, designed by Mikhail Kalashnikov, was created for the Red Army. It is now the most mass-produced weapon in history, with more than 100 million (including variants) in circulation. It's on the flag of Mozambique and was the standard rifle of the Viet Cong. It is the very symbol of the Cold War.

Fighting in Vietnam started with French colonial forces in the 1800s. It would continue on into the twentieth century and flare up again after World War II. Culturally and strategically, the country had no interest to America . . . except that because the rebels in the north had pledged their allegiance to the communist powers, America felt a line had to be drawn to stop the international spread of communism. That line was Vietnam.[1]

The Vietnam War is a complex story. It's a little like those impenetrable wars in Europe that bore everyone when mentioned: the War of Austrian Succession or the Crimean War, anyone? Their causes are unfathomable. In the long history of conflict, Vietnam is not a key war. It didn't change the world; it didn't involve many countries. It has been made to feel more important to everyone on the planet because America is obsessed with the war they lost. Hollywood keeps ramming this conflict down our throats, and the quality of the moviemaking is generally so high we keep eating it up.

To understand the conflict in Vietnam we must understand nineteenth-century French imperialism, we have to work out which countries were incorporated into French Indochina, and we have to understand the complexities of the Cold War and the domino theory.[2] But putting all that to one side, America keeps returning to the war they not only lost, but one that tore their own society to pieces. The story of America's involvement in Vietnam is a tragic one, but it is a hugely fertile source for all kinds of movies including war dramas, surreal odysseys, and comedies. Sometimes other wars are used as an allegory for this one; sometimes it is used as an allegory for something else. For a war that didn't involve most of the rest of the world, it's surprisingly well known, in no small thanks due to Hollywood.

THE GREEN BERETS (1968)

The first film about Vietnam was made during the war and is considered to be one of the worst films about the conflict. It all started in June 1966 with a trip by John Wayne to South Vietnam. He was impressed by what he saw, particularly by the Special Forces he met, and so he decided to produce a film as a tribute to them. His resolve was reinforced by the growing antiwar protests in America. Wayne was never going to be a pot-smoking, long-haired hippie; he was an old-fashioned Republican, and he wanted to create something patriotic that supported the war effort. He wanted to make something like *The Sands of Iwo Jima*, except he was layering that kind of simplistic good guy/ bad guy formula over a morally complex situation where, if anything, the Americans were the bad guys.

When the filming of *The Green Berets* began in Georgia in 1967, Wayne was over sixty, playing a colonel. He was about twenty years too old for the role, not to mention that a colonel would certainly not have been in the thick of the action depicted. The Department of Defense was delighted to have John Wayne on its side, and having read the screenplay, knew it had a great propaganda piece on its hands. When the film came out, it was action packed and a modest financial success. And that's the best I can say about it. All the Viet Cong characters are horrific stereotypes. They are brutal and cruel while the Americans are noble and good. There is an American/Vietnamese love story, presumably included to deflect charges of overt racism. The central battle is loosely based on the 1964 Battle of Nam Dong on July 5–6, 1964, when a mixed force of Americans, Australians, and South Vietnamese troops fought off a force three times its size. But what happened in 1964 and what is portrayed on screen bear scant resemblance to each other. In general, it's historically accurate to say that the Americans did better in pitched battles with the Viet Cong or the NVA (North Vietnamese Army); after all, this was what soldiers are trained to do, but it had far more difficulty and a lot less success with Viet Cong ambush tactics in jungle terrain.

The Green Berets, a story of American superiority, was filmed largely in 1967 but didn't come out until 1968. In January of that year the news reports of North Vietnam's shocking success during the Tet Offensive made many

Americans believe the war was likely unwinnable. This was a misreading of the situation. The US military for years had been failing to track the Viet Cong in the country's jungles, but when they attacked multiple urban locations in South Vietnam, it was exactly what US forces wanted. The mass attacks caught the Americans by surprise and significant gains were made by the Viet Cong; that part was reported in the news. But the media failed to notice or chose not to cover that the Viet Cong had nowhere to hide in urban environments. Within weeks, all their gains had been reclaimed, and the Viet Cong were destroyed as an independent fighting force. By the summer of 1968, it was the NVA that accounted for most of the combat troops fighting the Americans.

The intertwining between *The Green Berets* and the actual war is fascinating. The Department of Defense gave Wayne its full cooperation. The uniforms, equipment, and vehicles are all accurate because they are what US forces were using at the time and had been loaned to the production. The department provided the filmmakers not only with everything they needed to make a convincing war film, it also allowed Wayne to film on an operational Army base. At one point he shouts out to soldiers doing exercises on a field; they aren't extras, they are real recruits bound for the real war. The moviemakers returned the favor to the Army: when they had finished filming in the mock-up of a Vietnamese village, it was used for training for soldiers going to Vietnam. So, unlike all the others in this chapter, this film is part of the story of the war.

CATCH-22 (1970) AND M*A*S*H (1970)

In 1970 a huge amount of time and money were invested in bringing the sensational bestseller *Catch-22,* an ingenious antiwar novel, to the big screen. Mike Nichols directed this film about World War II bomber crews, with Alan Arkin in the starring role as Yossarian. The book was so influential it made the phrase "catch 22" popular; it's still in use today. The book was critically acclaimed; the film was not. Audiences couldn't relate to that war being hell on earth when another war was going on, one the Americans were losing. *Catch-22* bombed at the box office, and critic reviews were lukewarm at best.

That same year also brought a much-lower-budget medical comedy set during the Korean War. For decades World War II had been a hot box-office ticket. Nobody made films about a conflict dubbed "the forgotten war." But when *M*A*S*H* came out, it did all the things *Catch-22* was trying to do only better. And while the film is set in the Korean War, everyone knew it was really about Vietnam. As a final insult to *Catch-22*, *M*A*S*H* won an Oscar for the Best Adapted Screenplay; *Catch-22* wasn't even nominated.

M*A*S*H is unique in that it takes what is usually one scene in most war movies and turns it into a feature-length film (and later, an equally successful TV series). The field hospital is not the sort of place that gets a lot of coverage in war films; it's quite often used as respite from the front or where the epilogue takes place. The helicopters and equipment are era appropriate, but the long hair and moustaches are not. *M*A*S*H* makes no attempt to conceal the fact that it's appealing to a 1970s audience even though the war took place in the 1950s. If the counterculture must go to war, it won't be picking up a rifle to kill, it will be picking up a scalpel to save lives.

The other unusual thing about *M*A*S*H* is it's a black comedy. In and of itself that was nothing new. I've already mentioned Chaplin's *The Great Dictator*, and there was also Buster Keaton's silent movie *The General*, as well as many others. But just as movies like *Easy Rider* and *Bonnie and Clyde* took simple stories and developed them into something dirtier and more dangerous, *M*A*S*H* did the same thing with the war comedy. The doctors are often the worse for wear (but still capable), the tents are filthy, and the bodies gush with red gore. It even has female nudity, and it was exactly what audiences wanted from a film depicting the US military in 1970. Is it a realistic view of battlefield surgery in Korea? Absolutely not. Can it tell us anything about the history of the Vietnam War? Nope. But what it does do is reflect the contemporary attitudes of ordinary Americans, which now included hundreds of thousands of veterans, many of whom felt abandoned on their return from war. The attitudes are 100 percent historically accurate; they're just accurate about a different war.

As I briefly mentioned in the chapter on the world wars, Hollywood sometimes does not get the credit it deserves for its mature look at America. The Vietnam War was a disaster, and the way some of the troops behaved was abhorrent. It's something best forgotten, but it isn't because America dissects its failings in films that people want to see. I would challenge all the countries around the world that criticize American jingoism to show me ten big-budget movies from their own film industry that depict their soldiers behaving appallingly in a war they lost. In fact, show me just one. There won't be any because there aren't any. When I talked earlier about a Chinese movie set in the Korean War, you may have thought I was picking on China as an easy target because everything there must be approved by government censors; there's no point making anything negative as it would never be released. While this is true, the Chinese are more than happy to criticize American films that show China in a less than perfect light (although to get Hollywood films released in China, these sorts of overtly critical films are barely made anymore). Iran criticized the movie *300* for being offensive to Iranians, a legitimate complaint, but how many Iranian films show the Iranian armed forces raping locals and losing a war? *Platoon* portrays it all, but you will never see anything like that in Iranian cinema. Same with India, Korea, Japan, and Russia. These countries only portray their soldiers as brave and their armies as victorious; foreigners are not to be trusted. Such simplicity is neither historically factual nor very interesting. America turned its back on *The Green Berets* more than fifty years ago, but the rest of the world is still making this film.

Perhaps only Germany beats America when it comes to an objective view of its recent history. It's one of the few countries that openly teaches its past flaws and celebrates the victims of an unspeakable regime rather than the soldiers who perpetrated the crimes. In conclusion, it's safe to say that Vietnam movies are some of the most mature films in the whole of Hollywood's history.

GOOD MORNING, VIETNAM (1987)

While *M*A*S*H* is a savage black comedy made about Vietnam, it's not exactly packed with gags; it's more a case of a few funny scenes and some gallows humor. Arguably the funniest Vietnam film is *Good Morning, Vietnam*, with Robin Williams playing Adrian Cronauer, who "inspired" the events portrayed. Cronauer is real and he really did become a popular DJ on American Forces Radio during the Vietnam War. The soldiers liked him because he played the tracks they wanted to hear, rather than government-approved country and other music that interested no one. As depicted in the film, he arrived in Vietnam from a posting in Crete, and he did witness the army censoring stories, standard practice on military news. He also taught English to local people, but he was not an improv comedy genius rattling out jokes at the speed of an M16 firing on full auto. He didn't fall for a local girl, and he didn't befriend a member of the Viet Cong. Pretty much everything in the film is made up. Also, it was set in 1965 when some of the songs Williams plays hadn't yet been written and recorded.

Williams, however, managed to improv his way to a Best Actor Oscar nomination. As it was a comedic role he was never likely to win, but giving people belly laughs about elements of the Vietnam War is a slice of comedy genius. We still get the antiwar commentary, but it's not as anxious as *M*A*S*H* because by now the war had been over for fifteen years, so the tone is more antiauthoritarian. In the film Cronauer is the free spirit being crushed by Army bureaucracy and inflexibility, and it's one of the first times we see things from a Vietnamese perspective. Tuan may be the enemy, but he's human; he's doing things for relatable reasons, and the scenes of the

English classes with local Vietnamese people are touching and warm and show how people want to connect. It's war that stops that need to reach out and communicate.

THE DEER HUNTER (1978), RAMBO: FIRST BLOOD PART II (1985), AND PREDATOR (1987)

Good Morning, Vietnam could be the funniest film about war ever made. It's also honest in that this was a comedy vehicle written especially for Robin Williams. *The Deer Hunter* is the exact opposite. Starring Robert De Niro, this movie cleaned up at the Oscars, winning five, including Best Picture, Best Director, and Best Supporting Actor for Christopher Walken. Notable by their absence in that list are De Niro and Meryl Streep. The two titans of acting were beaten to Oscars by relative newcomer Walken; that's how good he is in this movie.

The story revolves around a group of young men from a small town in Pennsylvania who go to Vietnam to fight in the war. My mother always refused to see it because she's from a small town in Pennsylvania, and her brother served in Vietnam (more on him later). The film was too raw for her, but it came out to ecstatic reviews and did very well at the box office.

An interesting thing about Vietnam films is that they are, in general, seen as prestige productions. They usually get nominated for Oscars and almost always do at least decent business at the box office, but unlike World War II, there are no "action romp" style movies. I don't think there will ever be a *Where Eagles Dare* type of film set in the Vietnam War; the tone just isn't appropriate. Perhaps the two films closest to the type are *Rambo: First Blood Part II* and *Predator*, a couple of odd choices you might think. *Rambo* first: The film is not set during the war. This is 1980s foreign policy wish fulfillment, where a Special Forces soldier gets to go back and fight it out all over again. Indeed, "Do we get to win this time?" is asked at one point.

The other film is *Predator.* This one is also not set during the Vietnam War (and not even set in the country). I'm confident no aliens were involved in the real fighting, but an invisible enemy that keeps ambushing highly trained soldiers in the jungle and picking them off one by one . . . well, it's not exactly a subtle allegory, although it is a fun film.

The issue I have with *The Deer Hunter* is that while its portrayal of small-town life in America is realistic (we are introduced to the characters during a lengthy wedding scene, just like the opening scenes of *The Godfather*), once they go to Vietnam, reality takes a hit, and the story becomes a strange nightmare version of the conflict. Where they are and what's going on is vague, but De Niro, wearing a bandana, looks undeniably tough using a flamethrower even though infantry flame units were rarely used in the war. Showing the Americans as destructive is appropriate, but is the scene realistic? No, it isn't. This is another example of something added because it looks amazing onscreen and is, presumably, a metaphor for all the napalm dropped by the Americans during the war. It is a sad fact that a greater tonnage of bombs was dropped on Vietnam, Cambodia, and Laos than all nations dropped in the entirety of World War II. The Americans really did try to bomb the local population back to the Stone Age, and it is estimated that about 20 percent of Vietnam still has unexploded ordnance buried in it today. About five thousand people a year die from accidentally detonated explosive charges left over from the war, and that means more Vietnamese have died since the war ended than Americans died during the entire conflict.

Of course, if there's one incident in *The Deer Hunter* everyone knows, it's the Russian roulette scene when De Niro and Walken are forced to put a revolver to their heads after being captured by the Viet Cong. As they play this game of death, the Vietnamese watch and bet on who is going to die. Just because the Americans did despicable things doesn't mean the NVA were the good guys, and it is absolutely true that the Vietnamese treatment of American POWs was terrible. International laws about the treatment of prisoners were ignored as the men were beaten and tortured and sometimes summarily executed. For American servicemen unlucky enough to get caught, the privations they experienced can be compared to those the previous generation of Americans went through under Japanese incarceration in World War II.

That said, there is no evidence or eyewitness accounts of the Vietnamese ever forcing POWs to play Russian roulette; but putting that to one side, the scene is about as tense as any you will ever see on film. If you don't know how it ends, you will be hanging on for dear life. It was rumored at the time that to make the scene believable Walken genuinely played Russian roulette on screen; he didn't, but you can see why the rumor stuck. Many believe it was this scene that won Walken the Oscar. It is an amazing piece of cinema, but it is a made-up piece of "history," and because this film otherwise has the veneer of realism, I am going to put it in the same category as *Braveheart*. *The Deer Hunter* feels authentic and it's an incredible watch, but there's no historical authenticity to it, something viewers are less likely to understand because of the quality of everything else in the film.

JACOB'S LADDER (1990)

If *The Deer Hunter* is a nightmare, then *Jacob's Ladder* is full-blown horror. True story: I had just been dumped and wanted to cheer myself up. I'd been meaning to see *Jacob's Ladder* so went to Blockbuster and rented the video (yes, it was that long ago), not knowing anything more about it other than it was a Vietnam film. Let's just say it did not improve my mood. The film opens in Vietnam with Tim Robbins (a man so tall he would have been the first guy shot) and his platoon going through a village when they all start having seizures and begin frothing at the mouth before being rushed to a field hospital. Next, we see Tim back in America, where he meets a nice girl and tries to settle down to normal life, but he keeps having horrific visions even when he's awake. It is a good, if allegorical, take on the mental traumas these men took home with them. Many of them had been drafted and had no option but to go. The average age of a combat soldier was just nineteen, and these teenagers returned home to be spat at and called "baby killer." This war had no winners; every side of it looks bad at some point. I won't spoil the ending, but this surreal journey is a powerful metaphor for what so many young men experienced. It's what *Taxi Driver* would have been had it been directed by David Cronenberg.

TAXI DRIVER (1976)

Which brings me neatly to *Taxi Driver*. De Niro plays Travis Bickle, a Vietnam veteran so damaged by the war that he can no longer function in normal society. When he goes on a date with a nice young woman, he takes her to a pornographic movie; the date does not go well. He wants to protect an underage prostitute played by Jodie Foster and ends up wearing his hair in a mohawk and going on a shooting spree in a brothel. This is a more literal take on the psychological trauma of war. I would suggest that no matter how good your mood is, you do not watch this back-to-back with *Jacob's Ladder*.

PLATOON (1986)

Only one man who served in Vietnam has directed a major Hollywood picture about the Vietnam War, and only one filmmaker has ever made a trilogy of movies about it. That man is Oliver Stone. Stone served in various units in Vietnam in 1967 and 1968 and was awarded, among other citations, a Bronze Star with a "V" device for valor and a Purple Heart with Oak Leaf Cluster (so he was wounded twice). He was not someone who shirked his responsibilities while serving his country.

From Vietnam Stone went to Hollywood where he carved out a niche as a writer. In 1979 he won the Oscar for Best Adapted Screenplay for *Midnight Express*. From writing he moved to directing two poor horror movies. (One called *The Hand* starred Michael Caine as a comic book artist who loses his writing hand. A new one is attached and it comes alive and starts killing people. How Stone could make that after winning an Oscar is anybody's guess, although by his own admission he was doing a lot of drugs in the 1980s.) He also wrote the screenplay for 1983's *Scarface* and then, finally. got into his directorial groove with 1986's *Salvador*. It is an utterly bleak, unrelentingly honest portrayal of the civil war in El Salvador. As soon as he made that film and before it was released, he was working on his dream project: a movie inspired by his experiences in Vietnam. For this, he brought together a group of young actors and put them in a boot camp run by Dale Dye (who served multiple tours in Vietnam). Then he adapted *Faust* and thrust the idea of a good mentor and a bad mentor onto a young soldier who must choose which sergeant's advice to take. Will it be the wise and kindly Elias, played by Willem Dafoe, or the scarred god of war Barnes, played by Tom Berenger? The young soldier in the middle was played by Charlie Sheen.

Platoon is low budget; the napalm strike flown in by jets is more implied than shown. The film is largely troops trudging through jungles, no need for intricate sets and endless special effects. The film graphically portrays the tensions of search and destroy missions (later rebranded by military policy advisers to sound less aggressive as "sweep and clear"). The soldiers come into the village looking for trouble. Everyone is a suspect; there is no due process. The soldiers commit multiple crimes. Young Vietnamese men are found hiding and are killed by grenades. Sheen looks on in horror as does another young face in the platoon: blink and you'll miss Johnny Depp.

Platoon shows the day-to-day of infantry patrols in Vietnam. There are no mistakes with equipment, no made-up history. The film feels real because it's made by men who were there. Both Dye and Stone had to walk away from the set after the filming of the village scene; it was that traumatic for them. While the Faustian conceit may be artificial, this loose narrative plot allowed the audience to experience the terror of a nighttime firefight, the enemy wraith-like shadows, with their instantly recognizable AK-47s with the distinctive curved magazine with Elias creeping through the underground tunnel network regularly used by the Vietnamese to evade American patrols. Sheen's character is the rookie who is both the audience's and Stone's proxy. This feels real because Stone was re-creating his own memories. As a result, the film could be the most realistic depiction of history in this entire book.

The decision to use Samuel Barber's *Adagio for Strings* may seem an odd choice. It is, after all, a classical piece of music as opposed to something by the Rolling Stones or Jimi Hendrix, but this mournful piece of music played at several points in the movie takes a disturbing scene and rips it into beautiful despair. Its emotional heft is raw and uncompromising as it lays bare the realities of war and asks the audience to judge what it has seen. It is a truly poetic orchestra of emotion that enhances every scene in which it is played.

The film was a huge hit and won four Oscars, including Best Picture and Best Director. As a child I saw the poster of Elias on his knees, his arms stretched up to heaven with the tagline "the first casualty of war is innocence" (which I misread as "the first casualty of war is innocent" a subtle differentiator and probably just as true as the official version). It was the late 1980s, and all these Vietnam films were coming out to acclaim, but I couldn't see any of them as they were all rated 15 (R in America). I asked my mother why they couldn't make a PG version of Vietnam. I will always remember her response: "Some wars don't have a PG version." She was right. All that said, I did manage to play *Platoon* the video game, which bears little resemblance to the film. I didn't know that, but I really enjoyed it.

BORN ON THE FOURTH OF JULY (1989)

Oliver Stone was already well respected in Hollywood, but now he had two Oscars and was seen as the nation's authority on the war. He was offered almost anything he wanted to make another Vietnam film, so three years later, *Born on the Fourth of July* came out. Stone showed his serious intentions by telling a completely different story. Rather than doing another version of his first film, he made one that was less about combat (already done that very well), and more about the postwar impact on individual soldiers. This time he wanted to show the lasting effects of the war, how some men carry their wounds unseen, while others have to live with physical disabilities and pay the price for the rest of their lives.

The film starred Tom Cruise, who plays the real Vietnam veteran Ron Kovic. The young Kovic sees a Marine at his school give a talk saying the military can make you a real man. The Marine is resplendent in his dress uniform; everything about him is impressive, and Kovic is hooked. This is an example of someone (representing about half the country) who saw no shame in fighting for their country's freedom against the perceived spread of the communist threat. Kovic goes to Vietnam, where he enjoys the fight. Not all men are traumatized by war; some thrive in it, and Kovic is one of those men. But then he takes a round in the back during a firefight. He is dragged to safety and undergoes surgery back in the United States, where he is told that his spinal cord has been severed and he'll never walk again. Kovic's "can do" attitude will not accept this, and he gets better and better using his crutches, but his legs are still useless. He goes through a period of deep depression and gives up, feeling his country has given up on him.

Over time, Kovic's sense of futility turns into anger, and he becomes one of the long-haired antiwar protestors he once despised. Now he uses a wheelchair and goes on marches. It's all true, and Kovic was there on set to advise. At the end of filming, he gave Cruise his Bronze Star for his honest portrayal. I don't know this for a fact, but I would guess that meant more to Cruise than any industry award. Good job too, because while Cruise was nominated for a Best Actor Oscar and considered to be a frontrunner, he lost out to Daniel Day-Lewis for *My Left Foot* (Kenneth Branagh was also in the running for *Henry V*).

The film was a major change of direction for Cruise. Mr. *Top Gun/Cocktail/Rain Man* was now lying in his own urine with a beard and wild hair. It was a Cruise performance such as we had never seen before. The film won two Oscars, including a second Best Director Oscar for Stone.

HEAVEN & EARTH (1993)

So, after these two successes there was talk of the trilogy. The world was at his feet; Stone could have anything he wanted for a third project. But once again, he did not want to repeat anything he had done previously. He had said everything he could about the American experience in the war, so what was the angle? The answer was a bold one, just as bold as showing the rehabilitation process of a wounded soldier. He decided to tell the true story of a young Vietnamese woman who had struggled through the war. It was a noble idea, except Stone had never before had a female protagonist in a film; indeed, most of his films and scripts were overtly masculine.

In 1993 we got to see the end result in *Heaven & Earth,* starring Hiep Thi Le as Le Ly. Like *Born on the Fourth of July*, Stone took someone who had written a book about their experiences, but their story was not well known. There is nothing half-hearted about this movie. Stone was trying his best, and Hiep Thi Le, who had to carry an entire Hollywood production on her shoulders, is compelling throughout. Tommy Lee Jones plays the Marine she marries, and he is excellent in the role. The problem is that Stone is the wrong man to tell this story. Had it been given to a different (female?) director, they would have found the right pacing for it. It is by no means a bad movie and it is beautifully shot, with care and attention taken over everything, but the film is clearly the weakest of the three. It sank without a trace at the box office. Saying that, Oliver Stone had left us with an amazing body of work around the war. Two of the films are classics; the third film is a solid film. He is the cinematic master of this war.

TROPIC THUNDER (2008)

After looking at a filmmaker who experienced the war, let's take a look at the world of Hollywood make-believe with the comedy *Tropic Thunder*. The plot revolves around a bunch of Hollywood actors who want to make a super-realistic Vietnam war film and are dropped off in the jungle to film it "guerrilla style." What they don't know is they've been dropped into the territory of a dangerous drug gang, so the guns being fired at them are real. It's a case of Hollywood merges with real drama, with hilarious results. It's a basic setup that's been used loads of times, and you either get onboard for this loud, crass comedy with Ben Stiller as both star and director, or you don't. Is it puerile, with offensive jokes and a lot of shouting? Yes, I find that funny, and as it was a big hit, so do many other people, but I respect the opinion of those who didn't.

Regardless, alongside all the fart jokes and explosions, there are some very clever meta criticisms of Hollywood going on. Tom Cruise (again playing against type) is a fat, balding, utterly foul-mouthed movie producer called Les Grossman. He is a vile and angry man who thinks fury will fix every problem. Apparently Stiller and Cruise, who had both been in the business for years, based it on someone they knew, so while it's played for laughs, it's probably closer to the truth than any of us realize.

Stiller apparently got the idea for *Tropic Thunder* when he was filming Spielberg's *Empire of the Sun*. So, we have an actor in a war film planning another war film about how Hollywood always messes up war films. That sound you can hear is that snake eating its tail again. The film starts with a bunch of fake trailers to set the scene for what type of actor each of the characters is, and they are so perfect you can genuinely imagine those trailers being brought up in pitch meetings.

Ben Stiller may be the literal star of the show, but he is upstaged by Robert Downey Jr. (who in the same year starred in *Iron Man*, so that was definitely his comeback year). Downey Jr. plays Kirk Lazarus, a super intense Australian actor (obviously based on Russell Crowe) who is so dedicated to his role in the film that he had makeup for his character surgically added to his skin. Yes, we have a white man doing blackface, and yet he was nominated for a Best Supporting Actor Oscar for this role. (For *real*! This is not a joke.)

At one point Lazarus has a discussion with Ben Stiller's character, who tried to branch out from his action roles to do a heartfelt drama called *Simple Jack* that flopped and was utterly derided. Lazarus's advice is a completely accurate portrayal of Hollywood's views on neurodiversity.

Tropic Thunder then is a surprisingly smart film about Hollywood's attitudes about a number of complex issues, including the Vietnam War. It's also gorgeously shot. If you want to put your brain in neutral and fill your face with popcorn, then sit back and enjoy it.

DA 5 BLOODS (2020)

A lot of what has been discussed so far has concentrated on white men, but the reality was that during the Vietnam War, the draft disproportionately affected young Black and Hispanic men, with whites using their connections to escape to Canada or find doctors who would help them fake injuries. Let's look at that with *Da 5 Bloods*, directed by Spike Lee. It had a limited theatrical release due partly to the fact that COVID-19 was raging around the world and partly because it was a Netflix film. When it came out, it was so relevant to the situation in America that the movie felt like it had been made just a day earlier.

The organization Black Lives Matter has been around for years, but in 2020 it got a whole new level of attention after the deaths of Breonna Taylor, George Floyd, and Rayshard Brooks. So, to have a film about Black people that has several scenes with Black Lives Matter activists was electrifying at the time.

Da 5 Bloods is the story of a squad of Black soldiers both during the war and today. They are going back to Vietnam to find the gold they lost fifty years ago. It's a chance for the characters to atone and for Lee to educate the audience about the Black experience during the war. Delroy Lindo is phenomenal as a man slowly crumbling once he returns to the place that has haunted him over the decades. Narratives that take place fifty years apart would usually have a young cast and an older one. The trouble with that is the audience can't always work out who is who in the older roles. So, to stop that confusion, Lee decided to have the older actors play their young selves. You either go with it or you don't. The problem with that decision is compounded by the fact that Chadwick Boseman, playing Stormin' Norman Earl Holloway, dies during the war, so now we have this young man surrounded by, to be blunt, old men all pretending to be the same age. I understand the decision, but I found it jarring. Also, when you consider that the soldiers doing the fighting were generally in their teens or early twenties and Boseman is the youngest man there and he's still over forty, we are weirdly back to *The Green Berets* and men being way too old to be in the conflict portrayed onscreen.

Like almost all of Lee's other films, the focus on African American history is razor sharp and details are well researched. Everything looks correct, but the tactics are there to tell a story rather than to accurately re-create the Vietnam War. Lee isn't Stone: His goal is to make a movie about the Black experience in the war rather than a 100 percent accurate reproduction of combat in the jungles of Vietnam.

Another issue is that the film makes it clear that Boseman's character is not just a good squad leader, he is one of the greatest warriors in history, an unfeasibly brave man who is able to turn a firefight to his advantage because of his tactical brilliance. This is a great idea for a character, but Lee is more interested in social commentary than fighting, so although we keep being told how great this soldier is, we don't see him do anything that deserves those accolades.

I don't want to be too tough as this was one of Boseman's last roles, and at the time of filming he knew he had terminal cancer. He is a talent that was taken from us too soon. As so many Vietnam films are, this one is beautifully shot, and the footage tells us that there was always more to this stunning country than the war we dwell on. By changing the aspect ratio as they drive into the jungle-covered mountains, Lee leaves us gasping as the magnificent horizon stretches out in front of us. Many of the Vietnam films are from the 1970s and 1980s; Lee shows what the twenty-first century can add to intelligent filmmaking.

FULL METAL JACKET (1987)

My favorite ending to a film may be the one in *Scarface*, but my favorite opening is one in a Stanley Kubrick film. After showing everyone how to make the perfect horror film in 1980's *The Shining*, Kubrick showed us how to make the perfect war movie in *Full Metal Jacket*. The opening scene moves from young men having their heads shaved (to a country song called "Hello Vietnam") to a barracks with the young recruits standing by their bunks as Gunnery Sergeant Hartman walks slowly and purposefully around the room, verbally assaulting everyone in a perfect mixture of hilarious roast and pure malevolence. The sergeant is played by R. Lee Ermey. He had been brought in to coach the actor who had the role, but Ermey kept coming up with better and better ideas, so Kubrick brought him on to do the role instead.

Most of the scene is done in one continuous take, and Ermey is mesmerizing. The first half of the movie is there to show how military training techniques are designed to grind down the individual before building him back up as part of a fighting unit. It is unfortunate that young men had to go through this, but it is a necessary experience millions have had to endure to be ready for combat. By the mid-1980s, Kubrick had decided he wasn't going to travel far from his home in England, so the early scenes of recruits marching around in fields and on roads have a distinctively English feel for allegedly American locations.

The second half of *Full Metal Jacket* is set during the Tet offensive in Huế. For these scenes, rather than using Thailand or the Philippines (the two usual locations for Vietnam War films), Kubrick chose that obvious other location, the Docklands in London. To be fair, the fighting in Huế was urban combat, and at the time, the Docklands was the largest building site in Europe, so the two matched surprisingly well (with the addition of some palm trees to create that tropical vibe as opposed to that of a rainy October in London).

The film culminates in the squad getting pinned down by a sniper. The shooter is lethal and blood runs on the streets of London . . . I mean Huế. However, when the soldiers finally corner the sniper, they discover it's a teenage girl, who goes down fighting. One highly motivated teenage girl was able to terrorize a whole squad of US Marines, a memorable image to leave the audience with. Despite the unusual choice of location, Kubrick, as usual, has done his homework and then some. The training is accurate because the sergeant doing it is someone who did it in the 1960s (Ermey), and the battle is realistic because all the actors are wearing the correct uniforms and using appropriate equipment. Although it is not based on any specific incident, the scene with the sniper is intimate and believable.

I sat down with my uncle (the Vietnam veteran) to watch *Full Metal Jacket*, both of us for the first time. When I asked him at the end how realistic it was, he paused briefly before replying, "Not enough cursing." I asked him what he thought was the most accurate depiction of Vietnam, and he didn't hesitate in telling me it was Francis Ford Coppola's *Apocalypse Now*.

APOCALYPSE NOW (1979)

Much has been said about that film. Indeed, Coppola's wife made one of the best documentaries ever made about making a movie called *Hearts of Darkness: A Filmmaker's Apocalypse*, and it seems that to capture the scale and insanity of the Vietnam War it was necessary to wage war and go crazy. To quote Francis Ford Coppola himself at Cannes during the first screening in 1979, "My film is not about Vietnam, it is Vietnam."

Martin Sheen certainly committed to the movie by having a heart attack and then, captured on film, a drunken breakdown in all its visceral intensity. And that's how the film starts! When Sheen punches the mirror and ends up covered in a blood-drenched bedsheet, it's because he cut his hand for real. That's his own blood on the sheet. They only did one take.

Coppola initially had the idea to take the actors to Vietnam while the war was still on, to make it extra real, to give it authenticity. This was deemed unfeasible on the grounds that it's a war, and they have a habit of being unpredictable, along with a reputation for being hazardous to health. *Apocalypse Now* is based on Joseph Conrad's *Heart of Darkness,* a late-nineteenth-century novel that was a condemnation of the Belgian government's treatment of the people who lived around the Congo floodplain. It has absolutely nothing to do with a war on another continent sixty years in the future, featuring technology unimaginable at the time. And yet the basic story of traveling down a river, each part of the journey revealing more and more of man's inhumanity to man, fitted the situation in Vietnam perfectly.

Everyone knew that principal photography was going to take a while, and shooting began in March 1976 in the Philippines. To save money and ensure realism, the helicopter gunships are real and were in service, so there were times when they flew off mid-shoot to fight rebels in the mountains. In May, the set was hit by a typhoon and nearly 80 percent of it was destroyed. That wasn't Coppola's fault, but production and filming went on and on to the point where one industry trade paper ran the headline "Apocalypse When?"

In the end it took 238 days of principal photography to get the film in the can. Then began the mammoth task of editing. Some films are tightly scripted, with numerous storyboards; this one was not. There can be no doubt that the film was created/saved in the editing suite as the hours and hours of footage were beaten into some semblance of a narrative. No other film in this book had such a labored journey to the screen, but it got there in 1979. It should have failed but it didn't. The soundscape it created was overwhelming. The visuals are some of the most beautiful ever put on film. The scope is so gigantic Cecil B. DeMille would be impressed.

But because of its unwieldy editing process there are at least four versions. There is the original theatrical release which runs at two hours twenty-seven minutes. Then, in 2001, there was *Apocalypse Now Redux*, which when I saw it for the first time in the cinema with surround sound and a massive screen, I realized I had been watching the Diet Coke version on my home TV. That one is three hours thirty-three minutes long. Then there's *The First Assembly*, which can occasionally crop up on bootlegs; this one is four hours and forty-nine minutes long. Most recently, in 2019, and judging by its name, there is the very last version, called *Apocalypse Now Final Cut*, which is three hours and three minutes long. Which one should you watch? How long do you want to watch a movie?

The point about the film is that everything is real. It was hard to make, and it is battle scarred and weather beaten. It may be about a fictional mission to track down a fictional colonel, but it has a core of truth about it. If you want to see the insanity and brutality of war, this is the film that personifies it. At least, that's what my uncle thought, and he was there.

NOTES

1. Ken Burns, *The Vietnam War*, documentary series, 2017.
2. Ibid.

Conclusion

I would have loved to have included so many other movies, but you probably wouldn't have read a book that was double the length. My choices were made to illustrate the truth behind the Hollywood fantasies and are not intended to be a definitive guide.

Hollywood is there to take your money and entertain. If it has done a good job, we do not regret the price of admission and the ridiculously expensive popcorn. If we happen to get some genuine facts along the way, that's icing on the cake, nothing more. Hollywood does not check its facts, and its reach is far further than our history teachers in school. And while that sentiment is fine if the movie is about a superhero or the far future, it can become a problem when real people are brought in from history not to tell their story, but to tell a story movie moguls think will fill a theater.

This desire to entertain can lead to distortions of real events that everyone should know more about. The reality is more people will watch a film than will ever read a nonfiction book on the same topic, but to chastise Hollywood for doing what it does is like saying McDonald's is the cause of obesity. We have to take personal responsibility. If we watch a film that seems to be about real history, we can enjoy it, maybe take a moral message from it, and then, perhaps read something about it to determine what really happened. If we don't, that's on us, not Hollywood.

And, in the words of an animated pig,

"That's all folks!"

Bibliography

Abramovitch, Seth. "Oscar's First Black Winner Accepted Her Honor in a Segregated 'No Blacks' Hotel in L.A." *Hollywood Reporter*, February 19, 2015, https://www.hollywoodreporter.com/movies/movie-news/oscars-first-black-winner-accepted-774335/.

Adams, Maeve E. "The Amazon Warrior Woman and the De/construction of Gendered Imperial Authority in Nineteenth-Century Colonial Literature." *Nineteenth-Century Gender Studies*, Issue 6.1 (Spring 2010).

Alcott, Louisa May. *Little Women*. New York: Penguin Classics, 1989.

Anonymous. *The Anglo Saxon Chronicle*. Whitefish, MT: Kessinger, 2012.

Anonymous. *Cabala, Mysteries of State*. London British Library, 1694, 2011 (online).

Associated Press. "Iranians Outraged Over Hit Movie '300.'" March 13, 2007, https://www.nbcnews.com/id/wbna17599641.

Austen, Jane. *Emma*. New York: Penguin Classics, 2003.

Austen, Jane. *Pride and Prejudice*. New York: Bantam Classics, 1983.

Austen, Jane. *Sense and Sensibility*. Oxford: Oxford University Press, 2019.

Baring-Gould, W. S., and C. Baring Gould. *The Annotated Mother Goose*. Bramhall House, 1962.

Barker, Juliet. *Agincourt: The King, the Campaign, the Battle*, new ed. London: Abacus, 2006.

Beevor, Anthony. *Russia: Revolution and Civil War 1917–21*. London: W&N, 2022.

Benbow, Mark E. "Birth of a Quotation: Woodrow Wilson and 'Like Writing History with Lightning.'" *Journal of the Gilded Age and Progressive Era*, January 10, 2011, https://www.cambridge.org/core/journals/journal-of-the-gilded-age-and-progressive-era/article/abs/birth-of-a-quotation-woodrow-wilson-and-like-writing-history-with-lightning/320F8624D6FD74BE15443D8032FC7625.

Berry, Maria, director. *Spycraft*. Netflix, 2021.

Billington, Michael. "Henry V" (review). *The Guardian*, June 14, 2003.

Booker, Christopher. *The Seven Basic Plots: Why We Tell Stories*. London: Bloomsbury Continuum, 2019.

Brickhill, Paul. *The Great Escape*. London: W&N Military, 2000.

Brontë, Charlotte. *Jane Eyre*. New York: Penguin Classics, 2006.

Brontë, Emily. *Wuthering Heights*. New York: Penguin Classics, 2002.

Brosnan, Peter, director. *The Lost City of Cecil B. DeMille*. Random Media, 2016.

Burns, Ken, director. *The Vietnam War* (PBS documentary), 2017.

Caesar, Julius. *Commentaries on the Gallic Wars*, translated by Roscoe Mongan. London: Hardpress, 2018.

Carson, Annette. *Richard III: The Maligned King*, reprint ed. London: The History Press, 2009.

Chang, Iris. *The Rape of Nanking: The Forgotten Holocaust of World War II*. New York: Basic Books, 1997.

Collins, Nick. "How Wuthering Heights Caused a Critical Stir When First Published in 1847." *The Telegraph*, March 22, 2011, https://www.telegraph.co.uk/culture /tvandradio/8396278/How-Wuthering-Heights-caused-a-critical-stir-when-first -published-in-1847.html.

Cooper, James Fenimore. *The Last of the Mohicans*. New York: Midden, 2022.

Douglas, Kirk. *I Am Spartacus!: Making a Film, Breaking the Blacklist*. New York: Open Road Media, 2012.

Duducu, Jem. *The Busy Person's Guide to British History*. Seattle: KDP, 2013.

Duducu, Jem. *Deus Vult: A Concise History of the Crusades*. Gloucestershire, UK: Amberley Publishing, 2014.

Duducu, Jem. *Forgotten History: Unbelievable Moments from the Past*. Gloucestershire, UK: Amberley Publishing, 2016.

Duducu, Jem. *The Romans in 100 Facts*. Gloucestershire, UK: Amberley Publishing, 2015.

Duducu, Jem. *Slinkys and Snake Bombs: Weird but True Historical Facts*. Gloucestershire, UK: Amberley Publishing. 2021.

Duducu, Jem. *The Sultans: The Rise and Fall of the Ottoman Rulers and Their World: A 600-Year History*. Gloucestershire, UK: Amberley Publishing, 2018.

Eveleth, Rose. "The History of Cone-Shaped Medieval Princess Hats." *Smithsonian*, December 30, 2013, https://www.smithsonianmag.com/smart-news/medieval-cone -shaped-princess-hats-were-inspired-by-mongol-warrior-women-180948217/.

Fallon, Kevin. "The Whitest Oscars Since 1998: Why the 'Selma' Snubs Matter." *Daily Beast*, January 15, 2015, https://www.thedailybeast.com/the-whitest-oscars -since-1998-why-the-selma-snubs-matter.

"First Black Oscar Winner Honored with Stamp." *Augusta* (GA) *Chronicle*, January 26, 2006, https://www.augustachronicle.com/story/entertainment/movies/2006/01 /27/mov-49935-shtml/14777279007/.

Frank, Anne. *The Diary of a Young Girl*. New York: Bantam, 1997.

Gachman, Dina. *George Lucas's Blockbusting: A Decade-by-Decade Survey of Timeless Movies Including Untold Secrets of Their Financial and Cultural Success*. New York: HarperCollins, 2010.

Gregory, Philippa. *The Other Boleyn Girl*. New York: Scribner, 2001.

Guin, Jeff. *Go Down Together: The True, Untold Story of Bonnie and Clyde*. London: Simon & Schuster UK, 2012.

Harr, Kara. "'Hidden Figures': 10 of the Film's Stars and Their Real-Life Inspirations." *Hollywood Reporter*, January 30, 2017, https://www.hollywoodreporter.com/lists/ hidden-figures-10-films-stars-real-life-inspirations-964715/.

Harvey, Brett, director. *Inmate #1: The Rise of Danny Trejo*. Universal Pictures, 2019.

Holburn, Vanessa. *The Amritsar Massacre: The British Empire's Worst Atrocity*. London: Pen & Sword, 2019.

Holland, Tom. *Persian Fire*, new ed. London: Abacus, 2006.

Iorizzo, Luciano. *Al Capone: A Biography*. Westport, CT: Greenwood Publishing Group, 2009.

Kazhdan, Alexander, ed. *De Ceremoniis*: *The Oxford Dictionary of Byzantium*. New York and Oxford: Oxford University Press, 1991.

Keneally, Thomas. *Schindler's Ark*. London: Hodder and Stoughton, 1982.

Lee, Harper. *To Kill a Mockingbird*. New York: Harper, 2015.

MacLean, Alistair. *The Guns of Navarone*. New York: HarperCollins, 2019.

Marlantes, Karl. *Matterhorn: A Novel of the Vietnam War*. New York: Atlantic Monthly Press, 2010.

Matheson, Sue. *The John Ford Encyclopedia*. Lanham, MD: Rowman & Littlefield, 2019.

McCoy, Alfred W., with Cathleen B. Read and Leonard P. Adams II. *The Politics of Heroin: CIA Complicity in the Global Drug Trade*. New York: Harper & Row, 2003.

Miller, Julie. "*BlacKkKlansman*: The True Story of How Ron Stallworth Infiltrated the K.K.K." *Vanity Fair*, August 10, 2018, https://www.vanityfair.com/hollywood/2018/08/blackkklansman-ron-stallworth-true-story-spike-lee-kkk.

Mims, Bob. "Did Butch Cassidy and Sundance Kid Die in Bolivia? Yes, But." *Los Angeles Times*, January 14, 1996, https://www.latimes.com/archives/la-xpm-1996-01-14-me-24474-story.html.

The Myth of Troy exhibition, British Museum, 2004.

Newsome, Matthew. *The Early History of the Kilt*. Franklin, NC, Scottish Tartans Museum, March 2015.

Nitobe, Inazo. *Bushido: The Soul of Japan*. New York: Merchant Books, 2009.

Nolan, Frederick. *The Wild West: History, Myth & the Making of America*. London: Arcturus, 2020.

Northup, Solomon. *Twelve Years a Slave*. New York: Heritage Publishing, 1853.

OHCHR Assessment of Human Rights Concerns in the Xinjiang Uyghur Autonomous Region, People's Republic of China. August 31, 2022.

Osmond, Louise, director. *Richard III: The King in the Car Park*. Banijay, 2013.

Nayaka, Jayant Pandurang, and Syed Nurullah. *A Students' History of Education in India (1800–1973)*, 6th ed. New Delhi: Macmillan, 1974.

Pargeter, Edith. *A Bloody Field by Shrewsbury*. London: Headline, 2016.

Peel, Dan. *The History of the Civil Rights Movement: The Story of the African American Fight for Justice and Equality*. Solihull, UK: Sona Books, 2020.

Pennell, C. R. *Bandits at Sea: A Pirates Reader*. New York: New York University Press, 2001.

Petersen, Wolfgang, director. "Audio Commentary." *Troy*, Warner Bros. Pictures, 2004, 2005 (DVD).

Pitt, Ingrid. *Darkness Before Dawn: The Revised and Expanded Autobiography of Life's a Scream*. Baltimore: Midnight Marquee Press, 2008.

Plutarch. *Plutarch's Lives: Translated from the Original Greek, with Notes, Critical and Historical, and a Life of Plutarch.* New York: Derby & Jackson, 1859.

Remarque, Erich Maria. *All Quiet on the Western Front.* New York: Random House, 2013.

"Revealed: The Scot Who Inspired Dickens' Scrooge." *The Scotsman*, December 24, 2004, https://www.scotsman.com/news/revealed-scot-who-inspired-dickens-scrooge-2470097.

Rhodes, James Ford. *History of the Civil War 1861–1865.* Independently published, 2016.

Richie, Donald. *The Films of Akira Kurosawa*, 3rd ed. Oakland: University of California Press, 1996.

Robinson, Anna, and Matt Reigle. "The Truth About Clark Gable's Relationship with Hattie McDaniel." *Grunge*, July 13, 2022, https://www.grunge.com/764140/the-truth-about-clark-gables-ralationship-with-hattie-mcdaniel/.

Ryynanen, Timo. *James VI: The Demonologist King: Demonic Descriptions and Their Context in James VI's Daemonologie.* Dissertation, Univ. of Eastern Finland, 2010.

Scott, Ridley, director. "Making of Documentary." *Gladiator*, Dreamworks, 2000, 2001 (DVD).

Shakespeare, William. *Antony and Cleopatra.* New York: Simon & Schuster, 2020.

Shakespeare, William. *Henry V.* London: Penguin Classics, 2015.

Sherriff, R. C. *Journey's End.* London: Samuel French Ltd., 2010.

Shetterly, Margot Lee. *Hidden Figures: The American Dream and the Untold Story of the Black Women Mathematicians Who Helped Win the Space Race.* New York: William Morrow, 2016.

Singh, Sunny. Hist Fest conference, 2018.

Smith, Helena. "Legal Threat Over 'Gay' Alexander." *The Guardian*, November 22, 2004, https://www.theguardian.com/world/2004/nov/22/film.filmnews.

Sparks, Hannah. "'Mulan' Star Liu Yifei's Support for Hong Kong Police Sparks Disney Boycott." *New York Post*, August 16, 2019, https://nypost.com/2019/08/16/mulan-star-liu-yifeis-support-for-hong-kong-police-sparks-disney-boycott/.

Stowe, Harriet Beecher. *Uncle Tom's Cabin.* Herfordshire, UK: Wordsworth Classics, 1999.

Szpilman, Władysław. *The Pianist.* New York: Picador, 2019.

Tallis, Nicola. *Crown of Blood: The Deadly Inheritance of Lady Jane Grey.* London: Pegasus Books, 2016.

von Tunzelmann, Alex. "The Other Boleyn Girl: Hollyoaks in Fancy Dress." *The Guardian*, June 8, 2008, https://www.theguardian.com/film/2008/aug/07/1.

Zebrowski, Carl. "Why the South Lost the Civil War." Historynet, August 19, 1999, https://www.historynet.com/why-the-south-lost-the-civil-war-cover-page-february-99-american-history-feature/.

Index

About the Author

As far back as Jem Duducu can remember, he has loved two things: history and movies. So, writing *Hollywood and History* fulfills a lifelong dream. As the author of more than a dozen nonfiction books and historical novels, he loves uncovering the lesser-known personalities and events from history. Jem is a firm believer that the past can teach us many valuable lessons about the world today and can help guide us to a better future.

Jem's previous nonfiction books include *The Busy Person's Guide to British History*, *The British Empire in 100 Facts*, *Deus Vult: A Concise History of the Crusades*, *The Romans in 100 Facts*, *Forgotten History: Unbelievable Moments from the Past*, *The Napoleonic Wars in 100 Facts*, *The American Presidents in 100 Facts*, *The Sultans: The Rise and Fall of the Ottoman Rulers and Their World: A 600-Year History*, and *Slinkys and Snake Bombs: Weird but True Historical Facts*. His historical fiction novels are *Silent Crossroads*, *Echoes*, *And God Watched*, and *Edge of Life*.

Jem works and lives in London with his wife and two children and is slowly losing the battle for the TV remote.